Dangerous
Words

Dangerous

Talking about God in an

Words

Age of Fundamentalism

Gary Eberle

TRUMPETER

Boston & London 2007

TRUMPETER
An imprint of Shambhala Publications, Inc.
Horticultural Hall
300 Massachusetts Avenue
Boston, Massachusetts 02115
www.shambhala.com

9 8 7 6 5 4 3 2 1

First Edition
Printed in the United States of America

∞ This edition is printed on acid-free paper that meets the
American National Standards Institute Z39.48 Standard.

Distributed in the United States by Random House, Inc.,
and in Canada by Random House of Canada Ltd

Designed by DCDESIGN

Library of Congress Cataloging-in-Publication Data
Eberle, Gary.
Dangerous words: talking about God in an age
of fundamentalism / Gary Eberle.—1st Trumpeter ed.
p. cm.
Includes bibliographical references.
ISBN 978-1-59030-432-7 (alk. paper)
1. Language and languages—Religious aspects. 2. God. I. Title.
BL65.L2E24 2007
210.1'4—DC22
2007001718

To Sue

In principio erat verbum . . .

Contents

Acknowledgments xi

Introduction xiii

1 : Words   3

2 : Modernism   11

3 : Truth   32

4 : Fundamentalism   58

5 : Myth   85

6 : Religion   110

7 : Tradition   127

8 : God   151

9 : Silence   180

Notes   205

Selected Bibliography   219

Index   225

Acknowledgments

I WOULD like to offer special thanks to the following: Aquinas College for granting me a sabbatical to write this book; Lisa Johnson, for help on preliminary research on people's attitudes toward the word *God*; Fountain Street Church, Rabbi Albert Lewis, the Aquinas College Emeritus Program, and Christ Community Church of Grand Rapids for offering me the chance to pilot these ideas in workshops; Dr. Stefan Davis for early help in biblical research and Christian mysticism; Rev. Fred Wooden and Rev. Colette Volkema DeNooyer for suggestions on various parts of the draft; Dr. Deborah Wickering for use of unpublished material; Dr. Chad Gunnoe for sources of information on the Reformation; David O'Neal, my editor; and, as always, my wife, Suzanne, my first and best reader, for criticism, support, and encouragement.

Introduction

W HY am I writing this book?

All writers get asked this question, and the answer is never easy.

Much of my reason has to do with the lamentable world situation. In my fifty-plus years, I have never felt as powerless and hopeless to do anything about the world I live in. A new ugliness and brutality have come into both national and world politics, much of it driven by various forms of religious fundamentalism. As a result, a war of words is taking place in this country—a battle, some would say, for the soul of America. In the past twenty years, a new politically active style of conservative Christianity has risen up that is challenging America's traditional separation between church and state. At the same time, liberalism seems to have lost almost all touch with religion and has adopted a kind of fundamentalist secularism that, to many people, seems to be trying to separate religion from public life altogether. Internationally, terrorism, preemptive wars, and the bloodbaths among Israelis, Palestinians, Hindus, Muslims, Sikhs, and Christians continue in various parts of the world and show very few signs of abating in our lifetimes. As a person who considers himself spiritual, I find it very distressing to see people dividing themselves along religious lines for the purpose of killing each other.

Like many other people who may consider themselves good Christians or Muslims, I have felt both angry and insulted when far-right extremists have claimed to be the "real" spokespersons for Christianity and Islam. At the same time, I have not felt comfortable with the response to religion offered by strict secularists who would deny religion any place in public life. Because of the prominence in the media of the extreme voices on both ends of the spectrum, and because of the relative silence of more moderate religious voices in recent years, these extreme points of view have come to control the terms of our religious conversation. We have let the strict fundamentalists and the strict secularists define emotionally loaded words such as *truth, religion,* and even *God* in a narrow, rigid, and literalistic way, and the rest of us have let ourselves be cowed into responding on their, not our, terms, as if our approach to religion, not theirs, were an aberration of what religion is and has been.

In the United States, traditional moderates and liberals seem to have lost their voice and focus, virtually conceding both flag and God to conservative religionists. As a local minister recently put it in a sermon, gatherings of liberals today seem more like reunions than forward-looking political rallies. Having forfeited a vision of the future, they grumpily munch on the bones of the past, remembering the heady days when they, too, had political and social influence. Even liberal political gains like the Democratic midterm victories in 2006 will not likely alter the essential nature of the cultural debate. Mainstream moderates seem to think that a wishy-washy relativism is an adequate response to militant conservatism and strict secularism, but it isn't. In a time of heated political and social unrest like ours, voices of moderation urgently need to articulate a clear and sharp defense of their position and hold it with some passion. This, I think, we have so far failed to do.

As a writer and teacher of literature and humanities, I decided to study how we are using language in all this, for language forms the underpinning of both politics and religion. As I have listened to political and religious arguments over the past ten years and heard what passes for intelligent discourse on talk radio and on television commentary programs, I have come to the conclusion that we live in an age of polluted language, and that nowhere has it become more polluted than in the tumultuous waters where religion and politics meet. Two generations ago, George Orwell famously warned us of this danger in his "Politics and the English Language," but even though we know the dynamics of linguistic distortion, large numbers of people are still succumbing to political and religious demagoguery throughout the world.

At this perilous moment in history, we may need reminding once again of just how language can go wrong. This book, therefore, represents an attempt by a citizen and layman to understand what's going on in the crazy world in which we find ourselves. Watching events unfold on the evening news, I have sometimes felt like an inhabitant of a world that has gone mad over religion and has set loose the dogs of war in the names of its various gods. We do not fully understand the dynamics of the energies we let loose when we invoke the name of God as a cause of war. I feel, as I watch, the way I would feel if I came upon a child playing with matches and sticks of dynamite.

Religion is arguably the most complex of all human behaviors. In fact, it might even be called a "meta-behavior," for it transcends any single sphere of human life and connects them all together. As the twentieth-century historian Arnold Toynbee pointed out, religions were not by-products of the historic world civilizations, they were their very foundation. Throughout history, spiritual beliefs have had tremendous power to shape the physical and social world. In ancient Egypt, for example, belief in the divine power of the pharaoh and in the afterlife moved millions of tons of stone to form the pyramids. In the European Middle Ages, spiritual beliefs motivated people to erect massive stone and glass cathedrals. Similar monuments to our species' religious impulse—Angkor Wat, Borobudur, the great mosques of Islam—stand throughout the world. Even a quick survey of world history shows that religion has exerted tremendous power to create art, culture, civilization—and, let's be honest, war.

For another grim truth of human history is that we have apparently always used our gods as divine sanction to slaughter our enemies who believe in other gods. Unfortunately, belief in the absolute truth of one's own gods may make all other people who believe in other gods something less than human. We call them "infidels," unbelievers, and, because they do not believe in our particular deity, we, in effect, "de-speciate" them, making them less than human so that we may kill them with impunity.

Today, in a world torn by wars and conflicts of varying intensities, religious rhetoric is being used by all sides to justify their carnage. Many people, myself included, find this repugnant, whether the language is used by an Islamist suicide bomber or a premillennialist Christian who sees in the current struggles in the Middle East the necessary (and welcome) violent conflict before the Second Coming of Jesus.

And here is where this book may serve a purpose. It is an attempt to study and understand "God-language." Though the term *God-language* is a more or less direct translation of *theology* (*theos* + *logos*), this book is not about theology. Rather, it will look at the way people use and misuse language about God and ultimate realities, and it will suggest another way of understanding God-language than the current tendency to look at it as operating in the same way as other kinds of language.

By studying God-language—its etymology, rhetoric, and dynamics—perhaps we can enter into the religious imagination of a teenage suicide bomber and understand what motivates him. Perhaps we can understand why a self-professed Christian would shout insults at the families during the funerals of dead soldiers killed in Iraq or why some "Christian" Web sites call for the cold-blooded execution of doctors who perform abortions. Is this really what embracing religion leads to? Is a strict secularism the only possible answer? If our religions cannot bring us to understand each other better and to change the way we think about each other, then are we simply doomed to continue the slaughter in the names of all our gods?

My argument in this book is addressed to both religious moderates and religious liberals who are looking for a way to use religious language again in the contemporary world. I believe we all, fundamentalists included, need to develop a new way of understanding our own religious language. By studying language, I hope to show that, in fact, fundamentalism is not a return to "that old-time religion," as fundamentalists themselves might think, but is actually an anomaly in religious history. I will also try to demonstrate why a literal interpretation of scripture may actually lead to distortion of scriptural language rather than clarity. I also hope to show how, paradoxically, fundamentalists have actually adopted a modernist worldview. That is, in attempting to reject the modern scientific way of looking at the world, they have actually adopted that worldview as their own. As we'll see in chapter 4, fundamentalists, without realizing it, have applied scientific-style modernist thinking to a realm it was never intended to enter, and indeed over which it has no sway whatsoever. The result has been, as in the cases of calls for "creation science" or "Intelligent Design," neither good science nor good religion. In doing this, I hope to show religious moderates, and even conservatives, how they may continue to have a Bible-based theology without falling into the trap of strict literalism.

For liberals who have grown somewhat squeamish about using words like *God, truth,* or *belief,* I hope to show how we can reappropriate those words that are so necessary to meaningful human life but whose meanings are now being controlled by the religious right. Liberalism has grown more secular over the past twenty years, but religious language contains valuable words, words that are, in fact, irreplaceable, for they name realities of our human experience that otherwise would remain nameless. Liberals need to reclaim these words and start using them again as they have in the past.

Perhaps nothing, ultimately, can ever be done to stop human beings from slaughtering each other, but I would at least like to start to remove the gods from the list of causes of war. When we invoke the gods, we call into ourselves a divine madness, and we become possessed by a daemon, or energy that is intoxicating and seems superhuman, even though it is often really only infantile in its primal urge to express its power by destruction. The Greeks, of all their gods, hated Ares most, because of the destruction he wrought.

My hope is that by examining the language we use to talk about God, religion, and other matters of what Paul Tillich called "ultimate concern," we may become more conscious of how the tremendous powers of religion may be harnessed for good and creative, rather than evil and destructive, ends. If we are to keep religion from destroying the world, then we must move beyond religions (plural) and understand how the religious impulse, shared by all our species, finds its rich expression in the many vocabularies we use to _____ ___. The greatness of God transcends all names. Most trad_____ now we must decide either to find a common lang_____ each other or to continue our war of words and live in a post-_____ world of confusion.

Dangerous Words

1 : Words

LANGUAGE is regarded by many as the distinctive characteristic of the human species. Certainly the complexity of our linguistic abilities and the way language encompasses virtually all human behaviors is far beyond the signaling capacity of other species on the planet. Language is not perfect by any means, but it is, by far, the best method we have to move ourselves forward, to figure our way out of our problems, and to articulate our human condition. So when language becomes polluted, as I think it has in contemporary debates about religion, politics and science, then we need to set about analyzing just where the source points of the pollution are and try to clean them up or else we risk further poisoning the religious environment in which we live.

The words by which we call things do matter, and so the struggle today over who owns religious vocabulary is of vital importance. If *family values*, for example, can mean only the values of a traditional nuclear family living according to a rigid patriarchal interpretation of Christian scripture, then what can we say about all the other families we may know who have definite values, like tolerance, inclusiveness, and compassion, but who don't fit into the narrow fundamentalist mold?[1] Similarly, if we allow the word *truth* to mean only literal truth, then how can Judaism, Islam, Christianity, and all the other world religions be, as their followers believe them to be, "true," even when they seem mutually contradictory in some ways? If *truth* can only mean one thing or be interpreted in only one way, as strict fundamentalists would claim, then conflict over this word is inevitable. This is not good. On the other hand, the liberal solution to the conundrum presented by the word *truth* is not very satisfactory either. If *truth* is only relative and can mean whatever a believer wants it to mean, then how do we avoid chaos? So, we need to figure out what exactly we mean when we say that a particular religious tradition and its scriptures are *true*.

As these examples show, being clear about what we mean when we say things is vital, especially today when so many people seem to be talking but so few seem to be listening. Trying to be clear should be the first thing that a book on language attempts to be. Therefore, a word about the methodology used in this book is in order.

Religious language, by its very nature, is highly volatile. All words come loaded with histories, emotional connotations, and powerful resonances, but religious words are especially heavily freighted with both personal and cultural meanings. Religious words are the linguistic equivalent of an unstable explosive such as nitroglycerin. Unlike ordinary words, say *dog* or *tree,* a religious word like *God* stirs deep emotions in us, emotions that are hard to articulate because they are so complex, so deep-seated, and so intertwined with our fundamental conceptions of what we, and the universe we live in, are all about. So, one problem in approaching religious language is simultaneously to acknowledge its emotional resonance and also to be able to analyze it objectively. This is an extremely difficult balancing act, but by using a linguistic approach to God-language rather than a sectarian one, we can maintain a dual focus on words' emotional connotations and on their use within a larger language context. By focusing on God-language as language, we can avoid, for a while, arguments over orthodoxy and truth and thereby free ourselves to look more or less objectively at how we use certain words.

Another problem with studying religious language today is that most of us don't understand the scriptural languages of Hebrew or Arabic. An even more pressing (and interesting) problem, however, is that we may not really understand certain words when we use them in English. When we use the word *God,* for example, we think we know what we mean by it and we assume that others who use that word will understand us also, but in reality we often end up speaking past each

other. When President George W. Bush indicates that God called him
to run for the presidency, or when he uses words from moral theology
(*good versus evil,* for example) to characterize his foreign policy, we
need to ask exactly what he understands by those words. It is one thing
to say, as most believers of most faiths would, that they believe a divine
providence oversees their lives; it is another to believe that the Judeo-
Christian God literally spoke to one, as if one were a biblical prophet,
singled out for a special role in history. Even if we limit our study of
God-language to the English language, we find ourselves entering
strange linguistic territory.

Not only laymen, but even professional linguists have difficulty
with religious language. To their consternation, they find that, perversely, it operates by different rules than everyday language does. To
use the succinct comment of British linguist and bishop Ian Ramsey
from fifty years ago, religious language gets "odd." It functions according to different principles than everyday discourse, and is wildly different from the way we use language in science and academic disciplines.
Obviously, analyzing religious language is an enormous and important
task, but there has been surprisingly little work done by professional
linguists in this area, especially in recent years. Perhaps this is because
it is so problematic, or perhaps it is due to the increasing secularization
of the academic world, but clearly the field is not exhausted. Some research was done in the mid–twentieth century, and a new term, *theolinguistics,* was even coined around 1986, but since the 1980s and the rise
of semiotics, the topic seems to have been dropped. At least in my research in sources such as the online Modern Language Association bibliography, the American Theological Library Association (ATLA)
database, and other sources, I could not seem to find much linguistic or
theological research on God-language since the spate of activity in the
1950s and '60s. In light of increasing cultural conflicts that are arising
around the use and misuse of religious language in the contemporary
world, the time seems ripe for scholars to return to the subject.

Before starting, however, I should first make what journalists call a
disclosure. Though I studied some historical linguistics and rhetoric in
graduate school, and now regularly teach a college course on the history of the English language, my professional work has been mainly in

the field of literature and humanities. I am not a professional linguist. Neither am I a professional theologian, though I studied much theology in two years in seminary and as an undergraduate. I have relied heavily on the insights of trained linguists and theologians in reaching my conclusions, but my thoughts in this book remain those of a lover of words and a teacher of language who is upset at the misuse and abuse I see in the way religious language is being tossed around today by many extremists.

In order to keep the scope of the book manageable, I will focus primarily on the usage of words in English. When reading scripture, I rely, like most people, on the competence of translators, but I also regularly use a Bible that has extensive language footnotes, since these often give the connotations of the original Hebrew, Aramaic, or Greek, and I also find it helpful to keep several historical translations of scripture handy so as to compare how English words are used over time. There are numerous excellent books on the original languages of the scriptures, but this book will focus primarily on the use of religious language in English, since the cultural debate I am engaged in is happening in the English-speaking world of America, even though it has parallels in Arabic- and Hebrew-speaking cultures.

That being said, we are ready to move ahead. This book will use a historical and etymological approach to language and words. English, like any language, is similar to a layer cake or an arrangement of geological strata. By digging down through the history of a word from the present, we come upon earlier layers of meaning, some of which are quite surprising and enlightening. Each word in our language has its own history. Each one came into the language at a particular time, in a particular place, and under a particular set of circumstances, and it filled a niche to name something or some quality or some action at that time. Language, however, is in constant flux, and new cultural influences bring new words into it. English is amazing in its spongelike ability to take in words from other languages. In its long history, it has absorbed Celtic, Latin, Anglo-Saxon, Norse, Danish, French, and Greek words, to name only its most prominent sources. Today, English is receiving an influx of words from Arabic because of our recent, how shall we say, "cultural contact" with the Middle East. Words such as *jihad, fatwa,* and *mullah* are entering our everyday conversation and will eventually be absorbed into English, just as earlier Arabic words, such as *algebra, alcohol,* and *zenith,* were hundreds of years ago. So, the meanings of words in English are colored by where they came from, their provenance.

In addition, we need to remember that words in a given language change their meanings over time, so that what a word meant in one century may be completely different from what it means in a later time or place. (One can compare, for example, the use of the word *promiscuous* a hundred and fifty years ago, when it simply meant "a variety of things in the same place together." Today, a "promiscuous gathering" might call things to mind that would never have occurred to someone in 1850.) Not only that, but some words mean different things in different places. A quick comparison of the everyday British and American meanings of the words *lift, subway, jumper,* or *biscuit* will show that what a word means often depends on where it is spoken.

All of this is by way of saying that language is conditioned by time and place, so the more we know about a particular word's previous usage, the more we can understand layers of meaning in it that at first might not be apparent. Historical and etymological dictionaries are invaluable tools in this process; fortunately, they are readily available for speakers of the English language, and I have used them frequently.

The chapters are organized around words such as *truth, God,* and *religion,* words that seem to me to be particularly loaded with emotions and around which much of our current cultural debate is clustered. In the course of examining these loaded words, each chapter also examines other, related words, such as *sacred, faith, belief,* and *holy,* in order to show how religious words, taken together, form a constellation of meaning that is much more complex than could be indicated by simply labeling them *true* or *false.* Religious language, we will find, treads a middle ground, a gray area, as it were, between those loaded words *true* and *false,* and, as such, it fills a needed linguistic space. It cannot, however, be read, heard, or spoken in quite the same way as other language.

In analyzing language this way, I hope to show how, ironically, readings of sacred scriptures that insist on their literal truth ultimately distort the very texts that strict fundamentalists claim to value. In doing this, our goal is to awaken scriptural literalists to the richer and more profound truths expressed in religious language.

The cultural debate of our time, however, is not just being determined by fundamentalists of the religious kind. There is another fundamentalism abroad in the world today that goes by the name of modernism. Modernism, also sometimes called secular humanism, most often offers itself as a rational alternative to religious fundamentalism. As we'll see, modernism's hallmark is a secular and scientific view of the world. As such, it is intellectually compelling, and its accomplishments are impressive, but a completely secular worldview can be emotionally and spiritually unsatisfying, and, taken to an extreme, strict modernism can be as narrow and unyielding a form of fundamentalism as the religious kind. If there is to be an effective counter to the religious fundamentalism that is sweeping America and the Middle East, it really can't come from secular modernism. Rather, the answer to religious fundamentalism must come from a truly religious perspective, one that offers a healthy and life-giving antidote to the extremes of both religious fundamentalism and total secularism. In order for that to happen, we must find a new way of thinking and talking about religion in the modern world, a way that will offer us a means of speaking civilly to one another again about this most important aspect of our life. We might say the fate of the future depends on it.

Throughout our evolutionary history, human consciousness has used language to grope into the intellectual darkness. Of course, we have always used language to explain what we already knew, but, more importantly, we have also used it to reach toward what we did not yet know or understand. Like children who are always reading above their grade level, we human beings are always stretching our language into the still-unarticulated and unexplored areas of our own consciousness and our interaction with the world. That gives us hope that some day our God-language may be used to unite us rather than to divide us. As we strive to understand the dynamics of God-language and its use in the contemporary world, perhaps we will come to see that all of us—Christians, Jews, Muslims, Buddhists, Hindus, and even atheists—are engaged in the same quest, to find the name of the unnameable and to understand our existence in its light.

The following chapters set out to reexamine several "troublesome" religious words and to rescue them for use by everyone, not just religious extremists. At this point in history, it is vital to examine the nature of our religious discourse and see if we can find common ground, for if we cannot, then we risk bringing the whole tower of our world civilization down around our ears.

Religious language is powerful and is capable of rousing us to act out the best or the worst of our human nature. A quick look at the headlines will show us how horrifically we can behave in the various names of God, but, usually on the back pages, we find that religious language can also inspire us to rise to the heights of human compassion and understanding. It can send us off to the far corners of the earth to alleviate hunger and disease, and it can lead us to lifelong growth in the spirit. Religious language has the power to overturn lives and hearts for good or ill.

Today, the consequences of continuing to talk past each other instead of to each other are very high. With modern explosives, modern methods of travel, and weapons of mass destruction that will inevitably include nuclear weapons as part of terror's arsenal, the time has come to talk with each other again or face even more slaughter in the names of our gods.

We live in a strange time. The twentieth century, with its modernism, attempted a bold experiment. For the best of reasons, brilliant thinkers advocated a purely rational life, in which the religious or spiritual realm was either invisible or terribly truncated. Rational life, modern life, grounded in reason and science, would rid us of superstition and provide a solid foundation for building an ideal future. One hope among many others was to avoid religious wars like those that had afflicted the past. As we can now see, the experiment, while noble, was in many ways a failure. Secularism was not enough to stop religious wars. If for nothing more, we must thank the fundamentalists for helping us to see that. The tremendous upsurge of fundamentalism in Christianity and other religions is evidence that people have a hunger for the life of the spirit, and that they are not satisfied with mere materialism or an improved material standard of living. But given the events of the past ten years both at home and abroad, it should be just as clear that religious fundamentalism is not a type of religion the human race can afford to live with for very long. Religions of fear, based on hatred rather than compassion, founded on seeing other human beings as different from us and therefore worthy of slaughter, simply cannot be allowed to become the future of world religion.

This book will attempt to present a new—or actually very old—way of talking about God and the gods that may provide a starting point for further, more peaceful conversation. We cannot continue to live in the post-Babel world. We must learn to speak the same language again so that we can help one another reach out to that ultimate Being that will bring us to our full potential as human beings. That is simply another way of saying we must all turn to God and address God by all God's many names.

Religions are, above all, constructed of words, and wars of religion are, in many ways, wars of words. In the following pages, we will examine, in turn, several words that seem particularly troublesome today. In the end, perhaps thinking about these words will move us that much closer to naming what, finally, will be unnameable.

This cultural debate is taking place in countries where the modern world is coming into conflict with traditional worlds, and the world's religious fundamentalisms seem united in their opposition to *modernism,* so it is with that strange and troublesome word that we will begin.

2 : Modernism

Modernism has many definitions. In art, it defines the period from the late nineteenth through the first three-fourths of the twentieth century, in which artists experimented with many different styles. In architecture, *modernism* came to mean a clean, geometric structure where form followed function. Modernism's iconic buildings were glass and steel towers like the Seagram Building in New York, the Hancock Center, or Sears Tower in Chicago, and, of course, the World Trade Center. For purposes of this book, however, we want to use *modernism* in a wider sense. We will use the word to denote a particular mind-set, or way of looking at the world, that came into full flower in the early twentieth century in the Western world and has spread, along with Western technology, to the rest of the world in the intervening hundred years. It includes modern art and architecture, and much else besides.

Modernism, as a worldview, has its roots deeply sunk in Greek rationalism, but it really rose up out of the Enlightenment thinking of the seventeenth and eighteenth centuries. During that period, which followed the more theocentric Middle Ages and Renaissance, a new way of thinking about the world came into being, and the result was a peculiar constellation of social, technological, and intellectual changes that constituted a remarkable transformation in human consciousness. The modern way of thinking also had spiritual dimensions, and, like all comprehensive worldviews, eventually permeated every aspect of life. Taken all together, the changes made up what we now call the "modern" world. As paradoxical as it may seem, even contemporary Christian fundamentalism, as we'll see below, can be understood as an offshoot of modernism.

A tentative definition would say that modernism is a worldview that has shaped and was shaped by the massive social, technological, and intellectual changes that have taken place since the Scientific Revolution; it is characterized by rationalism, a focus on the outer, rather than the inner world, and it has an obsession with time and history over eternity. Richard Antoun writes that the modern way of thinking and being "values change over continuity, quantity over quality, and commercial efficiency . . . over human sympathy for traditional values."[1] For the most part, this worldview was greeted triumphally when it debuted. It was the worldview that would overcome ages of superstition; the modern world would become the age of science and would see the triumph of reason; the modern period would be the age of progress and would lead to the ideal human future.

In many ways, modernism fulfilled this optimistic vision. The twentieth century saw enormous advances in human knowledge, particularly in the sciences, but it also saw massive wars, tyranny, and environmental destruction on a scale never seen before in human history. The end result was that many of the most aware and sensitive experienced a feeling of exhaustion and of things breaking apart. As the twentieth century came to a close, there was a widespread feeling that life was faster, more fragmented, and more alienating than it had ever been before.

The conclusion seemed self-evident to many. We can take virtually any aspect of what we call "modern" life today—the television, radio, cell phone, computer—and see in it virtually the same pattern. Everything we call "modern" has its value because it is faster, more powerful, and more efficient, but the price we have paid for all this is an increasing feeling of being fragmented and hurried, torn in all directions. While cell phones, for example, seem to connect us to one another, they also cut us off from our immediate environment. While television and computers may give us constant access to the world at large, they also tend to mask from us our local neighborhood. Real communities in our lives have been replaced by virtual ones, such as anonymous online chat rooms, and in our actual communities a dreary sort of sameness has set in from town to town and region to region. The modern strip city that has developed around major urban areas is the architectural expression of the outer limit of modernism applied to community development, an urban conglomeration laid out in a straight line, efficient for automobiles but neglectful of some important human needs. A look at the world modernism has created shows that we have become willing to trade off more traditional values, including family cohesiveness, religious sentiment, and interpersonal relationships, for a higher material standard of living.

So, let's begin by conceding that the world's various fundamentalists have a compelling and legitimate point—the world created by modernism is, in many ways, a confusing mess. Its glamour and flash can blind us to the fact that it is, in many essential ways, superficial and dehumanizing. The fact that religious fundamentalism can be so attractive to so many people today, and that it can spawn so much violent upheaval worldwide, is evidence in itself that the modern, technological (that is, "Western") lifestyle leaves many people greatly dissatisfied. Religious fundamentalism is often regarded as a problem in the world today, but perhaps it is merely a symptom, a sort of allergic or toxic reaction to the negative aspects of modernism.

In fact, scholars of religion who have studied the matter agree that the worldwide upsurge of religious fundamentalism in the twentieth and twenty-first centuries is actually a by-product of a widespread discontent with contemporary life. The fact that fundamentalism could arise in the midst of modern or modernizing societies reveals that many people in many cultures hunger for something more, but the "more" that would satisfy their hunger is clearly not more of the same. Fundamentalists are not clamoring for more of the material goods that modernity can give them; rather, they desire more "immaterial" goods, such as an acknowledgement of the spiritual realities and moral values that they see lacking in the modern secular world. And their case is compelling. It seems that every culture that modernism has touched has experienced the same cycle: as modernization and its values enter in, the culture experiences a breakdown of traditional family structure, a sense of historical and cultural discontinuity, and an erosion of traditional spiritual values. Thanks to modern mass media and international business, changes that took the Western world a couple of centuries can now happen virtually overnight.

An anthropologist friend of mine has traced the transition, in just twenty years, of a Sinai Bedouin group, the Tarabiin, from being a traditional nomadic herding tribe to being a group of settled "hoteliers" running a small tourist resort on the Red Sea. Twenty years ago, they trekked into the mountains with camels and goats, had a dynamic oral culture, and lived by deeply embedded folk customs. Today, when they are not waiting on foreign tourists, they watch American soap operas on television and are quickly forgetting, within a generation, the essential lore their people had passed down for a millennium. Though they still take tourists on camel treks into their former mountain haunts, they are aware that these excursions are mere shows, not a lifestyle, and the children, newly literate, are losing the old stories and skills that once bonded the people together and gave them identity. The older (really only middle-aged) people, who have lived through the entire cultural transition, admit that the old days were harder, but they are also acutely aware of the price they have paid for their modern ease.[2]

Similar stories can be told of many indigenous peoples. A Canadian Broadcasting Corporation documentary I used to use in a class showed the rapid social breakup of an Inuit group as it allowed satellite-beamed television into its remote Arctic Circle village. Within six months, families were struggling with "modern" problems—dissatisfied teens, people staying in their homes, individuals isolating themselves from the community, a discontent not there previously. The traditional stories of the people were getting replaced with the violent and sensationalized stories from the land to the south. These stories did not represent Inuit reality. In fact, they did not even represent what had been Inuit fantasies. Suddenly their world and the world of their ancestors was not good enough anymore. They were becoming, in a word, modern.

What makes these cases so fascinating is that they play out, in microcosm and at fast speed, the changes that occurred in the Western and modernized world as a whole over a longer period of time.

An epitome of modern life and modernism is the airline terminal, that place of temporary meeting and permanent transit. Airports are efficiently and rationally laid out to meet the needs of our machines. They are places that have many amenities, but ultimately they are places where no one wants to stay. In these places of no place, we all become mere passengers, human cargo, being ferried to other airports that will be virtually the same.

In a sense, our modern world has become a giant airline terminal, a world characterized by a creeping sense of anonymity, impermanence, sameness, and overwhelming bureaucracy. People living their lives in this world move geographically from place to place quite often in their lives in order to proceed vertically in their careers. As a result, the sameness of exurban development—the cookie-cutter subdivisions with their McMansions, the big-box stores along identical commercial strips—becomes the only continuity in the lives of people who may not stay in any one place for very long. Tradition, a sense of place, rootedness, and history all go missing. I have written elsewhere that living modern life is like living in a permanent state of jet lag.[3]

Of course, one more manifestation of the modern mind-set was and is the international style of modernist architecture. Based on grid-like arrangements of metal and glass, it offers us towering, impressive, and overpowering buildings that somehow remain soulless, creating an urban landscape into which no one ventures much after work hours.

In that sense, the World Trade Center was an extreme embodiment of modernism, both in its design and in the scope and function of its twin towers. Though it had wry references in its architecture to cathedrals in the bracing of the lower levels, it was, like all modern skyscrapers from the Woolworth Building down, essentially a "cathedral of commerce," that is, a construction devoted to the making and getting of money, the *lingua franca* of the modern world.

On September 11, 2001, two airplanes, hijacked by Islamist fundamentalists, slammed into the two WTC towers in the name of God and brought them down, killing thousands. Though at first the world was confounded as to a possible motive for this horrendous crime, there is now little question that the twin towers of the Trade Center had come to represent for the terrorists and their mastermind, Osama bin Laden, the quintessence of modernism, a symbol of all that they were threatened by and fighting against—secularism, materialism, Western civilization, and globalism. If they wished to strike a symbolic blow against the center of modern life, they could not have chosen a better target.

When the twin towers were opened in 1972 and 1973, they were not immediately regarded as symbolic of anything in particular. They were simply an international center for import and export. Begun by David Rockefeller as a way of spearheading redevelopment of lower Manhattan's financial center, the buildings were described by at least one architectural critic as examples of "colossal dullness."[4] Eventually, like other arguably ugly structures—the Eiffel Tower comes to mind— they came to represent an entire city, in this case New York City, with all its power and allure as a center of international finance. Finally, the World Trade Center became iconic of commercialism and materialism, especially in the minds of those who wished to strike a symbolic blow against the modernist world. The first attack against the building occurred in February 1993, so the building has carried its iconic significance for some time among Islamic extremists, who see their traditional culture and values threatened by everything the towers represented. The evil brilliance of the 9/11 attack, requiring many years of planning and complicated coordination, and the reaction it brought from the United States, showed that both the perpetrators and the victims attached powerful emotional significance to the icon. That such an act would also claim thousands of innocent lives seems not to have been an issue to the supposedly religious terrorists, nor was the fact that such an act utterly failed what we might call the "compassion test" by which we may safely judge the value of any religion. Driven by ideology, fueled by religious rhetoric, these Islamist fundamentalists were obviously capable of destroying any number of other human beings in the name of God. The modern world, in the form of the George W. Bush administration, was swift and overwhelming in its retaliation. It unleashed the massive destructive power of the modern world's high-tech weapons and apparently won quick military victories in Afghanistan and Iraq, only to find itself occupying territories whose residents refused to admit they were defeated. Nothing could better illustrate the clash between modernism and fundamentalism.

How we organize our cities, and where we put our financial, emotional, and artistic resources reveals our core values in a way that is sometimes literally concrete. And here we should dwell a little more on the depth of symbolism involved in the 9/11 attack and its aftermath. The modern city, of which New York is the paragon, is actually something of an anomaly in history. The most ancient cities in the world, those that sprang up on the plains of Mesopotamia and were probably the models for the story of Babel and its tower, were built around temple complexes that featured ziggurats, which were artificial mountains where the priests offered sacrifice to the gods. The tops of these towering temples were, in fact, regarded as gateways to the gods, as the biblical name Babel suggests.[5] Until fairly recent times, human communities in both the Christian West and throughout the world were built around sacred complexes that represented, for the people who lived near them, the very center of the world, that is, the place where heaven and earth met, that formed a model, as it were, of how the world was put together. The temple complex formed an *axis mundi*, or world axis, which provided a metaphysical stairway to the realm of the gods. The vaulting spires of a cathedral or the towering minarets of mosques pointed upward to remind us of the divine function of the buildings to which they were attached. The sacred center formed a focal point for the spiritual, economic, and social life of human communities. In Islam, for example, the Kaaba in Mecca forms a center not just for the city but for the entire Muslim world, indeed the whole physical universe, and every believer is enjoined to undertake a pilgrimage, or *hajj*, to this sacred center at least once in his or her life. Furthermore, every mosque throughout the world has its *mihrab*, or niche, which points to the Kaaba. Every day, every Muslim is enjoined to bow down toward this sacred center five times.

In the same way, medieval cathedrals were situated to remind believers of where the center of their lives should be. They were typically oriented to the East, symbolic of Jerusalem and the direction from which Christ will come again at the end of time. Like the Muslim, the Christian believer, in participating in daily life, would always know where the eternal center of his or her life was located. Whether it was a church, a mosque, a Greek temple complex, or a sacred mountain, human communities have virtually always had a sacred site as their psychological and physical center.

But the modern city that emerged in the twentieth century represented something new and unprecedented, a city that was purely secular in its organization and whose common life revolved around economic rather than spiritual values.[6] Modern cities and their skyscrapers were monuments only to their own magnificence. They did not point to anything beyond themselves. They were not gateways to the gods but only to the world of finance and capital, the common religion of modern times.

Insofar as traditional religious values played a part in the life of the modern city at all, they were considered private affairs, and as the century wore on, religious matters shrank into the background of daily life. This arrangement could be called the "American Solution," for, as far as I know, the new United States of America was the first place where religion was, by law, dis-established from the state, where the leaders were not believed to have their power directly from God or the gods but where power in the now-secular state resided in the people and gravitated upward. In the First Amendment to the United States Constitution, the rationalist founding fathers decreed that there would be no law abridging the free expression of religion in this country, and in Article VI, section 3, they explicitly decreed that there would be no religious test administered as a prerequisite to holding office in the government. After witnessing hundreds of years of brutal European religious wars, this separation of church and state seemed like a welcome relief, as did founding a nation on rational thought rather than religious dogmatism.

Far from becoming an irreligious country, however, the United States remained a surprisingly religious one, but religion was separated from participation in civil government. The American model functioned reasonably well for over two hundred years. An American civil religion developed, classically articulated and analyzed in Robert Bellah's brilliant 1967 article "Civil Religion in America."[7] A compelling historical case can be made that in America, public utterances about religion have tended to be generic rather than sectarian. For example, though every presidential inaugural address has used the word *God,* and even though our currency bears the motto "In God we trust," one can search the founding documents of the government in vain to find a reference to *Jehovah* or *Jesus.* That is, though the Declaration of Independence speaks of inalienable rights being endowed by a "Creator" and we often read synonyms for God such as "Providence," "Supreme Judge of the World," and so on, the founding documents pointedly do *not* use proper names of God that belong to a particular religion or sect. The word *God,* as we'll see in a subsequent chapter, is unique in being both a proper and a common noun, grammatically speaking. This creates certain linguistic problems, of course, but it also gives us a word broad enough to encompass a variety of beliefs while allowing each believer to supply his or her own specific image of God when the word is spoken or read. It allowed Americans to go through two hundred years of history without significant religious strife.[8]

By the mid–twentieth century, however, the political-religious landscape had changed significantly in the United States and throughout the world. Secularism had risen in prominence. Attendance and participation in mainstream historical religions shrank, the rhetoric of religion left daily life, and, more and more, human beings met each other only in business transactions. The "cash nexus," as the Victorian Thomas Carlyle called it, had come to dominate human affairs, that is, others were of interest to us only as potential customers or potential business rivals. *Value* came to mean only economic value. Modernism—the secular, rational, merely material worldview—had triumphed.

One does not have to be a religious fundamentalist to admit that the lives we lead today and our much-vaunted Western lifestyle are almost exclusively measured and evaluated in material terms. To say that contemporary American culture is a secular materialist culture is merely to state the obvious. By the late twentieth century, science, the brainchild of the Enlightenment, had come to dominate every aspect of life and, in its more hubristic moments, even claimed sovereignty over all other ways of knowing.

The lifestyle that resulted was overwhelmingly seductive for millions of people, both in the United States, where it was pioneered, and throughout the world. It is flashy, attractive, and convincing. In a sense, the modern way of looking at the world has solved many of the problems human beings traditionally turned to religion for. Modern science peered into the origins of the world and of life on earth. It came to understand the universe both on a macrocosmic level, with its manned and unmanned space exploration, and on a subatomic level. Knowledge underwent a huge explosion in the last fifty years of the century, and worldwide access to information through the Internet made it seem possible that some day all questions would be answered by that electronic "universal library." Modern commerce, with its stepsister Science, brought not only material prosperity to many people, but also vastly improved health, increased life spans, and gave us the promise of a world without either psychological or physical pain. Such advances of modern medicine as transplants, in vitro fertilization, and new drugs to combat disease did indeed appear as "miracles" to those who remembered life before them. Telecommunications abolished distance, and we did in fact seem to be living in a brave new world, where life before 1900 seemed as remote as life in fifth-century B.C.E. Athens.

But as modernism gained momentum through the century, discontents began to arise. Many cultural critics pointed out that in spite of our material plenty, we seemed to suffer a spiritual poverty relative to previous ages. In what became widely known as the Age of Anxiety, cultural critics of all stripes noticed a fairly precipitous decay of the traditional social fabric, the erosion of traditions, and a sense of anomie. Statistics could back them up, showing dramatic increases in urban violence, drug abuse, and the breakup of traditional family structures. In the world of entertainment, films of extreme violence became the norm, and images entered the cultural mainstream that would have been labeled pornographic only a few years before. So-called "point of view" shooting games became, literally, child's play, and the vision of "normal" human sexuality, as presented by the media, was of a life characterized by multiple sexual flings with no commitment and no emotional entanglements, sex without procreation or even relationship. Many perceived there to be a general coarsening of daily life, manifested in a decline of manners, rituals, and customs. Environmental degradation, including loss of huge tracts of rain forest, evidence of global warming, overpopulation, and a persistent hole in the earth's ozone layer, added to the mix.

The attempt to create a "counterculture" in the late 1960s was just one manifestation of discontent with the modern way of life in the last third of the twentieth century. Young hippies, in this country and abroad, sought a more meaningful existence and "returned to the earth" in communes or found other ways to drop out of the dominant materialist culture. Finding their own religious traditions bankrupt or energy-less, they turned to Oriental traditions, drugs, or the psychotherapeutic approaches gathered under the heading of the "human consciousness movement." Though it was considered outrageous at the time, we can now see such behavior as a reaching out by young people for some sort of spiritual meaning in a world that had been presented to them as a soulless machine completely definable by science, where all needs could be satisfied by the purchase of material goods. The counterculture movement didn't entirely work, of course, but it was a spasm of activity that was symptomatic of a widespread discontent with the way things were, a manifestation of what Huston Smith called a "spiritual tropism" in the human species that reaches toward the spiritual the way heliotropic plants reach toward the sun.

Not much really changed in modern society after the 1960s, however, so, perhaps not surprisingly, the end of the twentieth century saw a significant increase in depression among young people, as well as a rise in the numbers of young people committing suicide, which the National Institute of Mental Health now lists as the third most common cause of teen death, after accidents (including auto) and homicide. Similar trends are also manifesting themselves in Japan and several European countries.

By and large, people in modernized countries seemed to look on these social and environmental ills as an acceptable, if unfortunate, price to pay for the blessings of what were, in effect, the new gods of the age, progress and material prosperity. One's comfortable material lifestyle was to be the compensation for suffering the slings and arrows of outrageous modernism, and for the rest there was television to divert us and now, or soon, a new pill to elevate our mood or dull the pain.

But not everyone was content to suffer social and spiritual malaise in exchange for a few new widgets.

In the United States, after the turmoil of the 1960s, there was a surprising late-twentieth century upsurge in religious fundamentalism that had its roots in early twentieth-century movements. The current phase of fundamentalism gained steam through its effective use of radio and television, and finally manifested itself in an increasingly visible way in politics after the 1980s. Many commentators and historians agree with Richard Antoun, who wrote that fundamentalism was "a reaction, both ideological and affective, to the changes in basic social relationships that . . . occurred on a worldwide basis as a result of the social, organizational, technological, and economic changes introduced by the modern world and as a result of the historical shift in power relations that has occurred over the last two hundred years in that world."[9] Even more than reacting, then, simply to events that were occurring in the late twentieth century, fundamentalists of all stripes were responding to the entire Enlightenment and its great transmutation of Western civilization from an essentially religious society to an essentially secular one. Though these fundamentalists believed they were calling people back to "that old-time religion," as in Jerry Falwell's nostalgically named *Old Time Gospel Hour,* this fundamentalism was something fairly new and even, ironically, modern.

It's not just Christian fundamentalists, of course, who are discontent with contemporary civilization. Similar fundamentalist movements have risen up in Judaism and Islam, and for essentially the same reasons. Even secular humanists are not blind to the shortcomings of the modern world. But "fundamentalism" is the name of a particularly strong and peculiarly religious reaction to modernism. In all three of these major world religions, at about the same time, there emerged elements bent on "developing a militant form of piety whose objective is to drag God and religion from the sidelines, to which they have been relegated in modern secular culture, and bring them back to center stage again."[10] Each one had its unique spin, of course. Islamist thinking is reacting violently to the Islamic world's political colonization by Europe for over two hundred years, and Jewish fundamentalists see themselves in a pitched battle against the enemies of Israel and against the secular world, which sometimes includes the secular state of Israel. While the focus of this book is on Christian fundamentalism in America, it is important to remember that what we call the fundamentalist mind-set has similarities across the three religions. (Karen Armstrong's encyclopedic *The Battle for God: The History of Fundamentalism* gives a comprehensive history of the movements in all three traditions and shows how all are united in their rejection of modernism.)

Although Christian evangelicals and fundamentalists in the United States began as fringe movements on the edges of "liberal" Christianity around 1900, they eventually gained considerable political and cultural power. After being politically marginal since the Scopes trial in the mid-1920s, the religious right began to emerge as a distinct political force in the Reagan years with the Moral Majority, and through the 1990s Christian evangelicals and fundamentalists gained seats on local school boards, in state legislatures, and in the U.S. Congress. They were even given credit for swinging the 2004 presidential election in favor of George W. Bush, a man whose life story of failure, alcohol abuse, and subsequent rebirth as a Bible-reading Christian perfectly fit the trope of the born-again Christian who suddenly sees the light and goes on, through the grace of God, to achieve greatness. Even after President Bush leaves office, the religious right is apt to remain a significant, even if not dominant, part of our social and political discourse.

Even before the destruction of the WTC, this group was gaining strength and momentum, but after it they gained even more, and seemed to become more strident about calling America, as a nation, back to what they saw as its specifically Christian roots. The already quick growth of evangelical mega-churches in the American exurbs picked up more steam in the past five years, and astonishing numbers of otherwise modern people were suddenly proclaiming a belief in the literal truth of the Bible. The fact that many of these people worked in science or technical areas, the chief new areas of the postindustrial economy, only added to the paradox of a reactionary religious world-view coming to the fore in modern times.

The ramifications of this movement were felt through the whole society. "Creation science," a Bible-based alternative to evolutionary science, laid siege in several states to the science curricula of school systems, and from the federal government, as the War on Terror gained momentum, we began to hear rumblings of language reminiscent of the Book of Revelation. Fundamentalist historians, looking at the origins of the United States, claimed that the founding fathers intended America to be a specifically Christian nation, lifting quotations out of context and ignoring much evidence to the contrary. Legal battles over courthouse displays of the Ten Commandments included arguments about the specifically Christian foundation of the American legal system, as if the tradition of British common law had never existed. Within the armed services, the influence of evangelical Christianity became an issue as well.[11] In 2005, a chaplain at the Air Force Academy resigned during an investigation into allegations that the academy was putting undue pressure on cadets to accept evangelical Christian religion. A blue-ribbon task force concluded there was no "overt religious discrimination" at the academy, even though they noted incidents that included a football coach putting a "Team Jesus" banner in the locker room, and cases of Jewish cadets who claimed individual, if unofficial, harassment. The panel concluded that the academy, while not overtly evangelical, had "failed to provide full accommodation for the religious needs of non-Christian and nonevangelical cadets."[12] The New York Times also reported that there had recently been a great increase in the number of military chaplains who would identify themselves as "evangelical." At the same time, Catholic, Jewish, and mainstream chaplains declined in numbers, leaving service people of those denominations to be increasingly ministered to by the evangelical preachers. The problem in this trend was the tendency of these new chaplains to evangelize, if not proselytize, Mormon, Jewish, Muslim, and other nonevangelicals in the military, encouraging them to embrace their conservative Christian, often fundamentalist, approach to religion.

On other fronts, creation scientists continue to challenge modern science head on with Web sites and textbooks that treat the creation of the universe in biblical terms, a sort of science based on the theory of

Intelligent Design, that seems very strange indeed to those trained in traditional scientific method. In addition, there has been an increase in the number of and enrollments in evangelical and fundamentalist institutions of higher education. Adding itself to the traditional bastions of fundamentalist and evangelical learning such as Jerry Falwell's Liberty University and Bob Jones's eponymous university, a new college called Patrick Henry College in Purcellville, Virginia, was established in 2000. Its Web site proclaims that its explicit mission is to "prepare Christian men and women who will lead our nation and shape our culture with timeless biblical values" in order "to aid in the transformation of American society by training Christian students to serve God . . . through careers of public service and cultural influence."[13] Many liberals and non-Christian Americans may feel a chill at that rhetoric, which strikes them as a code for an underlying agenda of injecting an explicitly right-wing Christian interpretation of religion into our governmental structure and our legal system, but these Christian institutions are well funded and growing.

In fact, most liberals during the 2004 election cycle seemed shocked that around half of their fellow citizens seemed suddenly to be speaking a language and using a vocabulary that only a few years before had belonged primarily to what they considered insignificant fringe groups of the far right.

Of course, the emergence of fundamentalism into the mainstream of American culture was not really sudden, though it may have seemed that way to liberals who were watching other things for the past twenty years. The way of the modern evangelicals had been prepared for over a hundred years by Christian fundamentalist preachers and theologians, who began reacting against modernism as early as the late 1800s.[14] American history is shot through with religious rhetoric, from the writings of the earliest Puritans through the various Great Awakenings that swept the country with religious fervor from time to time, but the current rhetoric is something new. Though it may remind some of the fulminations of the seventeenth-century Massachusetts divines, the recent wave of religious fervor has a distinctly modern, antiscientific spin that makes some liberals long for the relatively progressive thinking of Cotton Mather.

How do we account for the fascination with fundamentalism, with its attendant belief in creation in seven calendar days and in a horrific culmination of history in an apocalyptic upheaval? Even more perplexing, especially to traditional or liberal religionists, is the question of how so many modern people can be attracted to a form of religion that, to them, seems the very antithesis of religion. That is, the heart of Jesus Christ's gospel message, as he himself expressed it, is to love God and love even your enemies, but from the outside, fundamentalism seems to manifest itself as hatred, divisiveness, and revenge. The paradox is not unique to Christianity. Every chapter of the Koran refers to "Allah the merciful," and Judaism's emphasis on ethics is exemplary among world religions, and yet, in each of these religions a group has risen to prominence whose ideologies and interpretations of their sacred scriptures seem to promote fear, hatred, separation, and even murder. The fundamentalist traditions in all three sects, writes Karen Armstrong, "have neglected the more tolerant, inclusive and compassionate teachings and have cultivated theologies of rage, resentment, and revenge" that now, according to extreme Islamists, sanction even the most horrendous acts of terrorism.[15]

Perhaps what happened was something like this: in the past fifty years or less, enough people became disgusted enough with the confusion, anomie, and secularism of modern culture that, in desperation, they turned to those who seemed to offer a clear path out. One verse of scripture, John 3:16, would suffice to solve all the world's ills. It is a seductive idea: "Believe thou on the Lord Jesus Christ" and all personal, political, and economic dilemmas go away. While some would say this approach avoids the real complexity of the world we have created, fundamentalism does offer its adherents a clear, inflexible standard for values and behavior in a world that offers little but modernist relativism and confusion as an alternative. Fundamentalism's simplicity is attractive in itself.

As Martin Marty, Nancy Ammerman, Karen Armstrong, Gilles Keppel, and many others point out in their scholarly works on fundamentalism, what the various fundamentalist movements in world religions all have in common is that they are reactionary in nature. All of them evolved as reactions to the confusion and secularization of life, which they see as inevitably intertwined with modernism. In the case of Islamic fundamentalists, this was complicated by centuries of often-brutal foreign intervention in the form of colonialism, a colonialism that was racist in nature and smug in its confidence that the modern, Western (read "white") way of life was superior in every way to the primitive "infidel" lives of the colonized people.

Islamic fundamentalism's rejection of the cultural hegemony of the West, therefore, is not just a religious movement. It sees itself as involved with cultural and ethnic preservation, an attempt not to lose the Islamic world's fifteen-hundred-year tradition of learning, scholarship, art, and religion to the tsunami of Western cultural values that continues to enter and dominate their society through television, McDonald's restaurants and Western fashions, even after the apparent fall of colonialism as a political enterprise.

Jewish fundamentalism in Israel is also, at root, a rejection of the modern worldview in favor of a religious worldview. It was tempting to see the establishment of the modern state of Israel as a reincarnation or culmination of the biblical narrative of God giving the land of Palestine to the ancient Jews and to assume that the modern state should occupy the exact same geographic space as the biblical land, as if the Bible were a real estate deed rather than a wisdom book. Thus, history seemed destined to repeat mythology in a literal way.

The ultimate irony of this situation, of course, is that the most fervid enemies in the current international cultural and military wars—the Islamic, Christian, and Jewish fundamentalists—in fact have the most in common. Hard-line Islamic, Christian, and Jewish fundamentalists all reject the secular materialistic worldview of modernism and are trying to replace it with a religious worldview based on their idiosyncratic readings of their own scriptures. The problem, of course, is that as they currently perceive their missions, their worldviews are not mutually compatible and may even call for their enemies' destruction.

Complicating the world situation even further, we need to note again, is the fact that it is not only religious fundamentalists who are disappointed in and angered by modernism. Many liberals, too, even atheists, see the shallowness and vulgarity of the modern world and yearn for deeper, more spiritual values, but for the moment they have lost their way and even their voice. They seem to have accepted the use of the word *liberal* as a pejorative, and have been unable to recapture the key terms of the cultural debate from the fundamentalists, who, on all sides, seem to be growing increasingly militant, whether that militancy takes the form of verbal invective on talk radio, individual suicide bombers, or national armies fueled by the rhetoric of Armageddon. Somehow liberals have allowed words like *God, religion, truth,* and *values* to be appropriated and narrowly defined by the religious right, who insist that their interpretation of these words is the only allowable one.

In a sense, the situation in our post–9/11 world is similar to the one that existed after the destruction of another famous tower, that of Babel. Before the destruction of that tower, the people of the world spoke only one language. They came together on a large plain and built a city of brick and, to make a name for themselves among the people of the world, they built a great tower with which they hoped to reach the sky. And God, watching from heaven, saw that because humans spoke with one voice, there would be nothing they could not do. So he came down from heaven and confounded their language and scattered them over the face of the earth. The people were forced to stop building the tower and, babbling languages others could not understand, they were dispersed.

The story of the tower of Babel takes up only nine verses in Genesis (11:1–9), but it is one of the best known of the early biblical narratives because in its short, swift drama it seems to illustrate so much about human aspiration and arrogance, about the power of God and about human limitation. That it is also an etiological myth, explaining how the various people of the world came to speak different languages, seems almost incidental, but in fact, for our purposes, it is the crux of the story as we try to figure out the confusing Babel that today surrounds our talk about God.

In a sense both literal and figurative, modernism built its own tower of Babel. The iconic building of modernism was the skyscraper. The name itself is hubristic, and architects throughout the twentieth century competed to see who could construct the tallest one. The Empire State Building reigned supreme for many years, then the World

Trade Center towers, until they in their turn were replaced by the even higher Sears Tower in Chicago, which was kicked out of first position in 1996 by the Petronas Towers in Kuala Lumpur. Earlier in the century, Frank Lloyd Wright even drew speculative designs for a mile-high tower. Freudian critics comically spoke of these towering skyscrapers as being a penis display on a massive scale, but perhaps a biblical criticism could bring us closer to the mark of what lay behind this urge to build toward the sky.

If modernism was the triumph of scientific thinking, the ultimate extension of Protagoras's old maxim, "Man is the measure of all things," then the skyscraper was the expression of just how far humans could extend their reach toward the realm of the gods. Modernism was the "one language" we spoke in common, an international language of commerce, materialism, and technology. Coldly rational, driven by the bottom line, it was a transcultural language. Listening to progressive modernists speak, one could sense the same feeling of arrogance that the inhabitants of ancient Babel showed. Nothing is impossible to human initiative, runs the modernist dogma. One day science, that is, the unaided human mind, will solve all life's problems and dilemmas; we will explore all corners of the universe; the book of all knowledge will be opened to us. Some even speculate that we will be delivered from our ultimate human destiny, death, through the eventual triumph of science.

We should know better than to think like this. As the story of Babel, not to mention the ancient Greek tragedies, shows us, whenever the human ego gets this inflated, the gods exact a terrible vengeance. From the modernist perspective, the God of the Babel story could be seen as a frightened bully who gets nervous, even jealous of his own creation, as that tower approached his heaven. But if we read the account of Babel as a cautionary tale about human, not divine, hubris, then the action of God in the story is similar to his revelation of himself to Job in the thunderstorm. That is, it is the business of the divine to remind us humans that we are not the whole show, that we are not the measure of *all* things. Some things may measure us.

When the short story of Babel concludes, we recognize the human world as it is, confused, scattered, and stuck on the plain of existence, not living in the heavens. It is as if humans need reminding, constantly, that we are, after all, human. We can forget that so easily, and one function of the gods is to remind us of that unalterable fact continuously. When we neglect the gods, they will come looking for us, and they will be implacable.

And so, when we say that the various fundamentalisms that are rising up today are intimately linked to modernism, this is what we mean—that when human hubris grew too great, when the human ego got overinflated by what it thought it could do, some message had to come from the realm of the gods to demonstrate to us the limits of our own powers. Sometimes nature provides that reminder in the form of earthquakes, tsunamis, and hurricanes that, like the theophany in *Job* and the story of Babel in *Genesis,* remind us of our status by simply overwhelming our engineering marvels and scattering human beings and our human constructions like straws. Sometimes, however, it is the other side of our own human psyche that speaks with the voice of this jealous God. As Jung pointed out in his works, the human psyche, or soul, seeks balance and wholeness. When one side, or one function, of the self gets too overdeveloped, too powerful for its own good, it calls forth its opposite, as it were, to restore balance.

Applying this principle to the upsurge of fundamentalism, we could say that just so far as modernism reached toward a godlike status for itself, it called forth its opposite, fundamentalism, to redress the imbalance. Insofar as modernism was scientific, fundamentalism would be antiscience; insofar as modernism was rational, fundamentalism would fly in the face of rationality and insist on faith alone. As modernism would be material, fundamentalism would be spiritual. And so on. It is like a law of physics, with each action calling forth an equal and opposite reaction, as if the collective human mind would not allow the modern world to go on ignoring religion any longer, and so, to get the modern world's attention, the religious function of the psyche had to emerge in the strident, absolutist form that it has in various world religions.[16]

If this is too speculative, then we can at least say that, like the people after Babel, we no longer speak the same language when we speak about religious matters. Even though many of us use the same words, like *God, religion, sacred, evil,* we do not understand anymore what we mean by those words. When I hear fundamentalists say *God,* I wonder what that word has to do with the God in whom I believe. Their God seems to speak to them clearly, mine in more cryptic terms. Their God seems to be a literalist, mine seems to be a poet. So whose *God* is God? Which usage of the word names the deity? Fundamentalists claim exclusive ownership of *God* and other words related to it, and their ironclad certainty can intimidate those whose religious function is weak or atrophied. Modernists don't seem concerned with who or how *God* is used. They believe that, eventually, religion will pass away and that God will be seen as a fiction, so we may as well dispense with religious vocabulary altogether. Religious language, they say, is simply an archaic way of saying things we can say better through science. But what are we who are neither extreme fundamentalists nor extreme modernists to do? What about those of us, a majority I suspect, who find ourselves stuck in the middle of this horrendous war of words? Deprived of religious words' broader meanings by those who would define them narrowly, what shall we call our understanding of the ultimate power or being of the universe? And if *religion* can mean only what the extreme right wants it to mean—a narrow, dogmatic straitjacket—or what the strict modernists mean—mere superstition—then how can the rest of us be "religious" as we most desperately need and want to be? It all hinges on the way we approach the loaded word *truth,* which we will take up next.

3 : Truth

THE CONFLICT between fundamentalism and modernism forms a kind of geological fault line beneath our contemporary cultural conversation. As with the tectonic plates hidden beneath the earth's surface, there is a constant tension between these two powerful ways of thinking about the world. They press against each other with enormous strength, usually holding each other in check. Occasionally, however, the cultural pressure becomes too great, resulting in seismic tremors around certain key "earthquake zones," such as evolution versus creation science or anti-abortion versus pro-choice. Because of the way we have structured the debates around these issues, there can only be two sides, so, like citizens on the West Coast, we live ready to dive under the nearest table when the temblors start.

We have reached an intellectual impasse because each camp has decided that it, and it alone, possesses truth. But *truth* is a notoriously slippery word. We sling it about as if we knew what it meant, as if it were plain and simple, when, as Oscar Wilde quipped, it is rarely, if ever, either.

In order to understand the intellectual trench warfare going on between modernism and fundamentalism, it helps to move back in time and trace a radical shift that took place in our perception of what *truth* means. This shift took place in fairly recent times, and it resulted in a profound change in the way we understand the troublesome words *true* and *truth*. In order to understand that change, we first need to look at larger linguistic changes that have taken place in the past five hundred years. The word *truth* has been around a long time, but the linguistic context in which the word is used has changed profoundly, as has language itself.

Simply defined, language is an oral signaling system. People may supplement their vocal sounds with gestures and facial expressions, but language is primarily spoken. In those cultures that become literate, like ours, writing derives from oral language, and, at least at first, tends to reflect patterns of speech. Linguists make a distinction between cultures that are primarily oral and those that are primarily textual, and that distinction is vital to understanding how the word *truth* has gotten a new meaning in modern times.

Through the vast majority of human history, primary orality was the rule. First of all, most human languages never developed literacy, and in those that did, when writing came in, it was modeled on speech. The earliest epics of the Greeks, for example, derived from generations of oral storytellers who passed heroic tales down through the centuries. As a result, the *Iliad* and the *Odyssey* contain large numbers of oral tropes and memory tricks that are the stock-in-trade of the oral storyteller, catchphrases like "rosy-fingered dawn" or formulaic descriptions of the "wily" Odysseus, which help the storyteller link the pieces of the epic in memory. Even the written *Dialogues* of Plato are influenced by speech, taking the form of simulated transcripts of conversations between Socrates and his interlocutors. Similarly, the earliest portions of the Hebrew scriptures were based on oral traditions handed down between 1900 B.C.E. and about 900 B.C.E., when they were written down, complete with all the redundancy, poetry, and contradictions that we notice in print but that pass by our ears without comment. Likewise, the earliest versions of the Christian gospels were based on the *kerygma*, the oral transmission of the story and spoken words of Jesus down from the apostles through the next generations. With the exception of his once leaning down and enigmatically tracing something, probably letters, in the sand, Jesus himself did not write anything (cf. John 8:6). Though he was apparently literate, the most common refrain in the gospels is "Jesus said," and we are to "hear" the word of the Lord, not read it. In secular writing as well, we notice a marked tendency for letters and poetry written prior to the invention of the movable-type printing press to follow oral patterns and to be remarkably careless about such print conventions as spelling, punctuation, and regular grammar. Simply put, people wrote as they spoke, and if their accent had a burr in it, so did their writing.

The reason for this is that prior to mass literacy, which really only gained ground after the Reformation, most writing that existed was meant to be heard rather than read. The written record was to assist oral performance. There is evidence, for example, that Chaucer performed his early works aloud to court, and there are many medieval illustrations of people, often women, sitting in a circle listening to someone read out loud from a manuscript. Even private reading was apparently meant to be heard rather than seen. Augustine, writing in the fourth century C.E., remarks on an odd quirk of his friend and teacher, Ambrose, that he habitually read in silence rather than out loud. The fact that Augustine felt this worthy of comment is evidence that even when reading alone, one was expected, as a rule, to vocalize.[1] In Islam, medieval Muslim scholars decreed that in studying the Koran one had to *hear* the sounds of the holy text, even if reading to oneself.[2] In fact, the very word *Koran* means "recitation."[3]

Today, however, one of the first things we say to children learning to read privately is "don't move your lips." Reading has become primarily visual, not aural. Obviously something has changed, and the historical crux of it was the invention of the movable-type printing press in 1450 and the gradual, but inexorable, shift of Western culture from primary orality to primary textuality.

In his groundbreaking study of oral versus written language, the linguist Walter Ong exhaustively parses out the differences between these two related but distinct modes of communication.[4] The oral-aural man's "whole response to actuality is . . . organized differently than typographic man," says Ong.[5] Oral cultures and print cultures have quite different orientations to language, and, therefore, to social and physical reality.

For starters, the spoken word requires *presence.* That is, both speakers and listeners must be present to one another in space and time. The spoken word is a social event that takes place in time and is ephemeral. The spoken word begins, continues, and then ends, and when it ends, it has disappeared except as remembered by the hearers.

Those in the present audience are not simply passive; they engage in dialogue with the speaker, answering back, asking for clarification, responding with gestures, sounds, and affirmations. In nonliterate societies, information transmission relies on memory, so the language of nonliterate people tends to be full of mnemonics. Oral speech contains familiar tropes, repetition, rhymes, dominant rhythmic patterns, and narrative in order to aid the memory in retaining what was said. "In an oral culture, the mnemonic procedures which we today ordinarily associate with verse are not only part of ordinary . . . verbalization but actually determine thought structures as well," says Ong.[6] In order to retain information, one must learn things "by heart." To learn by heart calls on us to internalize information in a way that storing learning in written form does not. We all know people who can recite lines of poetry from memory but who sound like digitalized recordings, rattling out the verse like mechanical parrots. Those who have truly learned the verse "by heart," however, infuse the remembered words with all the passion and emotion that the phrase "by heart" implies. It is a holistic way of learning and knowing. In an oral culture, one speaks from the heart, the center of the self, not just the head.

As a result, oral language tends to be highly personal. It is impossible to separate the words from the speaker. As the performance poet Kurtis Lamkin says, "The muscle of the tongue is connected directly to the heart."[7] And because spoken language relies on memory and repeated oral transmission, it is highly malleable. Information transmission in oral-aural cultures is somewhat like living in the midst of a constant game of Telephone, where messages get transmuted from teller to teller. Though anthropological studies show a surprisingly high degree of continuity and constancy of messages, even in long memorized passages of epic poetry that may amount to thousands of lines, there is no absolute method of verifying the accuracy of transmission of messages.[8] The message is only as accurate as the messenger's memory. This is both good and bad, of course, from our point of view. The negative is that much is lost. When languages go extinct with their last speakers, as happened with Cornish in the eighteenth century and with some Native American languages more recently, entire bodies of cultural lore go extinct with them. On the other hand, from the point of view of our study of religious truth, the orally transmitted story may adapt and change to meet changing realities since it is not locked into the rigid form of a copied text whose cultural references may be a thousand years out of date. This is another sense in which the oral word is *present;* the orally transmitted story is always contemporary, even if set in the dream time of the beginning.

Much religious language was originally experienced as spoken word. The gods spoke, they did not write to humankind. In the early books of the Hebrew scriptures, God *calls* and *speaks* directly to Adam, Noah, and Moses, who engage in dialogue with him. Muhammad is overwhelmed by a vision of the angel Gabriel and then, because he himself could not write, dictates the revealed words of Allah. For over twenty-one years, he spoke his visions and created the Arabic language's classical masterpiece. The Buddha's teachings, like Muhammad's and Jesus's, were originally oral, only later being written down in the Pali canon and the Dhammapada. The Upanishads take their title from the Sanskrit word *sad,* which means "to sit," implying that a learner sat at the feet of a teacher and heard his teaching. The texts that follow in these traditions, though written down, follow the conventions of orality, that is to say, they are poetic rather than scientific, using metaphors, mnemonics, and narrative to convey their truths. When we try to approach them as written texts, that is, as texts that were meant to be read with the eyes rather than heard with the ears, we can fall into all sorts of problems, of which, as we'll see, literalism is only one.

The shift from primary orality to primary textuality was a slow one. Because literacy and orality existed side by side in Western civilization for so long, the change is also incredibly complex, but reviewing the transformation, even briefly, will help us understand why the word *truth* is giving us so much trouble today.

Writing as such was invented by the ancient Sumerians about 3,500 B.C.E. for the purpose of keeping track of grain brought into the cities as a primitive form of taxation. (Poets and novelists invariably cringe when they realize that writing was invented, in effect, by accountants, but it is true.) Whether in cuneiform, hieroglyphs, pictographs or a true alphabet, written language has certain characteristics that set it apart from oral communication. For starters, writing creates a more or less permanent record of communication. As the ancients said, *Verba volant, scripta manet,* "spoken words fly, but writing remains." Thus, the most salient characteristics of orality, physical and temporal presence, are no longer necessary. Writing allows the communicator and his intended audience to be distant in time and space. Indeed, in the case of recovered archeological fragments, the distance may be thousands of years. At first, and for a very long time, as we've mentioned, writing tended to follow the conventions of speech, serving mainly as a record of talk. Among the ancient Greeks, who had an alphabet from about 700 B.C.E., we can see the beginnings of the shift to textuality. Even though the *Dialogues* of Plato are written in a pseudo-dramatic form, the logic in them is more linear, less discursive than real dialogue would be. It is clear that Plato simply sets up a bunch of fall guys who punctuate Socrates' arguments with questions and dumb replies. But we have not made the move to primary textuality at all. Greek education remained based on memorization of the epics, and as Aristotle's *Rhetoric* shows, one was expected to hold forth in oral, not written, argument in the public square. This was true for the Romans as well, and we read in Cicero how important it is for a man of affairs to be able to carry himself well in public speech and debate.

After the fall of the classical world, the European Middle Ages continued with only marginal literacy. Pockets of literate monks and nuns preserved manuscripts, laboriously copying them and transmitting them in a painstakingly slow way, but by and large, even among some low-level clergy, literacy was a rarity. As a result, the experience of the Word remained largely oral in the Middle Ages, and we see evidence of primary orality in the Gothic profusion of legends, extrascriptural folk tales of Jesus and the saints, and a credulity about miracles that astonishes the postscientific mind. The truth was spread by the emerging preaching orders, such as the Dominicans, the *ordo praedecares,* who became famous for their sermonizing, not their writing. The fluidity, imagination, and creative innovation of the times show that it was not, by any means, a dark age at all, but it was definitely not an age of the book in our modern sense. It is true that books held great prestige as objects. The value placed on medieval manuscripts, reflected in their ornate covers and magnificent illuminations, was tremendous, but such books were rare. Nobility invariably had their portraits painted with their hands clasping a book, or their fingers tucked inside pages as if they were disturbed from their devotional reading, but books were items of conspicuous luxury. When Petrarch died, he had only a couple of hundred books in his personal library, and that was considered one of the largest libraries in Europe at the time. We were clearly not yet in the Age of the Book. That would have to wait until after the Renaissance and the invention of the printing press.

To understand the significance of the revolution wrought by Gutenberg and its effect on our understanding of what *truth* means, we have only to think about the amazing transformation of our own society in the past twenty years as a result of the personal computer and the Internet. A new means of communication comes on the scene and, almost overnight, everything about the getting and transmitting of information changes. Indeed, the very definition of *information* changes.

Gutenberg was not the inventor of printing. Woodblock printing existed prior to his invention of movable type, but it was a slow, labor-intensive process, involving carving out an entire page of print from a single piece of wood, in reverse, then inking the block and printing sheets of paper. Gutenberg's innovation in the mid-1400s was spurred by the Catholic Church's need for mass quantities of printed material, in particular printed indulgences, which, in light of this book on religious language, is yet another irony in our story, for the printing press and the spread of the Protestant Reformation were to be inextricably linked.

Gutenberg actually got his start in mass production by making souvenir mirrors for sale at the shrine at Aachen.[9] Like Chaucer's famous Canterbury pilgrims, those who came to Aachen were religious tourists, in the market for knickknacks. Medieval pilgrims could also receive an indulgence, a special dispensation guaranteeing time off from their suffering in purgatory. Indulgences were given for completing a pilgrimage to a holy place, for special religious observances, or, eventually, for simple cash donations to the church. To verify that they had completed their pilgrimage devotions and so had earned their dispensation, pilgrims received a piece of paper, also called an indulgence. Because of the volume of pilgrims, hundreds of thousands of these indulgences were needed. Printing them on woodblock, of course, was the only way to produce the necessary numbers prior to Gutenberg, but xylography, as it was known, had serious shortcomings. First of all, the blocks were difficult to produce, were prone to cracking, and wore out fairly quickly. One chipped letter meant recarving the entire plate. Gutenberg's genius was in realizing that movable cast-metal letters set in frames could be organized and broken down quickly to allow relatively speedy and cheap production of printed texts and books. He seems to have gotten the idea from the way playing cards were produced, using movable pips (hearts, spades, clubs, and diamonds) on a frame to produce the different numbered cards. Substituting the letters of the alphabet for the pips, he then devised a press that, according to legend, was inspired by a lever-driven wine press he saw. He set up shop in Mainz, called on his mass-production and marketing experience, and the rest, as they say, is history.

Within fifty years, printing had spread to virtually every country in Europe, and in the first hundred years, the period known as the *incunabula*, tens of thousands of volumes were produced. It was history's first truly mass medium.

As it turned out, Martin Luther, the great Reformer, had the good fortune to be born some thirty years after the invention of the printing press. Had he been born before it, his reform movement likely would have withered and died like those of Jan Hus in Bohemia or the Lollards in England, suppressed by the Church, sometimes violently. In fact, as it played out in the sixteenth century, the Reformation triumphed because of the evolution and rapid spread of printing. The theological movement and the technology of printing grew up side by side, like fraternal twins, to the extent that the Reformation as we know it would have been unthinkable without the printing press. And, in the symbiosis of the new theology and the new communication medium, Christianity was, in important ways, essentially changed, for it was during the Reformation and the succeeding Scientific Revolution that European society shifted from being primarily oral to being primarily textual, and the implications for what we call religious truth were profound indeed.

According to Elizabeth Eisenstein's study *The Printing Revolution in Early Modern Europe,* the Reformation was "a movement that was shaped at the very outset (and in large part ushered in) by the new powers of the press."[10] Earlier reform movements (Lollardism, Jan Hus) failed because the Catholic Church was able to contain the reformers' messages fairly easily. The reform movements were local in terms of geography, and the spread of the reformers' ideas could only take place through word of mouth or via laboriously copied manuscripts, both of which were fairly easy to suppress. Thus, the earlier movements were never able to gain traction.

The case of Luther, however, was different. The original piece of paper containing Luther's ninety-five theses could have been easily ripped from the Wittenberg cathedral door, torn up and forgotten, but the thousands of printed copies of his challenges that soon fanned out over Europe could not be so easily contained, and thus, metaphorically speaking, the wildfire of the Reformation began to spread. The Reformation was, from the beginning, a movement intimately linked with literacy. The primary problem it addressed was the corruption of the authority of the Roman Church as a source of authentic teaching about Christianity. If the authority was corrupt, then where could one turn for spiritual guidance? Only to scripture. The texts of early Christianity bypassed what the reformers saw as fifteen hundred years of intervening ecclesiastical corruption between Jesus and the present, thus allowing individuals unmediated access to the word of God.

Understandably, printing was described by Luther and others as a gift from God, a providential invention of the Germans for spreading the Gospel. It became a powerful weapon against the imperial papacy, because it allowed for the wide and copious spread of reform ideas.

The nature of print also led to significant changes in Christianity itself, however. Mass-produced identical texts meant that a subtle emphasis was now placed on uniformity in worship. Prior to identical texts, manuscripts had slight variations, and in the absence of an authoritative single text, local traditions tended to flourish. In a largely oral culture, teachings passed by word of mouth and ear, and they could be subtly adjusted in response to varying situations. Local saints and observances had a huge part in the Christianity of the Middle Ages, as witnessed in Celtic Christianity, for example, by the large numbers of holy wells and local festivals that were transmutations of pagan sites and customs. And since pre-Reformation Bibles were all in Latin anyway, the actual texts were available only to the literate clergy. But printing vernacular texts had a transforming effect. Luther's German Bible and the subsequent Protestant push toward mass literacy gave German-speaking people a uniform vernacular religious language. The changes did not occur just in the emerging Protestant realms. In the Catholic world, the universal use of Latin meant that the printed *ordo missae* would be identical from country to country, and each day in each church the rotation of prayers and readings would be, literally, the same. (Eisenstein feels that this "fossilized" the Tridentine Mass of the Catholic Church and prevented further evolution and variation.[11]) Even manuals of mystical meditation, the most highly individual form of prayer, became standardized.[12] The Catholic Church understood the power of print in spreading the Reformation and responded by developing its infamous *Index* and instituting the imprimatur to be sure of doctrinal uniformity in printed texts. (This, like all censorship, backfired. The *Index* became a boon to the Church's enemies, for it gave all those interested in the "forbidden" ideas of the reformers a ready list of books. The Church even did the reform-minded a favor by highlighting the passages that it especially did not want read.)

Western culture was on its way to becoming text-based. One side effect of increased literacy among laymen was that the clergy no longer had a monopoly on learning, even in the field of theology. Once a layman could read the Bible, he or she could read anything, and could become more knowledgeable than the local clergy, even in the field of biblical studies. In addition, scholars of antiquity and the technical arts also used the new medium of print and spread access to those pagan and secular ideas, so that increasing numbers of people came to see that there were other truths, other ways of seeing and understanding the world than those handed to them through the authority of Rome or even of Luther and Calvin. The Catholic Church's medieval control of acceptable knowledge was quickly eroding, but so was that of religion generally.

The practice of reading the Bible in the home moved religion out of the public sphere in which one had to go to the church to hear the word of God from a clergyman in a pulpit. Instead, scripture study now became a private, intimate affair, with the *paterfamilias* serving as a domestic cleric. With all the authority of religion directly speaking in the home through the father, patriarchal family structures were reinforced. The family Bible, passed down from generation to generation, containing a record of marriages, births, and deaths, became a kind of cult object, a book that possessed sacred power both in itself and in the message it contained. In a sense, then, while the printing press led to a decentralization of external church control, it paradoxically brought about an increase in a sort of inner control, in which religion, which had been primarily a public performance, now permeated the domestic sphere as well, and, because of the nature of reading, became intensely private. The voice of God was now experienced as a voice within the private self.

The private nature of reading, as opposed to the public nature of hearing the word of God at a church with others, may largely account for the fragmentation of sects that became typical of Protestantism, as individuals reading the Bible on their own come to interpret scripture differently from their co-religionists and so split off to form their own branches of Christianity. Eventually, of course, the print revolution ushered in an essentially modern paradox—on the one hand, a tolerance and acceptance of divergent points of view, and on the other, the closed-minded quality of literalism, in which the letter or word as interpreted by the individual or religious hierarchy becomes the ultimate authority.[13] This latter process will take a few hundred years, of course, and will be made possible by the next major movement in European thought, the Scientific Revolution, which followed, and some would say sprang from, the Reformation, for the Reformation and the printing process that spread it opened the Western mind and encouraged bold new ways of thinking that led directly to the boldest way of all—science. And science would provide us with a new definition of *truth*.

The printing house became the crucible in which the oral medieval mind was transformed into the literate modern mind. Eisenstein notes how printing offices became epicenters, as it were, of open and liberal thinking. Except for purely sectarian presses, most printers would print anything, from any persuasion. They were, after all, businessmen. Even if a particular press was sectarian, however, it still had need of translators, editors, people who knew Latin, Hebrew, Aramaic, and Greek, and thus, willy-nilly, the printing house became a place of cultural mingling. As the scientific revolution advanced, mathematicians, cartographers, and scientists of all stripes, not to mention the illustrators and artists who collaborated on the books, were added to the rich mix of print-house hangers-on. A printing office like Michael Florios's in London during Shakespeare's time must have been like an open university or an ongoing high-energy seminar. So, as Eisenstein points out, even though printing was essentially a commercial venture, "the enterprising publisher was the natural enemy of narrow minds," and the printing house became "an intellectual crossroads . . . a meeting place, message center, and sanctuary" for intellectuals of all kinds.[14]

The general openness of mind ushered in by the Reformation and printing thus set the stage for the Scientific Revolution, in which the Reformation ideal of individual experience of scripture and the primacy of individual conscience led to the idea of individual observation of nature and finding a method of ascertaining the truth of that observation. The scientific method amounted to a new way of looking at and thinking about the world and how to know what in it was true. The most important invention of science was science itself, and, as we've said, science radically redefined what was meant by the old English word *truth*.

As with the Reformation, the emerging scientific worldview was spread by print. Sentimental legend has it that Copernicus was handed a copy of the first edition of his *De Revolutionibus* on his deathbed in 1543. True or not, the story illustrates the almost mystical importance given to printed books by the sixteenth century. Books became the vehicles through which the Scientific Revolution dispersed itself, and the mass production of books made scientific ideas difficult to suppress. Thus, even though Galileo was forced to recant his mathematical proofs of the rightness of Copernicus's heliocentric theory and was put under house arrest for the rest of his life, his printed books escaped the control of Rome and made their way to Protestant northern Europe, where science was destined to blossom and flourish.

As part and parcel of this new way of thinking and disseminating ideas, a new attitude toward language developed. Since the language of science par excellence is mathematics, first scientists and then others desired that ordinary language have the same qualities as mathematics, namely, precision, accuracy, linearity, and logic, qualities more properly belonging to print than to oral language. Early on, scientists made some significant stylistic and linguistic decisions.

In 1667, Thomas Sprat, secretary of the Royal Society of London for the Promotion of Natural Knowledge, wrote *The History of the Royal Society,* which had just been incorporated five years before. In these early days of science, an extraordinary group of Englishmen had been meeting informally to share their ideas. Founding members of the Society included chemist Robert Hooke and architect Christopher Wren, and soon the organization was to include the astronomer Edmond Halley and later the incomparable mathematician Isaac Newton. The seventeenth-century membership list is a veritable who's who of early science. Eventually this group earned the patronage of Charles II and became what we now know as the Royal Society. It is no exaggeration to say that these virtuosi ushered in the modern scientific age in only a few years of astonishing activity and that the Royal Society set a standard for scientific investigation for the whole world. But it wasn't just in science that they had an effect; they also proved influential in the history of language and shaped how we think of language's relationship to what we call truth. In a section of his *History* entitled "Their Manner of Discourse," Sprat recounts a conscious decision on the part of the early British scientists to pare down and simplify their language.

Modern science was born in the age of baroque art, when aesthetic tastes ran to extravagant ornamentation, but the budding scientists wanted none of that. They were after a new way of looking at the world and so they wanted a new way of talking and writing about it. They wanted the language of science to be plain and simple. Previous scientists, like the ancient alchemists, often devised codes, including anagrams and private languages, to hide their discoveries from others. Other early natural philosophers followed the euphuistic style of the times and wrote in prettified and poetic ways. The members of the new generation of scientists, however, feared extravagant speech would only get in the way of good clear science. Sprat writes, "unless they had been very watchful to keep in due temper, the whole spirit and vigour of their *Design* had been too soon eaten out by the luxury and redundance of *speech*." Their goal was "to return back to the primitive quality, and shortness, when men deliver'd so many things, almost in an equal number of words." They were particularly against the use of metaphor. So the Society demanded a new style of writing from its members, "a close, naked, natural way of speaking; positive expressions; clear senses, a native easiness: bringing all things as near a Mathematical plainness, as they can."[15] Because the purpose of the Royal Society, and of science generally, was to share knowledge in a cooperative quest to unlock the secrets of the universe, their linguistic goals were accessibility, clarity, and precision. The collective pursuit of truth demanded clear, unambiguous communication.

We often think of style as a mere ornament to the content of what we speak and write, but linguistic style can also determine content. In this case, the stylistic decision of the Royal Society ended up having a profound effect, not only on the way we talk and write about the world but also on the way succeeding generations have seen and understood what is true about the world. In the end, the attempt to bring language to "as near a Mathematical plainness" as possible gave us a new notion of what the word truth meant, and, in an odd way, made biblical fundamentalism possible three hundred years later. It all hinges on the shift from primary orality to primary textuality, which became definitive during this period.

The fundamental difference between an oral and a textual society is that in a culture that operates according to primary textuality, written speech becomes the model for spoken speech, not vice versa. As the technology of printing evolved after 1450, and as literacy became the doorway to social advancement for greater numbers of people in commerce, religion, and science, attitudes toward language shifted. Whereas in an oral culture, there is wide variety in accent, usage, and even vocabulary, in written speech there is much less. Printers had to make decisions about whose language to use and, once set, the book froze that language. Soon, the idea of a standard language took hold. That is, between the invention of the printing press and the mid–eighteenth century, linguists can trace a definite trend in European languages to try to set a single standard among all the competing varieties of a given language. The standard variety, it goes without saying, would be based on the grammatical structures and lexicon of the ruling classes, particularly those that congregated around the capitals of London, Paris, Rome, and so on, for it is a general rule of linguistics that there exist "prestige" varieties of languages that those who wish to associate with or join the monied and power classes must adopt or imitate. In England, this involved a conscious decision on the part of William Caxton, who established the first printing press in Westminster in 1474, to set in type the language of Londoners, in particular those who were called "the better-brought-up sort." In effect, this meant the East Midlands dialect spoken in the linguistic golden triangle of Oxford, Cambridge, and London, the seats of learning and power. Once East Midlands was established as the print standard of the language, those living in Northumberland or along the Welsh border would be expected to imitate it, at least when they were writing.

Gradually, in a development that is directly linked to the Reformation's emphasis on reading and to science's use of printing to spread its ideas, writing became the model for speech rather than vice versa, at least in countries where mass literacy took hold, and subsequently primary textuality became the rule for understanding language. As a result, language would no longer be simply a record of speech, including all the verbal tics and accents of the writer. Rather, a new ideal of language emerged, an ideal that standardized the language, made it submit to rules, and in the end changed our attitude about the very nature of language itself.

As we saw in Thomas Sprat's extract above, the Royal Society explicitly desired the English language to come "as near Mathematical plainness" as possible. The problem, of course, is that words are never as plain and simple as numbers, and the early scientists sensed this. Language, when you look at it, is hugely imprecise. For starters, words change their meaning over time, as a quick check of the evolving meanings of words like *buxom, promiscuous, salt,* or *electricity* will show. In addition, language often does not follow logic. Shakespeare's use of double and triple negatives, his verbalizing of nouns ("uncle me no uncles"), and other tics would send a modern grammarian up the wall, and yet Shakespeare was a master of the language as it was spoken in his time. So scientists and others had to figure out how to be clear in their writing in the way that mathematicians were clear, where each symbol had a precise, unchanging meaning and where the connections among the symbols were logical, consistent, and governed by rules. So the Age of Reason, with its desire for order, rule, and logic, turned its attention to language.

In some countries, academies were founded to address this problem. The Accademia della Crusca was founded around 1582 to oversee the purity of the Italian language, and they published an early dictionary (1612) about the same time the first dictionaries were coming out in English. Cardinal Richelieu, in France, founded l'Academie française in 1635 "to labor with all possible care and diligence to give definite rules to our language, and to render it pure, eloquent, and capable of treating the arts and sciences."[16] In England and America, similar academies were proposed in the 1700s by Jonathan Swift and John Adams, among others, but no such academy was ever established. Rather, in English-speaking countries, the same end was achieved by independent publishers. All of these entities were striving to bring to language the clarity, sureness, and precision of mathematics.

The first problem was what to do about language's irritating tendency to change. Writers in the seventeenth and eighteenth centuries were acutely aware of the linguistic differences that separated their modern English from that of Chaucer and Shakespeare, whose works, even then, were becoming hard to read. Grammar evolved, words changed their meanings, and even pronunciation varied widely from century to century. The mathematics of Pythagoras, from the seventh century B.C.E., however, were still clear. Why couldn't writing be like that? Obviously somebody had to set a proper way to spell, speak, and write the language, and people would just have to conform.

Beginning in the late 1500s and accelerating in the 1600s, English publishers brought out dictionaries and, increasingly, grammar books whose intent was to help people speak "correctly," that is, according to rule. Simple word-list dictionaries like William Bullokar's *Bullokar's Book at Large, written for the Amendment of the Orthography of English* (1580), and Robert Cowdrey's *A Table Alphabetical* (1604), which gave only spellings and synonyms for words, eventually gave way to Nathaniel Bailey's *Universal Etymological Dictionary* (1721), an etymological dictionary that treated language like an archeological dig and sought out the ancient roots of words to ascertain their true meaning. Its goal was exhaustive and scientific. The title page claims that it includes difficult words from virtually all the arts and sciences, including "Anatomy, Botany, Physick, Pharmacy, Surgery, Chymistry, Philosophy, Divinity, Mathematics, . . . & co." The range of subjects, in keeping with the eighteenth-century encyclopedic impulse, is truly impressive, and note how smoothly "Divinity" is lodged there among the other sciences, just before Mathematics. Clearly Bailey and his readers believed that theological words and concepts could be defined as clearly as those in other fields of knowledge.

The move toward a scientific approach to words reached its eighteenth-century apex in Samuel Johnson's 1755 *Dictionary,* which had the effect of giving people the impression that words had a single precise meaning, and the work tried to ensure that the meaning of words would remain, henceforth, fixed or frozen. Looking at the English language prior to working on his *Dictionary,* Dr. Johnson found it "Copious without order, and energetick without rules."[17] Johnson was, of course, correct. Swift also noticed the need for a spelling guide, noting "the foolish Opinion, advanced of late Years, that we ought to spell exactly as we speak."[18] A casual look today at any word in the *Oxford English Dictionary* will show that Swift was right, too. Prior to Johnson's *Dictionary,* there were multiple spellings of virtually any word from *abase* (abesse, abasse, abace, adbass, abase) to *zodiac* (zodiac, zodiake, zodiaque, zodyak, etc.). Because of primary orality, people simply didn't care. Print had not yet gained its authority over the language, but people like Swift and Johnson certainly thought it should. So Dr. Johnson went to work, and when he was done, he had established his dictionary as an all-knowing authority to which people referred as they would refer to mathematical or chemical tables to find the "correct" spelling and usage of a word. The modern prescriptive dictionary was born. In America, the phrase "I looked it up in Webster's" came to have the same force as consulting the oracle must have had to the ancient Greeks, perhaps even more, since the oracle spoke in riddles while dictionaries spoke plainly and simply the truth, at least about the spelling and meaning of words. Henceforth, the dictionary would provide a written authority for a word's precise meaning, and people had better conform their speech to the dictionary definition and pronunciation, or else.[19]

Spelling was only one issue that had to be resolved. As anyone who's ever studied it knows, English grammar is an unruly mess, too. So, in the eighteenth century, grammarians set out to reduce English to rigid rules, a task that was ultimately doomed since English, like all languages, is notoriously resistant to rule. Generations of schoolchildren and foreigners have been frustrated by trying to learn the supposedly hard-and-fast rules of English, which, if pedants are to be believed, have all the universal validity of the Pythagorean theorem, even if each of them has multiple exceptions. Robert Lowth, in his *Short Introduction to English Grammar* (1762), wrote that grammar teaches us whether given phrases or constructions "be right or not," and "the plain way of doing this is to lay down rules and to illustrate them by example."[20] Only in that way could people learn to write "accurately."

This was all, of course, part of the great epistemological sea change of the Age of Reason, and the attempt to ascertain, fix, and refine the language was perfectly in line with the general intellectual goals of the period. Just as the early scientists were using mathematics to reveal the underlying and unchanging laws of the natural world, so too the early linguists were attempting to remedy the untidiness of English as it was spoken and bring it to resemble the rational way of thought they championed.

The next great goal of the eighteenth-century dictionary makers and grammarians, after ascertaining the true signification of words and setting grammar rules, was to "refine" the language. Like scientists refining ores, they wanted to purify the language, ridding it of "cant," their word for slang. Slang, of course, is primarily oral and it is highly evanescent, here today, gone tomorrow, except for those few words such as *fun* (which Johnson found to be "a low cant word") that eventually make it into the mainstream and become acceptable. What "refining" meant, practically, in the eighteenth century was making the language more Latinate, forsaking good old Anglo-Saxon words for Latinized imports. In this, they were following scientists who were coining new English words from Latin and Greek roots and suffixes to name their new scientific discoveries. Words such as *telescope, microscope, vertebra, atmosphere, incubate, forceps, pendulum, stimulus,* and *lumbago* all enter the language during this time. Such was the prestige of Latinate scientific language that lexicographers even went so far as to alter some spellings of solidly English words, such as *dette* and *dowte* to *debt* and *doubt,* to make them look as though they were descended from the more prestigious Latin *debitum* and *dubitum,* even though they were unable to change the traditional English pronunciations. (Thus the maddening and otherwise inexplicable silent *b.*) Part of this tendency to Latinize, no doubt, came from competition with the sciences, where Latinate vocabulary came to have a more learned and authoritative feel to it than Anglo-Saxon–derived words, so that a word such as *dissertation* became preferable to *book.* In the end, "refined language" came to mean writing that approximated scientific writing as much as possible, while scientific writing, as we've seen from Sprat, itself tried to approximate mathematics, the language in which scientific truths were expressed.

The final goal of the linguists and grammarians of this period was to "fix" the language, that is, to freeze it and keep it from changing further. Part of the motive for this was self-serving, in that writers like Dryden, Swift, and Pope were aware that the English language had changed significantly in the hundred years since Shakespeare's death, not to mention in the three hundred since Chaucer's. Should the language go on changing, they realized, people in the future would have as much difficulty reading their eighteenth-century works as they themselves had reading the ancients. But part of the desire to *fix* English must also have had to do with the general search for immutable truths, enshrined in the mathematical formulas and Latin text of Newton's *Principia Mathematica*. As Pope wrote, after Newton we could look up into the heavens and see "the chaste, inviolable law" of the universe. Jonathon Swift's envy of the immutable and unchanging laws discovered by science may be the first example of a literary person having what a late–twentieth-century wag called "physics envy," the desire on the part of humanists to speak and write with the clarity, precision, and apparent authority of scientists.

When all was said and done, a new attitude toward language and how words mean had come into being during these years. Between about 1450 and 1800, language, at least the language of the learned, lost the fluidity and flexibility of oral communication and became fixed on the page. The model for language became the printed text rather than speech. Rather than living, breathing flesh, the word had become text. By the end of the Age of Reason, the cultural shift from primary orality to primary textuality was virtually complete in the Western world, and modern humans had become, in Walter Ong's wonderful phrase, "intensely alphabetized."[21] The written, not the spoken, word became the model for all speech, and the written word was now presumed to be unchanging, clear, and precise, and to contain immutable truth in the same way mathematical formulas did.

This new attitude toward language—that the ideal text should have a single meaning that should be fixed and immutable for all time—was inevitably applied to religious language, even scripture. In his preface to his 1768 *Liberal Translation of the New Testament*, Edward Harwood wrote that his intention was to "cloathe the genuine ideas and doctrines of the Apostles" in proper language. His method was scientific. He tells us:

> I *first* carefully perused every chapter to investigate and discover the one true meaning of the Author with all the accuracy and sagacity I could employ. . . . When I apprehended I had found the *true* signification of the Original, and the *precise*

ideas of the writer at the time he wrote, my *next* study was to adorn them in such language as is now written. . . . Elegance of diction, therefore, hath ever been consulted, but never at the expense of truth and fidelity, which ought ever to be sacred and inviolable in an interpreter of Scripture.[22]

Note Harwood's own italic emphasis on words like *truth, fidelity, inviolable,* and *precise,* as well as the telling phrase "one true meaning." Harwood's preface reveals a religious mind aspiring to the validity of science. Never mind that Harwood's verbose translation of the Bible is overdetermined and full of lengthy Latinate expressions and that it pales beside the strong Anglo-Saxon–derived vocabulary of the Authorized Version; Harwood's had pretensions to being more "true."[23]

By the late nineteenth century, this desire for religious language to have the specificity and universal, eternal validity of scientific language had taken root, and people seemed to have difficulty accepting the fact that not all language operated according to the same rules. They would have difficulty separating the "truth" of scripture, which was essentially oral and poetic, from the "truth" of science, which was essentially written and rational.

The early virtuosi had hoped for a more congenial outcome. As they pioneered the invention of science, they hoped that their researches into natural philosophy would eventually prove that the view of the world presented in scripture was "true," in a scientific sense. The chemist Robert Boyle (1627–91) wrote, "the [scientific] knowledge of the works of God proportions our admiration of them, they participating and disclosing so much of the unexhausted perfections of their Author that the further we contemplate them, the more footsteps and impressions we discover of the perfections of their Creator."[24] (Note Boyle's use of the word *Author* to refer to God. God, who *called* creation into being with his voice in Genesis, is now conceived as the writer of a book, further evidence of a shift to primary textuality.[25]) As Boyle's quote indicates, many early scientists believed that scientific contemplation of God's Nature would eventually confirm that what we believed all along was "true," that is, science's calculations would prove that the Genesis account of creation and the Bible's picture of the cosmos would be scientifically proven to be accurate.

By the middle of the nineteenth century, of course, it was clear that the opposite was happening, at least if *true* had to mean "literally true." The increasing sophistication of science had driven a widening wedge between the Bible, on the one hand, and knowledge on the other. When Darwin's *On the Origin of Species* was published in 1859, it became immediately clear how far apart these two ways of knowing and perceiving the world—science and religion—had become. There was now a new definition of the old word *truth,* a scientific one, that would not allow for both the Bible and the scientific view of the world to be true. If one were true, the new definition of *truth* said, then the other must necessarily be false. In the famous 1860 debate between Thomas Huxley and Bishop Samuel Wilberforce, it became clear that the word *true* had two different and quite incompatible meanings. In front of a packed hall in the Oxford Union, Wilberforce defended the Bible against what he saw as the onslaught of a godless science. Calling on his considerable oratorical skills, he used sarcasm, humor, and not much logic to "refute" Darwin's theory, about which he apparently understood very little in spite of having written a review of it. He made much of the absurd, to him, Darwinian fact that humans were descended from lower life forms, namely apes. Huxley rose in his turn and simply laid out the scientific facts in a rational, logical, and convincing way, concluding, with his own rhetorical flourish, that he would not be ashamed to claim an ape as his ancestor, but that he would be "ashamed to be connected with a man [like Wilberforce] who used his great gifts to obscure the truth."[26]

There we had it, two different "truths" colliding in the modern mind.

This problem had not seemed to come up before in history, and the truth of scripture seems not to have been challenged in quite this way. Why did the contradiction between faith and knowledge emerge now? Why only now did we have to choose? Why could there only be one kind of truth now, with everything else being false? What had happened to the word *truth*?

Spending a little time with the *Oxford English Dictionary* and its entries on the words *true* and *truth* can be quite valuable in sorting out all the senses in which we now use this troublesome word. The *OED,* for those not familiar with it, lists all the uses of particular English words in chronological order. That is, the earliest and most common historical usage of a word is listed first, along with a representative selection of text that illustrates that usage. The oldest dated usage is presumably the first time a given word appeared in a manuscript or book in English, so the dictionary becomes a kind of archeological repository where we can watch a word's evolution over time. Under *truth,* we find that our current notion of the word, as being a virtual synonym for *factual* or the way things really *are,* is a fairly modern one.

Truth had multiple meanings through history, but, interestingly, most of them had more to do with the believer than the thing believed in. By far the oldest sense of the word is the sense of being *true* to someone, that is, being steadfast, loyal, and dedicated to another. Variously spelled, sometimes with the Anglo-Saxon letter þ, or thorn, as *triewþ, trywþ, trewth, trouthe, trouth,* and so on from the tenth century onward, it shares its etymology with the word *troth,* a now-archaic word that is almost exclusively used with the phrase "to plight my troth," or to offer to give oneself in marriage, and so *truth's* earliest meaning had to do with personal relationship.

In most of its earliest uses, truth was not located somewhere outside the self in the external world, but deep inside. One owned one's truth as a personal possession and could pledge it to a spouse, a lord, or a friend. We might almost say that, for most of the word's history, to be "true" involved not a falsifiable intellectual proposition but rather a holistic commitment of oneself to something or someone, its archetype being interpersonal love. Knights were described as "true" and as possessing "trouthe," by which was meant their chivalric honor. In the feudal order of vassalage, one was true to one's lord in the sense of pledging one's self in a solemn way, and thus being "false" meant being disloyal.

So *truth* originally meant faith, trust, and confidence in something or someone. You could offer your truth to another, and you could repose truth *in* someone else, trusting the person to be honest, upright, and honorable in his or her relations with you. What you could not do, of course, was prove, scientifically, that someone was true, for the kind of truth we're talking about is taken on faith. Truth involved making a commitment rather than proving anything empirically. If we contrast a statement like "Sheila is true to John" with "The Pythagorean theorem is true," we see the difference. "Believing in" someone is quite different from "believing that" something is factually true. The older, original sense of being *true* is personal, holistic, emotional, and multifaceted; the other, modern one is propositional, rational, simple, and falsifiable.

Our modern sense of *true* is obviously related to the older senses, but with a significant shift in the location of truth. When we speak of something as being literally true, we now mean that its truth is objective, out there in the world rather than residing in a person. The more modern sense of *true* means that something we say conforms to an outer, not an inner, fact. While there was always something of this in the older usages of *true*, this new connotation of the word really arises and comes into prominence only in the late sixteenth and into the seventeenth centuries. In other words, the modern sense of *truth* coincides exactly with the rise of the literate and scientific worldview as we've described it above. In this sense, it seems to have been a translation of or synonym for the Latin *veritas*, whose primary meaning was "conformity to external fact." Since the fourteenth century, the word *verity* served as an English equivalent, and to verify something meant to see if it did indeed conform to the situation in the outer world. It is in this sense that a level line or a square corner is said by builders to be "true." And in this sense, directional headings can be "true" as in "true North." In these cases, a scientific instrument like a level, plumb bob, square, or compass is used to indicate that something external to the observer is "true." Truth now lies in the object observed, and so *truth*, the word, assumes a depersonalized, objective quality.

From fairly early on, *true* was used in religious contexts, not surprising given its earliest meaning. One could be "true" to God and could swear, before God, to tell the whole truth and nothing but the truth, but in this earlier sense, telling the truth seems to have meant a pledge of one's honor (trouthe) before God to be honest about one's perception of things. Similarly, the "truth" of God or of scripture in early writings also had the earlier sense of the word. Prior to the scientific usage of the word, the Bible was "true" in the way that a knight would be true to a lord, that is, scripture was steadfast, reliable, loyal, and true in the way that a life companion would be. In the same way, the Hebrew word translated into English as *truth* was *emeth,* which also had connotations of trustworthiness or reliability. To be *true,* in the oldest sense of the word, meant to be in relationship with someone, open to whatever changes, challenges, and growth might come about during the course of a lifelong relationship. Truth thus could be, even had to be, flexible and adaptable to new situations. The truth of one's relationship could grow or diminish over time, and nothing about it was frozen.

Thus, in a surprising way, the modern idea of truth, as an empirically verifiable and unchanging factual reality is a rather late usage, and not really "true" to the original sense of the word. And when people say something is *factually* true, or that the events in the Bible are literally *facts,* they also forget that even the word *fact* is from the Latin *facere,* which meant "to make," a linguistic acknowledgment that what we construe as a true fact belongs as much to the observer as to the things observed.

So *truth* is often qualified with an adjective such as *factually,* or the more troublesome, but telling, *literally.* By now, it should be clear that what we call "literal" truth could only arise after the invention of printing and after the Scientific Revolution, for the word *literally* means truth "to the letter," that is, truth that, like printing, is permanent and unchanging, is reproducible, and is external to the self. Literal truth is actually an idea that could only have come about after the shift from primary orality to primary textuality, and the idea of applying this new notion of truth to the Bible could only happen after God ceased speaking to people and began writing to them. That is, somewhere around the Reformation, as the quote from Boyle showed, God stopped communicating orally and began to be considered as an Author who wrote to us, rather than a participant in a dialogue who spoke with us. People read rather than heard the word of God, and the repercussions for religion were immense.

To understand *truth*, in a literal sense, meant we had to understand truth as something that was as fixed and unchanging as a word on a printed page. *Truth*, a word with so many rich connotations of morality, ethics, emotion, and relationship throughout its long history, thus got severely truncated in its modern usage. A word that was flexible, pliable, and loaded with interpersonal overtones became shrunken and desiccated thanks to its narrow application by a scientific textual world. But such was the power of science to demonstrate truth in this new sense that the new meaning of *truth* moved from being its secondary signification to its primary one.

And so, by the late 1800s, deep into the age of print and the age of science, when the Western mind had become "deeply alphabetized," the stage was set for biblical fundamentalism, as we know it, to arise. That is, the Western world was ready for an ideology or approach to religion that, while on its surface, seemed antiscientific, actually depended on the scientific worldview for its notion of truth. In the late 1800s, a certain group of people began to search scripture rather desperately for a kind of truth that scripture was never intended to deliver, literal scientific truth rather than the old trouthe. Their goal was to persuade the modern world, on its own terms, of the truth of their religion. And so we arrive at the troublesome word *fundamentalism*.

4 : Fundamentalism

THE WORD *fundamentalism* is tossed around frequently in the media and is used rather imprecisely to lump together several movements in the Western, Middle Eastern, and Far Eastern worlds that seem to have in common a God-centered worldview and a desire to make others conform to their beliefs and theocentric ways. The various movements—Christian, Islamic, Jewish, Hindu—have their unique characteristics and resist generalization when you look more closely at them, but all of them have in common that in one form or another they reject modernism. In fact, the word *fundamentalism* makes no sense except in contrast to the word *modernism*. Modernism is the soil in which fundamentalism took root and flourished, and modernism is perceived by all fundamentalisms as the enemy.

Christian fundamentalists would like us to believe that they represent the real "old-time religion," and that they have a direct pipeline back to Jesus and biblical times. Looked at historically, however, we see that Christian fundamentalism is a modern movement that is really unthinkable without modernism, for not only did it rise up in conscious opposition to modernism, it also implicitly accepted modernism's new definition of *truth*. It is important to remember that fundamentalism's historical roots are fairly shallow. Scholars generally agree that neither Luther nor Calvin, the great sixteenth-century reformers, were fundamentalists in the modern sense, though both were thoroughly Bible-based. Luther, at least early on, practiced the traditional fourfold interpretation of the Bible handed down from the early days of Christianity, and, a brilliant translator, sensitive to nuance in language, he was also an exegete who was interested in the underlying meaning of scripture.[1] Calvin's approach to the world allowed science to continue its work, while the Bible was regarded as an attempt by God to impart truths about matters other than geology or astronomy in a language that was not literal but symbolic. He suggested that those who wished to learn astronomy go elsewhere than the Bible to learn it.[2]

If the essence of Christian fundamentalism is a literal reading of the Bible—that is, reading the language of scripture as if it were scientific language expressing factual truth—then one of the first stabs at a modern fundamentalist-style reading of scripture came at the beginning of the scientific age. In the 1600s Bishop James Ussher attempted to reconcile biblical chronology with a modern understanding of history. Ussher famously totaled up the ages of various patriarchs in the Bible to arrive at a chronology of biblical events and, counting back from the present, came up with a date for the beginning of creation, fixing it on an October night in 3963 B.C.E. His effort may seem absurd to us, but it did represent an early attempt to apply a scientific, or quasi-scientific, logic to religion. However, it was not fundamentalism as we understand it.

In those early days of science, it was hoped that as science progressed, and as the methods of science were applied to biblical texts, we would arrive at a grand unified theory of the material and spiritual world, with no contradictions between the two realms. What was formerly believed through faith would soon be known through science. The great physicist Isaac Newton spent much of his career speculating on theology. As it turned out, of course, science and religion continued to diverge after this hopeful start and eventually arrived at an apparently unbridgeable chasm, but Ussher's experiment aside, the seventeenth and eighteenth centuries were still a long way from what we know as fundamentalism.

The actual beginnings of the full-blown fundamentalist movement came somewhat later, in the nineteenth century. It arose as an explicit attempt to counter science, whose truth seemed increasingly incompatible with the truth of the Bible. By the late nineteenth century, traditional Christianity felt threatened from many quarters, and the advance of science seemed to leave it at least in confusion if not in disarray. Because *truth* had taken on a restricted meaning, and because science was becoming the dominant worldview, science was viewed as progressive and future-oriented, while traditional religion was seen as regressive, clinging to the past. The continuous stream of scientific triumphs in the 1800s pointed optimistically toward a bright future for mankind. The 1851 Crystal Palace Exhibition in London saw four million visitors pass through its gates as ordinary citizens came to gaze at pavilion after pavilion of scientific and technological marvels. When the bombshell of *On the Origin of Species* fell in 1859, many people felt it was time to make a decision between religion and science. Which was true? As we've seen, it was hard for them to imagine truth as a matter of "both/and" rather than "either/or," since *truth* was by then understood in its new modern sense. The problem was this: the scientific story of the earth's creation and life's evolution was intellectually compelling. There was real evidence in the form of fossils and bones and geological strata. True, the evidence was incomplete; there were gaps, but science was proving to be such a powerful engine of arriving at verifiable truth that people felt the theory would inevitably be proven beyond doubt. The more the scientific story was compared to biblical truth, the worse the old book seemed to fare. The more people put Genesis under the microscope of modern scholarly methods, the more the Bible seemed to be, as Emily Dickinson wrote, "An antique volume written by faded men at the suggestion of Holy Spectres."[3] Where was the hard evidence?

The scientific challenge to scripture was mainly on two fronts. The first, as we've seen, was regarding Genesis. The second had to do with reconciling biblical miracles with what modern science had discovered about how the world actually worked. If the laws of nature, as described by science, were universal and inviolable, as most intellectually sophisticated people were coming to believe, then clearly the miracles recounted in the Bible had to be fictions. When confronted with physical impossibilities such as God's stopping the sun so that Joshua could continue the battle against the Amorites (Joshua 10:13), or with accounts of Jesus raising the dead, not to mention Jesus's own resurrection, the scientific mind had to be at least skeptical if it did not outright deny that the event could have happened. According to the best science, the laws of the physical universe were inviolable and simply did not allow for divine intervention. Proof was needed before we could affirm the truth of scripture. This attitude was so new that a new word was needed to describe it, and the scientist and Darwin-defender Thomas Huxley provided it. He coined the word *agnostic.*

In Huxley's essay entitled "Agnosticism and Christianity," we hear the voice of a modern scientist defending himself and other like-minded thinkers against the charges that they were "infidels." His defense is that to say one is an agnostic is simply to say that one needs to see hard evidence before he will acknowledge the truth of anything, scripture included. Science believes in nothing, if belief means faith without evidence. The only creed of science, says Huxley, is "absolute faith in the validity of a principle," and that principle is "that it is wrong for a man to say that he is certain of the objective truth of any proposition unless he can produce evidence which logically justifies that certainty."[4] Thus, he reserves the right not to deny the truth of scripture but to suspend his judgment about that and about the existence of God until such time as hard, scientifically verifiable evidence appears. Until then, it cannot be admitted as "true."

The second development that caused the rise of fundamentalism had to do with the Higher Criticism, which applied methods of historical and literary criticism to scripture. Coming out of Germany, this method represented a "scientific" approach to literary texts and the humanities. Highly philological, it began asking new questions of the sacred texts, questions drawn from new methods of literary criticism. J. G. Eichhorn (1752–1827) was one of the first to suggest that, based on the language and literary styles used, the Bible might profitably be studied next to other Semitic literatures. Following that lead, Julius Wellhausen (1844–1918) analyzed the Pentateuch and was able to show that it evolved from oral tradition at a date later than the historical Moses. The Higher Criticism concluded that the Bible, far from being a unified text, as previously believed, was actually a compilation of separate stories written by many hands over a thousand-year period and reflected not eternal truths but historical mythologies.

The prevailing view before the Higher Criticism was that scripture was more or less dictated by God through Moses and the prophets. The Higher Criticism, however, showed rather conclusively that the different books of the Bible conformed to the standards of various ancient literary genres, were written over a long period of time by several authors, and contained cognate or source stories parallel to stories in ancient Middle Eastern myths such as *The Epic of Gilgamesh* where there is a clear source story for Noah and the Flood. In a word, they showed that the Bible was as *mythological* as the stories of other religious traditions that, since they were myths, were regarded by modern Western minds as outright fabrications or mere superstitions—that is, not *true*.

Uneasy compromises were attempted to unify science and religion. Edmund Gosse tells the story of how his Victorian clergyman father, Philip, attempted to reconcile the theory of evolution with the Bible by claiming that God had created the fossils during the six days of creation and placed them on mountaintops and elsewhere as a kind of game to fool scientists. The idea was hooted at by both scientists and religionists, and the elder Gosse felt humiliated by friend and foe alike. It quickly became clear that in this intellectual battle there could be no middle ground. The stakes were too high on both sides. Which of these two irreconcilable worldviews would triumph and lead into the future? Which would remain standing, science—representing progress—or Christianity, which the modern world was coming to regard as ancient superstition?

It was out of this context of intellectual and spiritual debate that Christian fundamentalism as we know it arose. The nineteenth century was a particularly crucial moment in intellectual history. As we saw in the last chapter, a new definition of *truth* had taken hold in these years, and it admitted no plural truths or contradictory truths. Truth was truth, and it had to be verifiable by facts in the outer world. That much was accepted by all.

Therefore, the religionists realized that any serious religious counterattack to science would have to be scientific itself, or at least have pretensions to science. Thus, Bible-believing Christians, in order to reject or refute modernism, would actually have to use a form of modernist thinking, treating biblical texts as if they were scientific documents rather than myths. They could not do otherwise, for they, along with everybody else, had already implicitly accepted the modernist's definition of *truth* that made *myth* synonymous with *falsehood*. This idea took hold in spite of the fact that the Bible had been interpreted symbolically and allegorically for most of its history. In the nineteenth century, Christians felt compelled to prove that the Bible was true. So, they gradually developed a strategy. Their faith demanded that they assume that the Bible was true, in the modern sense of *truth,* so what remained was to prove its truth factually, even scientifically. Most people sense a brittleness in the fundamentalist position, and it comes from this initial assumption. The fundamentalist worldview, as it evolved over the past hundred years, is based on a very fragile premise, an iron-hard "either/or" foundation which, if it once cracks, has to give way completely. The Bible must be true, or it is nothing; and every part of it must be true or the whole of it is nothing. That is why contemporary fundamentalists seem to remain impervious to what the rest of us think of as reason. If they give an inch, the entire edifice collapses.

At this point the focus of our story moves to the United States. The movement that would become modern fundamentalism was, at first, a primarily northern and urban American phenomenon. Much of the early activity was centered at Princeton Theological Seminary, where scholars laid a foundation for fundamentalist theology.

Charles Hodge, and his son Archibald Alexander Hodge (who took over his father's post in 1878) and Benjamin B. Warfield were early leaders of the movement. Charles Hodge wrote *Systematic Theology* in 1876, the title suggesting a scientific approach to talking about God and religion. In fact, in his introduction, Hodge develops an analogy between physical science and theology, saying that whereas the former studies nature, the latter studies the Bible, using similar methods. Just as the world contains specimens which the naturalist goes about collecting and classifying, "so the Bible contains the truths which the theologian has to collect, authenticate, arrange, and exhibit in their internal relation to each other."[5] His goal, like the goal of the scientists of the time, was to bring the phenomena he was studying under the discipline of a science. "We must endeavor to bring all the facts of revelation into systematic order and mutual relation. It is only thus that we can satisfactorily exhibit their truth, vindicate them from objections, or bring them to bear in their full force on the mind of men."[6]

One can hear in the language's attempt to be scientific an implicit response to Huxley and other agnostics. If you modern scientists want proof, hard evidence, we will supply it to you with our no-less-rigorous science of theology.

Alexander Hodge in his *Outlines of Theology,* writes, "Theology in its most general sense, is the science of religion . . . Christian theology is the scientific determination, interpretation, and defence of . . . Scriptures," and "theological methodology provides for the scientific determination of the true method, general and special, of pursuing the theological sciences."[7]

We may feel they protest a bit much here. Theology had always been "scientific." In the Middle Ages, it was even referred to as the "Queen of Sciences," standing at the apex of the university education, after the *trivium* and *quadrivium.* But, like *truth,* the word *science* had also undergone a change in definition. Derived from the Latin *scire,* "to know," the word came into English after the founding of universities and was used very generally to refer to knowledge; anything known was a "science." Thus Chaucer could refer to the "science of good works" in his translation of Boethius's *De Consolatione. Science,* as "knowledge," was distinguished from *con-science,* or *conscience,* "that which accompanied knowledge," such as a sense of morality. As the universities developed, the word shifted in meaning somewhat to denote primarily a branch of formal learning, and for many years the term "the seven liberal sciences" was used synonymously with "the seven liberal arts" to mean the same thing. By the 1600s, however, as the physical sciences were coming into prominence, *science* came to be distinguished from the arts. *Art* at that time meant something like a technical skill that could be learned and applied, while *science* was reserved to refer to theoretical knowledge.

In the 1700s, the meaning was restricted further to mean "knowledge of things learned through direct observation," and by 1867 the word had got its modern meaning. W. G. Ward in *The Dublin Review* of April 1867, wrote, "We shall use the word . . . 'science' in the sense which Englishmen commonly give to it; as expressing physical and experimental science, to the exclusion of theological and metaphysical."[8]

So theology, which had its own long history as a "science," now felt challenged to begin speaking what was, in effect, a foreign language, the language of empiricism. But where was the kind of proof that would satisfy a Huxley? In a tactic that was to become common as fundamentalism developed, theologians such as the Hodges looked to the Bible for proof of its own inerrancy. That is, to summarize and not really oversimplify the logic, they would say that the Bible is inspired by God because it was given by God through the Holy Spirit speaking through the prophets. Therefore, since the unshakeable assumption of the movement was that God existed and scripture was his word, the Bible and the religion it expressed had to be true.

Archibald Hodge, in 1878, published a defense of this literal approach to biblical interpretation in *The Princeton Review* that became widely influential in the late century as the fundamentalist movement gained traction.

About this time, the idea of "premillennialism" also arose and eventually blended itself into modern fundamentalism. In traditional Christian thinking, the end of time will occur when Jesus fulfills the promise he made at the ascension and returns to earth. The book of Revelation says there will be a thousand-year period of tribulation, and traditionally it was assumed this would take place before the Second Coming. One of the first to try to pinpoint when this would occur was a self-educated American millennial prophet named William Miller (New York, 1782–1849), who used a peculiar reading of the Bible, in particular the books of Daniel and Revelation, to predict the future. His method was similar in a sense to Ussher's, except that instead of reading the Bible backward to learn history, Miller read it forward, using the enigmatic final book of scripture to predict the exact time of the Second Coming, which, he calculated, was supposed to occur in 1843. When it didn't happen as prophesied, Miller's followers were briefly disillusioned, but Miller and others recalculated his figures, set a new, precise date at October 22, 1844, and waited. On October 23, the 100,000 Millerites were disappointed again. Miller's, of course, was only the first of many such attempts to predict the end of time over the past hundred and fifty years, and as we'll see, Miller's preoccupation with the end-times and his approach to accepting even the symbolic book of Revelation as factual, became hallmarks of modern fundamentalism as it developed. The next wrinkle to develop in end-times thinking was premillennialism, the idea that a period of time known as the Tribulation would occur before Jesus's Second Coming and that the elect would be taken up into heaven *prior* to the chaos, not after it.

John Nelson Darby (1800–82), a British member of the Plymouth Brethren, articulated this idea of "the Rapture."[9] Darby was not able to rouse much of a following in his native Britain, but, like Miller, he found many followers in the United States on six speaking tours he conducted between 1859 and 1872. Based on texts from Matthew 24:37–41 and 1 Thessalonians 4:15–18, premillennialists began poring over the book of Revelation looking for signs and portents of the end. Since they believed that this book, like all the books of the Bible, contains literal truth, they felt certain that the apocalyptic visions of Revelation were fated to occur; we only had to recognize the time as it approached by seeing in contemporary world events what had been prophesied to come. The interpretation of texts was not applied to the Bible, which was assumed to be inerrant; instead, assuming Revelation to be a true account of the future, believers had only to interpret the "book" of history as it unfolded, matching events in it to the prophesied (and inevitably true) future.

As the ideas about literal interpretation of scripture and premillennalism began to constellate around the antimodernist movement, large numbers of people grew interested, and the mass rally was born. In 1875, the first large conference, Believers Meeting for Bible Study, was held. This group decided to gather regularly, and moved itself to Niagara-on-the-Lake, Ontario, where it became known as the Niagara Bible Conference and became a venue at which the big names of early fundamentalism preached and taught. Men such as J. H. Brooke, William Eerdman, C. I. Scofield, and other Presbyterian and Baptist preachers held forth to growing crowds.[10]

Similar gatherings took place and grew in influence and popularity. In 1880, Dwight Moody's summer retreat Bible conference was held at Northfield, Massachusetts, and other conferences were held in New York City (1878), Chicago (1886), Boston (1901), Chicago (1914), and Philadelphia and New York (1918).[11]

The movement began to institutionalize early. In 1886, the Moody Bible Institute was founded. Magazines, books, and journals of opinion started up and grew in circulation. William E. Blackstone published *Jesus Is Coming* in 1878, and in 1894 J. H. Brooke founded a magazine called, significantly, *Truth*. Large numbers of people, feeling traditional faith threatened, turned to these new-wave thinkers for certitude.

In 1893, the General Assembly of the Presbyterian Church in America voted on a mass resolution which clearly articulated the essential premise. It read, "The Bible as we now have it, in its various translations and revisions, when freed from all errors and mistakes of translators, copyists and printers, [is] the very word of God, and consequently wholly without error."[12] Note the focus on language. If there were errors, they had to be human errors of transmission. The ancient root texts themselves were error-free.

From the beginning, the movement set itself up as scientific. In 1895, American Protestant author Arthur Pierson wrote, "I like biblical theology that . . . does not begin with an hypothesis and then warp the facts and the philosophy to fit the crook of our dogma, but a Baconian system, which first gathers the teachings of the word of God, and then seeks to deduce some general law upon which the facts can be arranged."[13]

In 1909 *The Scofield Reference Bible* was published and quickly became "the standard reference point for fundamentalists for most of the century."[14] The Scofield Bible was the King James, or Authorized, Version of the Bible, laid out with scholarly apparatus such as commentaries and footnotes. It is an impressive and scholarly-looking book, collating the work of many scriptural interpreters and theologians. The King James Version of the Bible is printed in dual columns, down the middle and in the margins of which are cross-textual references to relevant passages elsewhere in the Bible. Subheadings, a pronunciation key, a chronology, and such scholarly apparatus as introductions to the individual books, maps, footnotes, an index, and concordance made the Scofield a powerful tool for home Bible study and a formidable weapon against modernism's claims that religion was mere superstition. The Bible, which had been widely read as a sacred narrative since Gutenberg, was now read as a scholarly scientific text. The Scofield Bible remained popular through the twentieth century and was recently revised and updated.

The movement still had no name, but the watershed period in the emergence of fundamentalism was 1910–15 and the appearance of a series of pamphlets that became known collectively as *The Fundamentals*. Financed by the Stewart brothers, who founded the Bible Institute of Los Angeles, it was distributed free to over 300,000 members of the clergy and interested parties. The pamphlets' goal was "to provide intellectually sound, popularly accessible defense of the Christian faith."[15] These pamphlets were eventually gathered into twelve volumes, which remain in print in a newer four-volume set. In the spirit of the original, many of the original pamphlets are now available free online in full-text form.[16]

A quick perusal of the table of contents of the four-volume set gives an indication of the approach and scope of *The Fundamentals*. Many of them set out explicitly to counter the Higher Criticism and modernism generally. It is not really fair, however, to say that the original essays were truly antiscience or antimodern, because from the authors' own point of view they were offering an alternative form of modern science, one that was religious in nature, based on the inerrant foundation of the Bible. Those sciences and areas of scholarship most important to the fundamentalist approach—archeology, biology, history, theology, and philology—are represented. Biblical archeology, as in the later search for Noah's ark, owes much to the early fundamentalists, who were seeking to find hard scientific evidence of the Bible's truth.

Reading through them nearly a hundred years later, it is clear that these pamphlets were motivated by fear of what modern science was becoming. That fear, of course, was understandable, but the attempts by the authors of *The Fundamentals* to set up an alternate Bible-based science reveal, in retrospect, a desperation. An essay by David Heagle, professor of theology and ethics at Ewing College, reflects the all-or-nothing tone of many the pieces. Heagle's essay is entitled "The Tabernacle in the Wilderness: Did It Exist?" In it, he tries to make a case for the historical existence of the biblical Tabernacle, which, the Bible says, was the model for the Temple in Jerusalem. The Higher Criticism had revealed that, in fact, the portion of the Bible that refers to the Tabernacle the Jews had in Sinai during their wanderings was actually written after the establishment of the Temple in Jerusalem. This meant, according to the new criticism, that the story itself was written as an ex post facto justification for the design of the Temple and that the original had never really existed. If that was so, then the Bible was not literally, historically true. The essay's subtitle shows the importance of this, for it is "A Question Involving the Truth or Falsity of the Entire Higher-Critic." If Heagle could show, scientifically, that the ark antedated the Temple, as said in the Bible, then, he hoped, the entire edifice of the Higher Criticism would collapse.

Heagle wrote:

> The question as to whether or not the old Mosaic Taberna-cle ever existed is one of far greater consequence than most people imagine. It is so, particularly because of the very inti-mate connection existing between it and the truth or falsity of the higher critic theory in general. If that theory is all that the critics claim for it, then of course the Tabernacle had no exis-tence; and this is the view held by at least most of the critics. But if, on the other hand, the old Mosaic Tabernacle did really exist, and the story of it as given in the Bible is not, as the crit-ics assert, merely a fiction, then the higher critic scheme cannot be true.[17]

A kind of trench warfare subsequently set in. The inflexible foun-dation of *The Fundamentals* is biblical inerrancy. The Reverend James

Grey, dean of the Moody Bible Institute, threw down that gauntlet in his pamphlet "The Inspiration of the Bible—Definition, Extent and Proof":

> In this paper the authenticity and credibility of the Bible are assumed, by which is meant (1), that its books were written by the authors to whom they are ascribed, and that their contents are in all material points as when they came from their hands; and (2), that those contents are worthy of entire acceptance as to their statements of fact.[18]

From the start, the enemy was secular science and its spawn, the Higher Criticism, but the real *bete noir,* then as now, was Darwinism. It is surprising how quickly Darwin's theory of evolution became the flash point of the debate. Because natural history, including Darwin, had moved into the classroom as the public school system expanded in the late nineteenth and early twentieth centuries, the emotional issue of the formation of children got entwined with the more intellectual debate of competing sciences. In words that sound as if they come from today's court cases surrounding creation science or Intelligent Design, the pamphleteers roundly condemn, even demonize, Darwin and Darwinists. Their vehemence is striking. The Reverend Henry Beach, in the pamphlet on the "Decadence of Darwinism," sees the theory of evolution as undermining the foundations of society, not to mention endangering the soul. He says "the most deplorable feature of the whole wretched propaganda" is the way that this evil science has infiltrated the school system. Not to be outdone, the Reverend Philip Mauro, in his general diatribe against "Modern Philosophy," wrote:

> It may be that, somewhere in the dark places of this sinful world, there lurks a doctrine more monstrously wicked, more characteristically satanic than this, which is now installed in our seats of learning and there openly venerated as the last word of matured human wisdom; but, if such there be, the writer of these pages is not aware of its existence.[19]

A modern nonfundamentalist reader who dips further into the texts themselves can't help but get uneasy about the scientific claims and the arguments of the various authors. Much of the reasoning strikes us as circular. For example, one argument for the inerrancy of scripture is that the phrase "The Lord saith" appears over and over again in the Bible, two thousand times according to one scholar. Therefore, one is led to the conclusion that scripture is true because it says in scripture that these are the very words of the Lord and, since the Lord is not a liar, if the book says "The Lord saith," then these are the very words of the Lord we are reading. QED. This is hardly an exaggeration or parody of much of what is in *The Fundamentals,* as we see by the following quote from Rev. James Grey, dean of the Moody Bible Institute: "But the strongest proof [of the truth of the Bible] is the declarations of the Bible itself and the inferences to be drawn from them."[20] And C. I. Scofield's reference Bible said that the main proof of Mosaic authorship of the Pentateuch was the fact that Jesus himself gave testimony to that fact in the New Testament. From a scientific point of view, this sort of evidence was all internal, with no external verification. It proved only that the Bible was self-referential, but not, strictly speaking, that it was "true."

The movement toward contemporary fundamentalism was solidified when, in 1910, the Princeton Presbyterians laid down the five doctrines that would become the real "fundamentals" of the movement. The unmovable foundation stones were (1) that the Bible was inerrant; (2) that Jesus was born of the Virgin Mary; (3) that Jesus, by dying on the cross, atoned for our sins; (4) that he rose from the dead; and (5) that his miracles were factual and really occurred.[21] These had to be taken as literally true.

During World War I, fundamentalism received a real boost when the millennial and premillennial fundamentalists interpreted "the war to end all wars" as the beginning of the great struggle prophesied in Revelation. The Balfour Declaration in 1917, which called for a Jewish homeland in Palestine (and would lead to the eventual founding of the modern state of Israel in 1948), seemed to fit the pattern necessary for the prophesied coming of Christ at the end of times. Isaac M. Haldeman, wrote apocalyptically that Christ "comes forth as one who no longer seeks friendship or love. . . . His garments are dipped in blood, the blood of others. He descends that he may shed the blood of men."[22]

After the war, the fundamentalist movement gained more momentum. In August 1917, William Bell Riley had sat down with A. C. Dixon (1854–1925), one of the editors of *The Fundamentals,* and the revivalist Reuben Torrey (1856–1928) and decided to form an association to promote the literal interpretation of scripture and the "scientific doctrines of premillennialism."[23] These were promoted at a mass rally in Philadelphia in 1919 and were incorporated into a new organization called the World's Christian Fundamentals Association. The actual current usage of the word *fundamentalist* to mean what it means today seems to have been coined in 1920 by the editor of *The Watchman,* the northern Baptist newsletter.[24]

The postwar frenzy of fundamentalism reached its climax in the Scopes monkey trial in 1925, the details of which are fairly well known. In that famous trial, William Jennings Bryan, representing the prosecution and fundamentalists, and Clarence Darrow, defending Scopes under the banner of the American Civil Liberties Union (ACLU), went at it in what became a much-mythologized battle of worldviews. H. L. Mencken, the cynical but highly entertaining columnist for the *Baltimore Sun,* made sure Americans across the country were kept up-to-date on the trial, and in the process he managed to paint the fundamentalists as Bible-thumping know-nothings afraid of the modern world. The play and the film based on the trial, *Inherit the Wind,* which is the way most of us know about the trial, come off today as a bit smug in their secular liberalism. In fact, one has to have more sympathy for the fundamentalists. They honestly believed they were fighting for their, and their children's, eternal lives. In the so-called Monkey Trial, the fundamentalists were trying to save what they believed were their very souls from encroaching modernism, a not-altogether-unworthy goal, even if their means and their logic leave some of us cold.

After the Scopes trial, and the drubbing they took in the media, fundamentalists seemed to withdraw into the margins of American life. As we can see now, however, they were merely staging a temporary strategic retreat. Backing off from the public stage somewhat, they appeared to cede the religious arena to mainstream denominations, but behind the scenes they were getting themselves organized and were learning to use modern media to spread their message, and by the end of the twentieth century they would succeed in setting the terms of social and political debate in America.

The story is one of institutionalization and, ironically, "modernization." That is, fundamentalism succeeded, in the last half of the twentieth century, in creating an alternative but still modern society. Unlike the Amish, who have maintained their religious community by choosing to remain more or less locked in time, the fundamentalists were able to create an alternative modernism, a mirror world of mass media, businesses, schools—even, eventually, theme parks—all fully up-to-date and modern with the exception that they were thoroughly Bible-based.

They recognized early the potential of the new mass media. By the 1930s, fundamentalists were using radio to great effect. Early offerings included Charles Fuller's *Old-Fashioned Revival Hour.* Fuller and revivalists such as Charles G. Finney set out to save souls with plain talk, right from the Bible, using their broadcasts as, in effect, great electronic tent meetings.

By World War II, a distinction was being made between fundamentalists and evangelicals, with the result that mainstream evangelical Christians, such as Billy Graham, began to differentiate themselves from strict fundamentalists.

The founding of the modern state of Israel in 1948 gave momentum to the apocalyptic thinking that had already become part of the movement. Reading historical events in apocalyptic terms, the premillennialists couldn't help seeing the twentieth century—with its two world wars and the establishment of a modern Jewish state in the Holy Land—as "signs and portents." This interpretation of history only gained momentum after the 1967 Six-Day War and as the ensuing troubled history of the region played out. For those who had eyes to see, there seemed to be an escalating tempo of activity moving toward the end-times. Perhaps the thousand-year era of the Tribulation was upon us. If the Bible was true, who could doubt it?

The 1950s, with its widespread fear of "godless communism," encouraged many to accept the fundamentalist reading of history. In the context of the times, this is not too surprising. Religion was entering American public life in a new way. It was the 1950s that saw the motto "In God We Trust" put on United States coins, and during which "one nation under God" was inserted into the Pledge of Allegiance, which became part of every schoolchild's day. These were not fundamentalist initiatives, but came from mainstream Americans and showed how religious vocabulary was entering the public discourse in a new way to differentiate America from atheistic communist countries.

At the same time, fundamentalism proper was growing. J. Frank Norris, the "Texas Tornado," and pastor of the First Baptist Church in Forth Worth, led the formation of the Baptist Bible Fellowship, and withdrew from the Southern Baptist Convention. The conservative viewpoint moved onto campuses with the formation of the Campus Crusade for Christ, Intervarsity Fellowship, and Youth for Christ.

Then, during the 1960s and early 1970s, America went through a cultural sea change. The most obvious examples of it were in the counterculture, civil rights, and antiwar movements, the hippies, and the emergence of modern feminism. Landmark legal cases during this period—notably *Engel v. Vitale* (1962), the Supreme Court case that took prayer out of public schools, and *Roe v. Wade* (1973)—seemed to signal a creeping secularism and became focal points for religious, especially fundamentalist, opposition. The counterculture revolution of the 1960s, which looked like a turn toward chaos and anarchy, seemed yet another sign that the end was upon us.

In the spirit of the 1960s, perhaps, a Christian counterculture also took root. Large numbers of self-identified evangelical and fundamental Christians tuned in and turned on to God through the Bible, and, in effect, dropped out of secular society. Enrollment in evangelical schools increased sixfold between 1965 and 1983 until there were about ten thousand such schools.[25] Pastors and parents reasoned that if the 1960s youth culture, not to mention the creeping secularism of mainstream American, were luring children into a godless way of living, then it would be necessary to create a Christian counterculture to insulate them. The trend toward creating a Christian society within larger American society continued. Between 1989 and 2000, schools identifying themselves as "conservative Christian" saw enrollment increases of 46 percent, adding nearly 250,000 students to their rolls nationally.[26] By the year 2000, as America entered the new millennium, two generations of students who had been raised and educated in these schools were entering adulthood.

Gradually, as their voices grew more numerous and their use of media grew more sophisticated, the fundamentalist line of thinking moved from the fringes of American social and political life and came into the mainstream.

In the 1970s, Hal Lindsey's *The Late Great Planet Earth* became the first big "crossover" hit of fundamentalist publishing, selling some 28 million copies worldwide, according to the publishers, and being made into a 1978 film with a voiceover by Orson Welles.[27] It joined the popular secular genre of disaster movies such as *The Towering Inferno* (1974), *Earthquake* (1974), *When Time Ran Out* (1980), and a slew of airport movies to feed a widespread feeling of anxiety and dread about life in the frightening modern world. Even secularists experienced an apocalyptic nervousness about global problems such as overpopulation, pollution, and the threat of nuclear extinction. In a time of extreme uncertainty about humanity's fate, the idea that there was a book, the Bible, that foretold the future history of our times was extremely attractive to many people who otherwise felt powerless to withstand the social and technological forces working against them. In an age of mass doubt, someone was offering truth.

By the late 1970s, the fundamentalists had reached a critical mass and were poised to strike back at the secular society inside of which they had been slowly and laboriously building their own counterculture. In 1980 Hal Lindsey again produced a provocative best seller, this one called *The 1980s: Countdown to Armageddon*. In it, he advocated a political agenda that acted as if the final days were upon us, and encouraged electing officials who represented the fundamentalist point of view. The idea began to take hold that if America were to become a truly godly country (again), there might even be a possibility of a *national* dispensation. That is, when the end-times came, if America were truly Christian, in this fundamentalist sense, then the entire nation might be Raptured wholesale. There had always been a strain of exceptionalism in the American personality, from the Puritans forward, but this idea took it to a new level. However, only one thing stood in the way of that happening—secular humanism, which the fundamentalists saw as dominating American life. As the cultural debate continued, the so-called ideology of secular humanism, which fundamentalists viewed as a conscious organized movement, became the great Satan.

In 1979 and into the early 1980s, Richard Viguerie and Ed McAteer, along with Jerry Falwell, formed the religious-political coalition known as the Moral Majority. Other similar groups included the Religious Roundtable, the American Coalition for Traditional Values, and Christian Voice.[28] Much of their opposition hinged on proving that "secular humanism" was a religion. That was given a boost by a 1961 U.S. Supreme Court decision in a case, *Tarcaso v. Watkins,* in which a Maryland notary public questioned the legality of a state provision that he declare his belief in God as a requirement of his job.[29] The Court agreed that the law was unconstitutional, and in a footnote to the case, the term "secular humanism" was lumped together with a number of other nontheist religious orientations.[30] This obscure judicial footnote underlies the fundamentalist claim that secular humanism is recognized by the government as a religion. It was enough to ignite focused opposition.

Organized nationally through mass media and Viguerie's brilliant ability in direct-mail fundraising, fundamentalists and the "religious right" worked their way into the political infrastructure and inserted their terminology into the cultural debate. They began on a local level, often starting with school boards. The year 1981 saw the Texas textbook case. Mel and Norma Gabler led a campaign to "get God back into the schools." They didn't like the "liberal slant" of Texas schooling. By that they meant everything that liberals hold dear including:

> Open-ended questions that require students to draw their own conclusions; statements about religions other than Christianity; statements that they construe to reflect negatively on the free enterprise system; statements that they construe to reflect

positive aspects of socialist or communist countries (e.g. that the Soviet Union is the largest producer in the world of certain grains); any aspect of sex education other than the promotion of abstinence; statements which emphasize contributions made by blacks, Native American Indians, Mexican-Americans, or feminists; statements which are sympathetic to American slaves or are unsympathetic to their masters; and statements in support of the theory of evolution, unless equal space is given to explain the theory of creation.[31]

Of course, the fundamentalists' first great political victory came with the 1980 election of Ronald Reagan to the presidency. Though not a fundamentalist himself, Reagan seemed to seize upon some of the fundamentalist rhetoric, taking what had been a long-standing tradition of American exceptionalism and the providential mission of the United States ("the city on the hill" language that he used so effectively) and cast the Cold War in what seemed like apocalyptic terms.

In a brilliant long essay in *The New Yorker,* written at the beginning of Reagan's second term, historian Frances Fitzgerald traced the apocalyptic strain in American foreign policy, and how, in Reagan's first term, this had shaped our behavior in those ending days of the Cold War.[32] Seeing international politics in terms of an essentially Manichean struggle between good and evil, this view took something that had always been present in American political discourse, the "paranoid style," as Richard Hofstadter famously named it, and gave it a chiliastic spin. Since early in the century, fundamentalist preachers had interpreted the Russian Revolution and Soviet Communism as the biblical land called Ros, from which the Beast (as in the Russian bear) would appear in the end-times. That, with the ongoing troubles in the Mideast, as well as the Soviet Union's role in the possible worldwide spread of communism, made many people ready to hear Reagan's message. The story crafted by Reagan skillfully blended apocalyptic talk of the "evil empire" with brilliant use of patriotic imagery and Reagan's own carefully crafted persona as the epitome of the American myth. Reagan's great credibility, what made him the Great Communicator, was that he summed up so much of what Americans like to believe about themselves. He was, if we think about it, the embodiment of several American myths met in one man—the Midwestern all-American lifeguard and athlete who morphed from one American success story to another, being sequentially a romantic movie star, cowboy, TV personality, millionaire, governor, and finally president of the United States. What he offered Americans, in the end, was a clear narrative after some twenty years of social and political confusion. As Fitzgerald writes, "Most important, there was an aesthetic to Reagan's world. Instead of a chaotic mess, there was a story line, a single sweeping arc of narrative that bound all events together and made sense of them."[33] And Reagan's rhetoric made it clear that he believed the American narrative was a key part of the larger narrative of history, a history whose meta-story was told and foretold in the Bible.

By the early 1990s the fundamentalist vocabulary had fully entered the public discourse. Statistics showed that while 72 percent of Americans say that the Bible is the "Word of God," 39 percent say it is literally true. That is, more than half of all who believe the Bible is the Word of God are also interpreting it in a *literal* way. Similarly, 44 percent of those surveyed would describe themselves as "creationists."[34] Nearly half of Americans, in other words, now question or reject the scientific explanation of how life on earth developed.

During the 1990s, the fundamentalist point of view gained further political ground. Ronald Reagan and the Republican Party had successfully linked the word *liberal* with the phrase *secular humanism* in the 1980s, and now the fundamentalists were ready to take the counterattack to the next level by working to dismantle many of the liberal political victories of the post–New Deal and post-1960s eras. Writer Tim Lahaye in *The Battle for the Mind* (1980) had identified seven disturbing elements in contemporary society: the Equal Rights Amendment; attempts to limit parental corporal punishment of children; the Internal Revenue Service's questioning of just what a "religion" was for tax purposes; the movements to extend civil rights to homosexuals; humanist ideas such as "values clarification," which were being taught in schools instead of absolute values; the way government bodies were imposing certification requirements on Christian schools; and, of course, *Roe v. Wade*.[35] These, along with the old fundamentalist foe

Darwinism, formed a constellation of liberal "secular humanist" values that the religious right saw trying to exert control over the Christian world, and in the 1990s these issues became the focuses of the religious right's counterattack. Much, if not all, of this action took place from within the Republican Party and was influenced by such conservative organizations as Christian Voice and the Eagle Forum, the latter headed by the antifeminist Phyllis Schlafly, which had intellectual and financial ties to the party.

The sweeping Republican victories of 1994 ushered in an era of great change and unprecedented conservatism. Perhaps buoyed by their success in gaining political footholds after so many years in the wilderness, new fundamentalist groups known collectively as "Reconstructionists" began to emerge around the edges. The motto on the Web site of the influential Chalcedon Foundation is "Proclaiming the Authority of God's Word Over Every Area of Life and Thought."[36] The goal of Reconstructionists generally is to supplant the current government, which they see as dominated by secular humanists, with an explicitly Christian one, to gain "dominion" over the earth as promised in Genesis 1:26–28 and Matthew 28:16–20. A journal called the *Journal of Christian Reconstruction* was founded by R. J. Rushdoony (1916–2001), the intellectual patriarch of the Chalcedon group. Cornelius Van Til of Westminster Seminary provides much of the theology. The long history of American exceptionalism, going back to the Puritans and their city on a hill, was now taking what many nonfundamentalist Americans felt was a frightening turn. Some on the far left feared a sort of Christian Sharia or Christian Taliban was coming to power in the United States.

In the disputed presidential contest of 2000, Americans elected George W. Bush, a man who, like Reagan, embodied a story familiar to fundamentalism. Overcoming his early history of substance abuse and repeated business failures, he found God through a small Bible study group, and regenerated himself as a right-thinking Christian. That his religion is tinged with fundamentalism is clear, and many hear in his rhetoric the use of "code words" that are, on the surface, neutral enough, but which send clear messages to the fundamentalist faithful. To some, this kind of language is frightening, but to many

Americans it is apparently comforting and reassuring, for he was elected to a second term.

The 2004 presidential political campaign was suffused with the language of religion. Throughout the run-up to the election, the role of religion and religious language was commented on at length by major news organizations, including publications as diverse as the *Washington Post, The Christian Science Monitor,* and *The Nation,* and became the topic of several books and a PBS Frontline special called *The Jesus Factor.* They concluded that Bush's rhetoric was clearly targeting evangelical and fundamentalist Christians. From his claim that his favorite philosopher was Jesus Christ to his tendency to see the war against terrorism as a piece of the eternal struggle between good and evil more than just a political or economic battle, the president and his advisers often spoke in terms familiar to the Christian right. Many previous presidents, of course, had religious temperaments, but the particular language in which President Bush phrased his public and personal statements came from the general rhetoric and mentality of the conservative, evangelical arm of Christianity. No matter the president's real feelings, which he claims are tolerant of other faiths, Jews, other non-Christians, and liberal Christians heard in his rhetoric echoes of literalist-minded preachers who mixed politics and government with religion in a way they found disturbing.

The infusion of religious rhetoric worked. Analysts seemed to be in consensus that those identifying themselves as "white evangelical born-again" Christians, who represented about 20 percent of the electorate, voted solidly for George W. Bush and were due credit for delivering victory to him and the now-Republican-controlled House and Senate.[37] (Not all of these "evangelicals" were fundamentalists, but there was significant crossover.) The shift in 2006 to a Democrat-controlled House and Senate, or even the election of a Democratic president in 2008, will probably not do much to diminish the momentum of the movement. Such events may even re-energize the religious right. Previous electoral and judicial setbacks on such issues as Intelligent Design or abortion law have only prompted the right to alter their methods, not their objectives.

So far in the new millennium, there continues to be rhetoric that many find worrisome, such as the comment from evangelist James Kennedy, an ordained Presbyterian minister and head of a Christian mega-church in Fort Lauderdale, Florida, who said at a Midwest rally in 2004, "Things are going to change in America as godliness moves into a majority opinion. . . . [America] is going to be changed by the power of Jesus Christ. The victory is going to be his, and it is going to be soon."[38] In 1994, Kennedy founded the Center for Reclaiming America, sponsor of large "Retaking America for Christ" conferences each year.[39] Further from the mainstream, fundamentalist fringe groups called "Dominionists" proclaim they have a scriptural injunction to take over the United States government in Jesus's name.[40]

In the publishing world, the enormous success of Tim LaHaye's and Jerry Jenkins's *Left Behind* series reflects the growing, almost obsessive, interest in violent premillennarian ideas that were once on the edges of Christianity but now seem to be grabbing millions of readers and believers. LaHaye centers his ministry on the Second Coming of Christ, and he reads into contemporary events signs of the Tribulation, the bloody time leading up to the Rapture, when all true believers will be taken bodily to heaven, a time that will be followed by the interregnum of the Antichrist, during which those Raptured will look down on the earth and watch the suffering of those left behind. On his Web site, readers can read such articles as "Anti-Christ Philosophy Already Controls America and Europe," and "The Prophetic Significance of Sept 11, 2001."[41] On this site, LaHaye claims that 44 percent of American adults "believe that the rapture will happen someday," and 64 percent "believe that Jesus Christ will reappear on earth during the end-times."[42] In this same article he claims that "most public officials in the world" have rejected Christ and God.

By 2005, many commentators, including evangelical ministers and authors such as Jim Wallis, came to the conclusion that the religious right had successfully commandeered religious rhetoric and had effectively deprived liberals of using references to God. Wallis, who is head of the social service organization Sojourners, felt compelled to write about his concerns in *God's Politics: Why the Right Gets It Wrong and the Left Doesn't Get It*. In this book, he attempts to free God-language from those who have taken it hostage, but he does not let the liberals off easy either, for he challenges them to "Take Back the Faith" and stop being afraid of using religion in their rhetoric and their politics. It remains to be seen whether that will happen.

The reason so many Americans have proven so susceptible to fundamentalist rhetoric—and why liberals have backed away from it—is the fundamentalists' understanding of the power of religious language. They have taken words with heavy emotional overtones, words such as *truth, God, religion, family values,* even *the Bible,* and have defined them in such a way that they have effectively deprived others of using them. Nancy Ammerman wrote, "Drawing as it does on a biblical heritage that is deeply ingrained in the [American] culture, fundamentalism asserts a claim to be the rightful interpreter of the stories that shape American identity, and it offers a subcultural system in which those ideas can be nurtured and sustained."[43] Rather than be identified with that, the left has shrunk away from using religious language at all. (This in spite of such liberal religious men and women of God as Rev. Martin Luther King, Jr., Rev. William Sloane Coffin, Bishop Thomas Gumbleton, Sr. Joan Chittister, and fathers Daniel and Phillip Berrigan, who led liberal movements of the 1960s.) Because the fundamentalists speak with such apparent confidence, and use the word *truth* where others would dare not, many have chosen to follow.

In 2001, of course, Americans also became painfully aware that another kind of fundamentalism had been rising up, in the Middle East. On September 11th of that year, Islamic fundamentalism and extremism came into direct violent contact with an America where Christian fundamentalists, primed with premillennial rhetoric, had just gained unprecedented sway. Everyone, of course, was shocked by the events of that day, and spontaneous prayer meetings and displays of patriotism took place all over America and the world.

While secularists and religionists alike were universally appalled, the apparent knee-jerk reaction of some elements of the religious right was further upsetting. Many used the tragedy to link the 9/11 attacks to the fundamentalists' usual litany of complaints against contemporary secular America. Two days after the attacks, Pat Robertson interviewed Jerry Falwell on *The 700 Club.* During the interview, Falwell labeled the prophet Muhammad himself a terrorist, and during the conversation they put Muslims in the same category with Hitler and Nazism, not distinguishing between Islamist terrorists and other followers of Islam. A little later in the program, they linked Islamic terrorism to abortion, the ACLU, feminism, and the gay and lesbian movement.[44] Both men were forced to apologize, and we might grant them some leeway because the time immediately after the attacks was emotionally heated, but statements made by them since suggest that their initial spontaneous reactions reflect their general mind-set. Other organizations, such as Operation Save America, are even more explicit in their linking of 9/11 to America's cultural decadence. On its Web site, Operation Save America interpreted the attacks as the beginning of the end-times judgment on the United States for allowing abortion, banning prayer and the Ten Commandments from schools, and for the prevalence of homosexuality.[45]

Clearly this is a dangerous tendency and has to be taken seriously and countered. But, as Jim Wallis points out, such extreme fundamentalism cannot be effectively combated with secular rhetoric. The religious language used so effectively by the extreme fundamentalists has an emotional power and resonance capable of rousing us to action in a way that no other use of language can. And the only way to counter it is to use the same language. That is, those of us who are upset by such a volatile mix of religion and politics cannot continue to let the definitions of words like *God, religion, truth,* and *sacred* be established by people who would use them in ways that seem to us to turn religion from its true end, which is compassion, into a religion of intolerance, condemnation, and separation. In the modern, interdependent world we live in, many of us feel we can no longer afford to allow our religions to divide us or to be used as weapons of hatred by extreme elements. We must find a way to reclaim the power of religion to change the world in creative, not destructive ways, in ways that give life rather than take it. As Jim Wallis writes, this is the job confronting religious believers today. One way to begin that task is to define clearly for ourselves what we mean by the *truth* of our own religious beliefs.

And that brings us, by a roundabout way, to the troublesome word *myth,* which has to be rescued from oblivion, for we have forgotten what it means, what it can do, and how to relate to it. Fundamentalists claim their religion is *truth,* by which they mean literal and scientific truth. Secularists say that the fundamentalists' religion is *myth,* by which they mean falsehood. In fact, now that we have explored the myth of *truth,* it should be clear that both extreme camps are wrong. In fact, the only way out of our current conundrum is to rediscover the truth of our scriptures and to relearn how to relate to our sacred stories. And that will involve rediscovering the value of another often abused word, *myth.*

5 : Myth

EXTREME fundamentalism shows us what happens when people treat sacred stories as if they were *true* in a modern, scientific sense. A literalist approach to religion, strictly applied, seems to lead to a world at perpetual war with itself, a world where a human being's best hope is to be Raptured away from it before the thousand-year Tribulation begins. Surely religion ought to offer more than the prospect of being whisked off to a heavenly cloud from which we can look down at the warfare of the damned and say "I told you so." But how should a person be religious in today's world? In many ways, we have let fundamentalists define religiosity and religious life, and the rest of us feel forced to respond on their terms, backing down when they say they have the *real* old-time religion. The problem is that when they say they have the truth, we can only wallow in relativism and say, "Well, it may be true for you." In our hearts we know, even as we say it, this is not really an adequate reply.

Most of us who are not strict fundamentalists have made an uneasy compromise between secularism and religion, trying not to think about it too much, and perhaps we even secretly envy the confidence and certainty of the fundamentalists. Wouldn't it be nice to know the truth, that is, to really know the one and only true thing? If only life were that simple. Most of us know, intuitively, that the fundamentalist approach is unsatisfactory, but our response as to why is less clear. If we are going to answer the challenge of fundamentalism effectively, however, we must articulate a clear response, something beyond post-modern relativism, something that offers a real alternative to the ultimately divisive approach to religion that seems to prevail today.

Given all we've said about the changes in the Western mind-set over the past five hundred years, this will not be easy. But the starting point is clear; we must learn, or relearn, to read our sacred stories in another way, one that won't insist on taking them literally. In order to do that, we first have to get over our fear of the word *myth* and to get beyond the idea that it is somehow the opposite of *truth*.

Myth, like many troublesome words, is double-edged. Its meaning changes radically depending on who is using it. Surprisingly, linguists and etymologists seem unable to track *myth*'s ultimate origin.[1] The *OED* traces the word back no further than the Greek *mythos* and Latin *mythus*, where it seems simply to have meant "story." Some have tried to trace its roots back to an Indo-European word meaning "to think or imagine," but the ultimate etymology of *myth* remains uncertain.[2] It is clear, however, that the noun *myth*, as such, came into English surprisingly late. The *OED* gives its first usage as 1838. After our discussion of modernism, this should tell us something, for *myth* and earlier adjective forms (*mythic* and *mythical* date to the 1600s) came into common usage just as science was emerging and giving a new definition to *truth*. While it may be purely coincidental from a linguistic point of view, it is still interesting to speculate that the reason *myth* appears as a noun only in 1838 is that prior to that time we didn't really need a word in English to serve as an antonym for *truth* beyond words that already existed, such as *falsehood*.[3] The word *myth* came into the language at almost the exact moment that science laid exclusive claim to the word *truth* and had narrowed its original definition to something factual.

From the start, *myth*'s primary meaning was "a purely fictitious narrative usually involving supernatural persons, actions, or events, and embodying some popular ideas concerning natural or historical phenomena."[4] Prior to *myth*'s entering the language, supernatural stories were called by a number of other names, including *fables, legends,* and *tales,* all of which have an older linguistic pedigree than *myth*. It is clear that the word *myth* was used from the first to refer to things purely imaginary, having no basis in fact. Thus, in the science-dominated nineteenth century, *myth* became a pejorative for anything less than literally true.

Furthermore, since so many myths concerned themselves with etiology, or the origin of things such as geographical features, social customs, and the universe itself, myth came to be regarded as a kind of primitive science, "the science of a pre-scientific age," in the words of one nineteenth-century critic.[5] In other words, Victorians and early-twentieth-century people believed that mythology was how people understood the world before there was science to illuminate the way things really are. A myth, therefore, was no more than a childlike understanding of the world, a way of explaining things like physical geography and the origins of the universe in the absence of modern science. Now that human beings had the new scientific way of knowing the world, mythology was superseded by a far superior form of knowledge. For a modern person, to know a supernatural story about how rock formations came to be may have been charming or entertaining, but it was clearly no match for a geologic understanding demonstrable by scientific theory. Mythical knowledge was appropriate for very young children and for primitive races who could not yet master higher-level adult thinking, but we moderns would have none of it. To use other Victorian-era words, myths were nothing more than balderdash and humbug. They were entertaining for children and useful for antiquarians and classicists, but nothing more. A similar fate overcame what we now call "fairy tales." Originally tales told by adults to other adults, in the forms collected by the Brothers Grimm and other folklorists and linguists, they later became mere children's stories; to consider them seriously was beneath the sophistication of adults. Thus, in the nineteenth century, mythology, which had been the basis of classical religion and of Western education, could be effectively rejected. Modern education became increasingly utilitarian and fact-based, while fancy, imagination, and myth were banished to the nursery.

Of course, the modernists were partly right. Myths are, in part anyway, primitive science. They do represent beliefs about how the world came to be, and in oral cultures, they can contain huge amounts of cultural information, including practical and technical matters. Myth-ological narratives serve as powerful mnemonic devices for transmit-ting knowledge from one generation to the next because human beings find stories easy to remember. For example, in the Bambara tribe of Africa, blacksmiths and weavers hold special positions. Their crafts, so necessary to the life of the village, are passed down orally via sacred stories of the gods, who were the originators of the crafts. Memorizing the sacred story of the origin of the craft, and the rituals connected to it, serves as a major part of the apprenticeship of the young craftsman, and the story is inseparable from the technique of the craft. The loom used by a Bambara weaver consists of thirty-three parts, which must be assembled correctly in order to function. As part of each day's work preparation, the weaver must touch and name all the parts. The act of naming calls forth "the forces of life embodied in them."[6] As he oper-ates the loom, the movement of the weaver's feet is accompanied by a sacred chant that both invokes the gods and sets up the proper rhythm for the job. Similarly, the Bambara blacksmith enters his forge and becomes the Master of Fire who, like the original Master, transforms elements through heat. His craft is learned and remembered by means of an etiological myth of the god Maa Ngala, who initiated it, and he must recall this myth as he prepares for work and as he goes through his day. Each part of the forge is linked to the other parts via a sexual symbolism, the twin bellows being the testicles, the bellows' tube the penis, which is inserted into the womb of the furnace, where the new material is born. Each day's work repeats the original story of creation. Elaborate rituals connected with the creation myth precede the black-smith's work, and special clothing is worn reminiscent of what the god wore. Each of these craftsmen repeats the original work of the gods, given to mankind at the beginning of time, and the knowledge of the craft is passed down via story or myth.

Similarly, Australian aborigines have a very complex mythological way of mapping out their territories known as the Songlines.[7] The Songlines were laid out in the primordial "dream time" by the gods themselves, and each child is given a portion of the song by the elders to memorize and carry with him throughout life. Taken together, the tribal songlines form a web of "coordinates," as it were, for crossing vast stretches of Australian territory. Thus, a person carrying a song-line for a portion of land he has never been through can successfully navigate his way by "singing up the land." The narrative of the song-line helps the singer to know the directions by heart, a knowledge absolutely vital in an oral culture. Myths form a culture's collective knowledge and memory.

So myths, or sacred narratives, learned over time, do, in fact, serve as powerful teaching tools for passing down practical information, and sacred narratives and their accompanying rituals do serve techni-cal ends. In an oral society, strict and accurate memory is vital to cul-tural survival, and myths are at the very center of the transmission of important real-world knowledge. Myths are hugely valuable in that context. The invocation of the gods underscores in the mind of the young apprentice the importance of each step of an otherwise techni-cal process. But here's the corollary: if myth is *merely* a way of pass-ing down information, then all of the myths of a culture, and the rituals that surround them, become totally superfluous once people become literate and can read operating manuals and textbooks. At least that is what a truly modern person may think, given the modern view of mythological knowledge as mere *techne*. We can even prove it scientifically. Do away with what a modern person sees as mythologi-cal "mumbo-jumbo," and the quality of the cloth or metal produced by a Bambara weaver or blacksmith will not suffer. A literate Aus-tralian native can forget his songline and still find his way with a Rand-McNally or a hand-held GPS. Myth is not necessary, says the modern utilitarian. In fact, if the point of the enterprise is to produce high-quality fabric and strong metal bonds, or to not get lost, then we'd best get rid of the ritual hogwash altogether, teach the people to read, and bring in the machines. And that, in caricature, is exactly what Western colonialism did as it carried the white man's burden into what it thought of as the dark corners of the earth in the eigh-teenth and nineteenth centuries.

But, as we've seen, it wasn't just the colonial natives who suffered the loss of their gods. For demythologization was also taking place in Europe and America during the nineteenth century, and it was only a short step from seeing the gods of natives as superstitions to seeing the

God of Christianity as part of the same fabric of myth. Once the Higher Criticism revealed the mythological underpinning of Judaism and Christianity, then those religions, too, became myths to put beside those of Africa and India.

As we've seen, the fundamentalist effort to show that Christianity was not myth but truth was a desperate attempt to sidestep the dilemma brought on by the redefinition of *truth* and the nineteenth-century invention of *myth* as its antonym. Since we all agreed that *myth* meant falsehood, then once the Higher Criticism showed that the foundation of Christianity was mythic, fundamentalism or something like it simply had to arise to combat the inevitable conclusion that the Bible was false.

But does this conflict between the scientific and the mythic way of looking at the truth of the world have to be an either/or thing? Clearly we are uneasy with the chasm that has risen between the mythic and the scientific, but we have trouble understanding how both ways can be true. The human mind wants consistency at least, and both sides are trying to get it. The fundamentalists are attempting, rather uneasily, to meld the two kinds of truth together with Intelligent Design, and scientists are doing something similar when they wire people up with electrodes to study brain wave patterns during meditation, trying to find out what "really" goes on during prayer. Most of us don't try for unity. We compartmentalize our lives, believing the myth is true on the odd Sabbath we attend church or temple, then operating according to modern scientific truth through the other days of the week. Once in a while an ethics committee at a hospital tries to bring the two kinds of truth together, but mostly we insist on a wall of separation between the sacred and the profane. The Catholic Church's official approach is an example of the compartmentalization that most of us engage in. According to the church, science and religion represent "nonoverlapping magisteria," that is, the efforts of science are directed to the material world, while the teachings of religion are directed to the spiritual one. Thus, the Catholic Church has had less trouble with evolution than have Bible-based religions. It is perfectly proper for science to use its methods to understand the biological realm as long as it concedes that at some point in the evolutionary process God put a uniquely human soul into the human creature. As long as one believes that, then the process by which that creature evolved may be adequately described by science.[8]

The problem, of course, is that in contemporary society, the line between science and religion is getting grayer by the day as science moves into murky ethical territory with cloning experiments and issues regarding the beginning and ending of life, particularly as these become matters of government politics and policy. Science's capabilities clash with traditional religious teaching.

It would be immensely helpful if we could be clear about how the kind of truth we feel is inherent in our sacred traditions is related to the kind of truth we know is reached by science. The either/or model of truth, the model of simple falsifiability, has to be tweaked. But how?

Perhaps a helpful metaphor for beginning this discussion would be to think of science and religion as different lenses through which we look at the world. The unaided human eye is very good at perceiving things of a certain size, but when we wish to see things far away or that are very small, we need different lenses. Microscopes reveal what is invisible to the naked eye, while the telescope helps us see things far away. The microscope is useless for looking at the stars, while a telescope is worthless for seeing microbes. Similarly, each of us needs different eyeglasses to see well, and as we go through life, we need to readjust our lenses. Reading glasses help those of us of a certain age to see the fine print, for example, while nearsighted people need lenses to see details that are far away. What you see all depends on which lens you use, and you adopt one lens or another depending on what you want to see. It is still the eye that sees, and what you are observing does not change by being looked at, but what the eye sees will vary depending on which lens it chooses.

If we can think of mythology and science as two different lenses that we may put on or take off depending on what aspect of life we want to look at, then we will have gone a long way toward removing the either/or dilemma that both strict modernism and extreme fundamentalism put us in. The key to knowing which lens to use when, of course, is wisdom, and we can move nearer to that by getting a clearer understanding of the truth of myth and the myth of truth.

Human beings have a number of ways of knowing about the world, of which the scientific way is only one, albeit a powerful one. As Howard Gardner has shown in his work on multiple intelligences, we all possess not only cognitive intelligence but also intelligences that are social, kinetic, and emotional. I know an artist who "thinks with her fingers," that is, as she works at her art, her mind may be elsewhere, carrying on a conversation, say, or listening to the radio, while her fingers shape the figures she is working on. Similarly, when we watch Michael Jordan fly through the air toward a hoop ten feet above the floor or we observe an outfielder intuitively judging the arc of a fly ball and matching that with the speed of his feet and the reach of his glove, we are witnessing an intelligence at work that is not cognitive or quantitative in a strictly intellectual sense. Watching a "socially gifted" person at work shows us another kind of intelligence. Such a person knows how, within minutes, to put others at ease, link people together who will hit it off, and delights in nothing more than figuring out kinship relations going back several generations. Some people are gifted with spatial orientation, and others with incredible balance, knowing how to walk several hundred feet above the ground on a steel I-beam. Most of these other kinds of intelligence, or ways of knowing and being in the world, are undervalued in our society, for we have come to privilege the kind of left-brained knowledge that shows itself best in mathematics and science and that has become the model for our entire educational system, from preschool through postdoctorate work.

Now, as we've seen in the cases of the Bambara weaver and blacksmith and in the Australian aboriginal songlines, myths contain a certain kind of knowledge. Judged merely as information transmitters, however, myths come up short. Maps and technical manuals can communicate data and operating instructions more efficiently. But that kind of practical information is really only the most superficial level of the total knowledge conveyed by myth. If we go to myth only to find out the way the world was created or how to join metal, we will quickly abandon it in favor of the scientific story, which is far better at modeling the physical world. But before we abandon myth too quickly, we should look at what else it teaches us about the world. And here we need to contrast two ways of knowing that we can call, in shorthand, the scientific and the mythic.

The English poet Percy Shelley in his *Defense of Poetry* called these two modes by their ancient Greek names *to logizein* (analytic reason) and *to poiein* (poetic imagination). We could also use the Greek word *logos* to denote the scientific mode and *mythos* for the narrative. *Logos* meant "word" in Greek but also denoted a sort of rational organizing principle from which we get the root of our English *logic* as well as the various *–ology* suffixes of the hard and social sciences, such as geology, anthropology, and psychology. The names of the disciplines indicate the approach to knowledge taken in them. *Mythos,* on the other hand, means story or narrative, and it constitutes a way of knowing the world as valid as, but quite different from, *logos.* The contrast is best seen by sets of contrasting adjectives that describe each mode. Some of these are *analytic* versus *synthetic, logical* versus *metaphorical, mathematical* versus *poetic, material* versus *spiritual,* and so on.

Taken singly, these modes of knowing lead to only partial knowledge of the world. Taken together, they form complementary ways of knowing that serve to complete each other. While science excels at dividing things (think of dissecting a frog in biology lab), stories tend to bring things together, even things that appear, at first, unlike each other. That synthetic ability, of course, is based on metaphor, which contrasts with the logic of the scientific mode of thought. Science wants things to be either/or; metaphor allows them to be both/and. The primary language of science is mathematics, with its precision and complexity, but mathematics has severe limits in its range of emotional expressiveness. The primary language of *mythos,* on the other hand, is poetry, which in its own way is as complex as mathematical language, but its domain is the inner realm of feeling. Where science concentrates on the surface phenomena of the material world, the mythic mode probes below the surface, often reaching what has been called the spiritual. Thus, while the scientific way of knowing leads us to information and what we normally call "knowledge," the narrative or mythic mode leads us to the kind of knowledge, no less true, that we call wisdom. While the scientific mode can enumerate the world, the mythic mode can give it value. They have contrasting styles of operation. The scientific mode favors systems and regularity, but the narrative mode favors spontaneity, luck, serendipity, and surprise, even to the extent of physical impossibility. Where science has its applications in the worlds of business and industry, myth involves itself in a much larger world, a world that includes a particular kind of play that is often linked with creation.

In a distinction made in French but not so much in English, the scientific way of knowing the world provides us with *connaisance,* while the mythic provides us with *savoir. Connaisance* can be translated into colloquial English as "book learnin'," while *savoir* is best illustrated by the words *savoir faire,* a phrase usually translated as "to know how to do" something, though that translation makes it sound too much like "technique." Perhaps the best way to illustrate *savoir* is to remember how we learned to ride a bicycle. Someone, probably a parent, held you upright before you started and told you, "Do this, do that; pedal like so, hold the handlebars like so, steer like so, understand?" You nodded. You got the concept. You had *connaisance.* Then the whole thing was put in motion. Crash. You found out you had no *savoir.* Then, after many falls, you suddenly "got it." You knew somewhere in your bones, not your head, that this was how you ride a bike, and off you went and never forgot because it was deeply learned.

So now we return to the word *myth.* Myth teaches us *savoir,* to know, and the knowledge it imparts is far more complex than riding a bicycle, for what myths undertake is the terrifying task of teaching us how to be human, from cradle to grave, how to live on this planet, among these people, in this universe, how to grow into an adult, how to marry, how to give birth, how to age, how to grieve, how to die. The fiendish complexity and ambiguity of myth comes from its enormous task and its subject, which is nothing less than the whole project of being in the way that humans have to be. Myth, as a way of knowing the world, is as complex, multidimensional, and rich as life itself.

Many people feel a "flatness" in the extreme fundamentalist and modernist positions. This is because in their literalism they try to make the *savoir* of myth perform as mere *connaissance.* In the end, there is even a boring quality to both fundamentalism and modernism, as the same propositions get repeated over and over without real development. The world presented by extremists on both sides lacks nuance and shadow because it insists on literalism. It is divided too neatly into black and white, and we do not experience life that way. Interpreting scripture literally, both strict modernists and strict fundamentalists deflate the stories. They take the creator of the universe and make him fit inside a tiny box. Listening to them, we ask in the end, "Is your idea of God really that small?"

The contrast between the two ways of knowing—the scientific and the mythic—impressed itself on me one day while visiting the Menil Collection, a large private art museum in Houston. The eclectic collection included everything from ancient fertility figures to extreme modern art, and one room housed a large collection of Polynesian tiki figures. One in particular caught my attention. It showed the lower half of a man's torso protruding from the mouth of a shark. The figure was nearly life-sized and was oddly comic, with the man's legs splayed out froglike as if he were swimming directly into the shark. Hoping to get more information about the figure from the label, I found only the usual museum facts, scientific, modern, accurate, but dull. The label told me that the figure was wood, twentieth-century, Polynesian, and was called "Man Being Eaten by Shark." This told me next to nothing that I had not gotten from looking at the object itself. I knew there had to be more to it than that.

Referring to a reference book when I returned home, I quickly found that, not surprisingly, the shark plays a very large role in the mythology of the inhabitants of the Pacific Islands. Corpses of relatives are sometimes fed to sharks, a practice meant to transform the soul of the dead person into the shark. Kahunas, Hawaiian shamans, can identify who the shark was by the markings on the fish. Such *aumakuas,* as they are known, often become family pets, and when fishermen go out on the ocean, they feed their familiar shark in the belief that the shark will then drive fish into their nets or save fishermen who go overboard. Was the wooden figure in the museum an *aumakua* in the process of being transformed from human into shark? Or was it a depiction of a character called Tui-tofua, a young man who turns into a shark after being accused of bothering his father's second wives? Tui-tofua comes back to his home island and joins five other sharks in keeping the island's barrier reef clear of enemies. Or was I looking at Kukuipahu, who, Jonah-like, was swallowed by a shark and lived in its belly several days before emerging with no hair?[9]

If so, the figure in the museum would have been transformed from a rather comic depiction of a physical improbability (sharks most often attack their prey from the side, not the head) into a profound religious image of how oceangoing people contend with questions of life, death, immortality, Providence, and the power and mystery of nature. Knowing the myth or story, rather than just the art-historical "facts," I would have been able to comprehend the figure with a depth of meaning that would otherwise have left it a mere curiosity. The myths put art "objects" into a narrative context and made them come alive.

My wife (an art historian) and I had a similar experience walking through the Detroit Institute of Art with a Jewish artist friend who, in spite of a lifetime in the arts as a teacher of sculpture, had only a shaky sense of art history when it came to medieval Christian artifacts. As we walked by glass cases containing reliquaries and other "ritual objects" (to use the famous museum phrase), he would stop us and ask, "What's that for?" or "Who's that?" He was, of course, vaguely aware of the outlines of the Christian story, as anyone who lives in our culture must be, but the finer details of saints' lives, the apostles, Mary and Joseph—the details of the New Testament narrative—were foreign to him. Filling in the story from Nativity through Crucifixion and Resurrection as we went from case to case gave a level of meaning to the objects that the sparse museum labels ("gold," "ivory," "fourteenth-century France") could not. Those stories led us to tell more personal narratives, how as children the same sorts of objects were used in pre–Vatican II liturgy, how we used to have and display relics of saints in our homes. As we talked, I realize now, we were actually creating a story, one that encompassed not only the objects in the cases but also the long history of Christianity, and of our own lives as well. And, being with Irving, most of whose extended family was lost in the Holocaust, we also merged that larger story with his story, reflecting on the intertwined and often tragic narratives of the Jews and Christians in medieval and modern Europe. By the time our tour was done, our storytelling had illuminated more than just the art. This was true "musing," the origin of the word *museum,* and we left knowing more than when we went in—and I am not referring to what we read on the labels.

Cut off in their climate-controlled boxes, the ancient ritual objects, treated in a scientific modern art-historical way, were divorced from the myths that had made them meaningful in the first place. They became soulless *objects* of art, and one was left only to marvel at their possible monetary worth. ("All that gold!") Their "worthsip," the root of the word *worship,* was now measured only in monetary and aesthetic terms, not in spiritual ones. Which way of "knowing" the objects was more valid? Which was richer, the scientific or the mythic? Obviously, each illumined the objects differently, and to know or understand what we were looking at, we needed to practice both ways. But it should be clear by now that the narrative mode of knowing those art objects, that is, knowing them *mythically,* led us to a more "soulful" way of knowing them, a way that animated them with spirit that made them more than mere physical objects. We got to know them "by heart," as it were.

So, how can we reclaim this rich *mythic* way of knowing without becoming literalists? First, we must get over the idea that *myth* means "false." Fortunately, much of the way has been paved for us by twentieth-century thinkers who came to prominence at about the same time that fundamentalists were gaining ground in the United States. Before his death in 1961, Swiss analytical psychologist Carl Jung had laid a foundation for a psychological understanding of mythology and its role in our individual and collective inner lives. Departing from his onetime mentor Sigmund Freud, who in many ways regarded the religious impulse as symptomatic of neurosis, Jung explored the role of mythology in maintaining its adherents' psychological health. Far from being merely charming stories or mere superstitions designed as anodynes to life's miseries, Jung saw myths as emerging from deep in the human psyche, from the unconscious level of the mind, taking form as spontaneously as dreams, and providing a template, as it were, for the formation and growth of individual identity. That is, through mystical and imaginative participation in their culture's myths, the believers were provided with a model of human life.

Practiced over the course of a lifetime, mythologies and the rituals that sprang from them could, if understood correctly and enacted in a ritual context, provide individuals with rites of psychological passage through the various stages of life. This was not a rational process and did not depend upon logic. Rather, the effective process of engagement in the myth was through what anthropologists call *participation mystique,* or mystical participation, which perhaps can be best understood as active imagination. One enters imaginatively into the world of the myth, engages the myth on its own terms, and reemerges from the active-imagination exercise having experienced something archetypal, that is, something that is transpersonal, bigger than the self, something that has been encoded, as it were, in the story and its ritual enactment.

Before this gets to sounding too mystical and arouses our modernist skepticism, let's look at it another way. Traditional myths are narratives that have been passed down through generations, both as explanations of the physical universe and as guides to understanding and successfully negotiating major life events. Myths thus have a marvelous directness about them, for all the unessential parts of them have been stripped away over time. They say this is how the world began, this is how death came to humankind, this is how the gods interacted with our ancestors, this is how one should live, this is what makes a man, this is what makes a woman. These cultural values are transmitted through the myth, which becomes a model for life. In contemporary terms, the popular bracelets with "WWJD" for "What Would Jesus Do" are examples of myth at work. In life situations, one asks what would the mythic god do here? Model yourself on the character in the story and you will know how to behave. What is being modeled, as we will see in the next chapter, is nothing less than life itself. But the model is not the reality, and here is where the literalists go wrong.

Let's use the example of an orrery. Named after its inventor, Charles Boyle, fourth earl of Orrery, who died in 1731, an orrery is a mechanical model of the solar system with colored balls representing the planets and their moons. The device worked with a gear mechanism that, when cranked, put the whole mini–solar system into motion, showing the relative movements of the planets, the earth, and the moon around the sun. It was, of course, the archetype of the clockwork universe and reflected the eighteenth-century scientific understanding of celestial mechanics. But if we think about it, the orrery is an apt analogy for a mythology, for what the orrery showed us is a view of the solar system that actually is impossible to see. That is, there is no point outside the solar system at which we could stand and actually see what the orrery represents. Even if we could use space travel to get outside the solar system and look back, we still could not see what the orrery presents—a fast-action, compressed view of all the planets dancing around each other. For that, we need a model like the orrery. The model, by virtue of being a model, allows us to see something all together that otherwise we couldn't see, and it enables us to form in our heads a useful conceptual image of how the solar system works so that when we see the actual moon in a particular phase, say, or watch Mars move through the sky from night to night, we can relate that real-world phenomenon to the model and understand it in a larger context otherwise unimaginable and impossible to see. Without a model, we could not understand the reality we are looking at. The model works precisely because it is *not* the thing itself.

Mythology and religion could be said to operate in exactly the same way, except that what myths are modeling is nothing less than human life itself. Mythology's usefulness lies exactly in the fact that it is not the reality it represents. That is, perhaps the purpose of the outlandish quality of myth, its otherworldliness, its weirdness, if you will, is that it serves precisely to remind us that the story presented is *not* real life, though clearly it is related to real life.

Part of this is signaled by the formulaic openings of mythological stories. Such phrases as "in the beginning" or "at that time" remove the myth from the here and now and put it somewhere else. Great pains are taken to separate mythic time from profane time, as if to let us know that we are about to look at a model, something that lies underneath our daily reality, the skeleton, as it were, that supports the world as we know it. Some of the formulas for separating us from the time of the story are as simple as "once upon a time"; others are quite complex. One Irish formula goes, "Once long ago, and a long time it was. If I were there then, I should not be there now. If I were there now and at that time, I should have a new story or an old story, or I should have no story at all."[10] Clearly we are entering the time of no time, the time that is both here and not here, now and not now—in other words, eternity—a time outside of time, when truths may be told that are not dependent on time. One can see the effect of this "story time" when telling stories to children. At the magic opening "Once upon a time," they come forward on their seats, their eye-blink rate goes down, and their bodies have a slight tension to them. This tension, I think, takes us back to the root of the word *entertainment,* which comes from the French *entre + tenir,* that is, "to hold between." What the story does is suspend us, as it were, between our real outer world and the inner world of imagination. We are in a third place, neither here nor there, where transformations may take place that do not happen in the so-called real world. At the "happily ever after" you can see the children's bodies relax as they return to the present time.

Now, are we saying that the world's great myths are nothing more than children's stories? No, that is the modernist position. Mythology, as a genre, has many similarities with folk tales and fairy tales, of course, but what makes mythology unique is that its intent is not mere entertainment; rather, it seeks to connect us, in a profound and complete way, to matters of ultimate human concern, indeed to the life of the universe itself. Myths, and the rituals that accompany them, are also performative, that is, they effect changes in the hearers. They call forth what Ian Ramsey called a "discernment commitment," that is, a life change, a call to make a life commitment to live a certain way.[11] By undergoing initiation into a myth by a ritual like a baptism or bar mitzvah or the ancient Eleusinian mysteries, one sets one's life on a course that has an archetypal foundation designed to deliver one to wholeness and to sustain one through life's painful and joyful passages, up to and through death. This is no job for a "mere" story. Just as the function of the orrery is to orient us to our position in the physical universe, the job of the myth is to allow us to understand where we stand in the entire compass of our inner and outer life. Myth provides the narrative thread that guides us through the labyrinth of our lives.

Myths have several characteristics that set them apart from other types of stories and from the scientific way of knowing. Their language and form are always dramatic. Characters are caught up in dramatic actions that most often involve the supernatural in some way or other. As such, they are immediately evocative and unsettling, suggesting levels of reality not immediately apparent: bushes are on fire but are not consumed, people walk on water, the dead rise and live again, animals talk to humans, and so on. Myths speak these things directly; that is, unlike theology, which interprets myth, the story appears unmediated, telling itself in a language where metaphor and meaning have not been separated from each other. These stories operate according to their own logic, which is irrational and alogical. That is why the world of the myth strikes us as weird, uncanny. Gods appear and suspend the usual laws of nature. The hero journeys into the land of the dead, flies, speaks with spirits, and so on. In the case of cultural myths, the stories are often related to the identity of the group, providing it with a sacred origin and marking one group off from another. Most importantly, these stories are set in the "not now," even though, as the myth unfolds in our minds, the events seem strangely contemporary.[12]

The insistence on the "here/not here" and "now/not now" quality of the myth is the key to its meaning. The myth is pointedly not here and not now. The ancient Athenians set their tragedies in places and times that were clearly not present-day Athens precisely because removing the world of the plays from the everyday world the audience lived in allowed them to see their everyday world more clearly. By setting the events of *Oedipus Rex* in Thebes, in mythic times, the Athenians could look at the complex interworking of fate and human pride more clearly and, coming out of the dramatic time, return to their daily lives with more wisdom. Mythology is neither here nor there, which is to say it is simultaneously both here and there. If the individual is the microcosm, or small world, contained within the macrocosm of the physical universe, then the myth creates an imaginative "mesocosm" or middle world, which partakes of characteristics of the everyday world but which also has elements of the divine operating in it. The scientific mode of knowing relies upon human reason alone for its conclusions. The world of mythology relies upon human invention and imagination, but that is tinged with something that seems to have its origin elsewhere, outside the human self, given to us by what theologians call the process of revelation. Mythology is the realm in which divine revelation and human imagination come together and coexist.[13]

The world's myths can be understood as answers to some profound questions: How is the world put together? Why do we live? Why do we die? How should we live? How should we die? What is the context in which I can and should understand this universe and this life? This last question is most strange of all, for it asks, in effect, What context can I put the entire universe in? Clearly such questions stretch the human mind, and, not surprisingly, we find that the answers to these questions also stretch human language. Religious language becomes "odd." At the heart of its oddness is metaphor. We will be discussing metaphor and religion at great length in the next two chapters, but for now let us accept a simple definition that a metaphor is a comparison between two unlike things. The philosopher George Santayana was correct when he said that religious language was essentially poetry, and we must remember that poetry is not simply a dressed-up way of saying something that we could say more directly or simply in prose. Poetry, through its use of metaphor, creates a language that, in many ways, is irreducible. As the philosopher John Macquarrie put it, "In mythical discourse, what we recognize as 'literal' and 'symbolic' . . . have not yet been separated out. They are interwoven inextricably in an as yet undifferentiated matrix."[14] Out of this highly symbolic matrix come "the various forms of religious language and perhaps of other kinds of language besides."[15]

We have a tendency to want to explain the myth through psychology or sociology or theology, but we must remember that the myth is already its own explanation. As Walter Ong wrote, "Earlier man . . . found myth neither opaque nor distracting. We [moderns] find it both. We feel obligated to rationalize, to explain symbols which by definition and intent are themselves explanations."[16] In other words, myths simply must be believed. But, of course, *belief* itself is a slippery word.

What does it mean to believe a myth anyway? Clearly, belief is not knowing something as absolute truth. If it was absolutely literally true, it would be known and would not have to be believed. So what does *belief* mean? Originally, *belief* meant "to have confidence or faith in [a person] and consequently to rely upon, trust to."[17] The etymology of *belief* is fascinating, for it comes into English via the common Germanic word *glauben,* which ultimately is traceable to an old Indo-European root *lubh,* which is the same root as our modern English word *love.* That is, to believe something means basically to love it, or prefer it over something else, or to find it pleasing or satisfactory. Like the old meaning of the word *truth,* belief was a matter of trust, something inherent in a person, not a thing, as when we say, "I believe in John." In saying that, we don't mean that we believe that John exists. We know that. What we do mean is that we are satisfied that John is trustworthy, reliable, virtuous, genuine, and so on. To "believe" a person is to choose to accept his or her honesty, but belief cannot be proven as factual; it is a matter of *faith,* a word that itself comes from the Latin *fidere* meaning "to trust." In archaic English usage, we did not believe *in* something, we believed *on* it, suggesting a leaning upon some sort of foundation. This usage is in the King James Version of the Bible: "Believe ye on the Lord Jesus Christ." It is a phrase that is not falsifiable, unlike the phrase "I believe that the earth is flat," which is.

So we come back to fundamentalism, modernism, and a literal reading of the Bible. It should be clear by now that when I say the Bible is a myth, I am not denigrating it or indicating it is false. Rather, I am saying that the Bible contains tremendous truth, but it is truth understood in a particular way because the truths of the Bible are expressed through poetic language, which operates according to rules we may have largely forgotten.

As we saw in chapter 3, both science and religion accepted a definition of *truth* that located truth outside the self, in an object, or, in the case of literal interpretation of scripture, in a book. Ironically, they had both made the same mistake as regards the notion of truth and the way sacred stories convey their truth. The mistake was taking metaphors as expressions of literal truth rather than encountering them on their own poetic terms. They wanted religious language to operate the way regular day-to-day talk operated, but it was never designed to do that. Given the tenor of the times during which fundamentalism arose, this misunderstanding was probably unavoidable.

A poetic or metaphorical way of understanding something was seen as vastly inferior to the kind of understanding one could get through science and reason. As Earl MacCormac wrote, "the prevalence of metaphor in religious discourse" proved to scientists and logical positivists that religion "failed utterly as a mode of meaningful communication" for myth, like metaphor, failed science's test of "verifiability."[18] Thus the early fundamentalists' concern for finding the truth of the ark of the covenant or locating the remains of Noah's ark. If tangible scientific evidence could be found, then literalists could prove, in a scientific sense, the literal truth of the Bible. Chasing after absolute proof turned out to be a fool's errand for the religionists and scientists alike.

The apparent triumph of scientific thought lasted only a short time, of course. As twentieth-century science evolved, it became clear that its notion of itself as a pathway to absolute objective truth was mistaken. Werner Heisenberg taught us that there are even limits to what we *can* know. We cannot, for example, know both the exact location and the speed of an electron. We can know one or the other, but it is impossible to know both simultaneously. Neils Bohr showed us that the same entity could be either a wave or a particle depending on what we needed it to be and wanted to know about it. Science, like the rest of human life, contained a built-in ambiguity. By the 1970s, thanks to Thomas Kuhn's groundbreaking book *The Structure of Scientific Revolutions,* it had become clear that scientific facts were true only within certain paradigms. That is, any scientific theory or discovery could be said to be true only within a conceptual framework that operated very much like a poetic metaphor. The best we could say about something in the real world was, in effect, "It's like this. . . ." In other words, science, too, was forced to speak in similes and metaphors. Even scientists now admit that there is no such thing as unambiguous and absolute truth. This leaves extreme religious fundamentalists as the last holdouts of a seventeenth-century mind-set. Unfortunately, we have in the interim forgotten just how the language of metaphor is "true," and we have also not yet figured out that just because we say something is not "true" in the factual sense, we are not therefore saying that it must be "false."

Which brings us back to myth. What does myth have to offer us in the present age and how are we to understand it if not literally? If myth, operating as a model for human life, functions like an orrery, allowing us to get a view of the whole of life, where we only experience it in parts, then having a good grounding in one's culture's myth forms a kind of "tacit knowledge." Michael Polanyi, a twentieth-century philosopher, coined this term to name a sort of knowledge that encompasses other kinds of knowledge we may have. "Tacit knowledge" is implicit, largely unconscious knowledge that we gain through life experience and from our culture. As such, it forms a foundation for our actions and decisions, even if we are unaware of it. We use it constantly in making judgments about courses of action, values, moral issues. Since it is so comprehensive, it is difficult to articulate just what it is, but one knows it intuitively and senses it more in the gut than in the head. This largely intuitive way of knowing allows us to map the larger world and forms a kind of meta-knowledge. As A. S. Reber wrote in "Implicit vs. Explicit Learning":

> [It] is a cognitive state that emerges under specifiable conditions, and it operates to assist an individual to make choices and to engage in particular classes of action. To have an intuitive feeling of what is right and proper, to have a vague feeling of the goal of an extended process of thought, to "get the point" without really being able to verbalize what it is that one has gotten, is to have gone through an implicit learning experience and have built up the requisite representative knowledge base to allow for such judgment.[19]

This, roughly, is what a religion or mythological system should do. It provides us with a basis for judgment, especially in those (many) areas of life where the rational mind is of no or little use. But how do we know if it is "true"? We are back to that word.

Scientific truth depends on verifiability and, to use Karl Popper's term, falsifiability. That is, empirical evidence can be offered to show that a particular proposition is true, or an experiment can prove empirically that a hypothesis is false. In fundamentalism we have seen where asking for this sort of proof from religion can lead. The Millerite millennialists who used the book of Revelation to prophesy the end of the world in 1844 had their hypothesis falsified by experience. Similarly, creation science or Intelligent Design is not capable of providing credible empirical evidence of their position, nothing anyway that compares with the weight of evidence that can be provided to support evolution. When we ask a mythology to support itself with this kind of real-world evidence, it inevitably comes up short because the questions it asks are not of that kind. The empirical mind cannot answer questions like "Where is the home of the wind?" It says, "Show me the great spirit you say hovers over this lake. Where are the naiads and dryads? Show me one. Show me the remains of Noah's ark." It barks up the wrong tree. It is clear that when we apply empirical criteria to religion, religion is quickly reduced to absurdity. Looked at empirically, religion is all too easily falsifiable, but that doesn't mean it isn't true. It simply means that our definition of *truth* has become too narrow. It means we have mistaken religious language for scientific language and try to hold it up to the same standard, a standard by which it will ultimately fail.

But is there another kind of verifiability by which we can understand the solid truth of myth or religion? There is, but it is of a different order and subtlety than the scientific kind, for the ultimate criterion of the "truth" of a mythological system or religion is tested by human experience across the lifespan, and whether it is "true" in that word's older sense of steadfast, reliable, loyal, and dependable.

Think of the questions myths address, facing many of life's imponderables such as birth, death, the origin of things, the sense of it all. If myths are to be reliable models of all this, they must satisfy certain criteria, they must do a certain amount of "work" for us, and in the end we must have a sense of their truth, in the older sense. Earl Mac-Cormac wrote, "Religious language must be testable in the sense that common experiences must be available that are capable of interpretation in religious terms and symbols. Unlike science, these common experiences need not all be observable since much of religious expression involves feelings and desires."[20] Like all metaphorical speech, mythological systems must be confirmed by experience, except that it is experience of a different order than that delivered by isolated experiences.

Some of the basic questions we can ask when seeking the truth of a myth or religion are quite pragmatic:[21]

- Does it help us comprehend the world, not just the physical world we can sense but our inner world as well?
- Does it effectively help us negotiate the passages of life that we must go through, such as grief, pain, growth, joy?
- Does it bring together aspects of life that otherwise might remain separated and fragmented? Does it give a sense of wholeness? (As we'll see in the next chapter, this is the root meaning of the words *religion* and *holy*.)
- Does it provide a way of organizing and guiding our relations with other people? Does it teach us how to behave responsibly and compassionately in the world?

These are questions that can be answered, and insofar as they can be answered in the affirmative, our myth is "true," in the older and more profound sense of *truth*. So, the criteria are, in a sense, empirical. Does thinking of the suffering of Job or Jesus help us endure the suffering in our life? Does praying to God or offering a sacrifice give us a sense of coherence? Do the various stories of mythic heroes returning from the land of the dead with the elixir of life help us understand the mystery of death? Does the story we "believe on" enable us to live more compassionately?

Mythopoesis, the creation of myths, is a profound activity. The plastic, elastic, metaphor-making, living, breathing story-making capacity of human beings is perhaps the most powerful means we have of comprehending our world in such a way that we may live in it fully. It seems endless in its capacity to refresh itself, to make itself relevant through time and across cultures. When one system gets attenuated or grows brittle, another rises in its place. When traditional systems no longer speak to a generation, the mythic impulse gives rise to new stories, and story begets story endlessly.

We live today in a desacralized world, a world deprived of sacred stories, and both the fundamentalists, who try to make the story into science, and the modernists, who try to "explain" the myths or debunk them, have flattened the world we live in. Imagine living in the classical world, where every grove, field, hill, and stream, every well and fountain, had a presiding deity and a myth or story of origin. The gods, if not a God, would be omnipresent, if only in the sheer abundance of their numbers. To live in a storied world, in which our personal life story merges with the larger story of the universe, a universe with meaning and cohesion, is the goal of mythology and religion. If myth is ambiguous, it is so because so much of life is ambiguous. Anything less than the ambiguity of a story is not adequate to deal with the complexity of life as we experience it. If myth is to be a mirror of life, if we are to judge it by its ability to lead us through the labyrinth, then we must allow it to have the same ambiguity as life itself.

In ancient Norse legend, Odin, the chief of the gods, went forth to seek wisdom. He traveled through the entire world questioning those he met. He even went to the magic spring of his uncle Mimir, which was located at the base of the world tree Yggdrasil and sacrificed an eye to drink from it to gain wisdom. Finally, he impaled himself with a spear on Yggdrasil to face death itself. Nine nights and days he hung on the tree, writhing in pain. His shuddering caused twigs to break off the world tree and they fell to the ground beneath him. Gazing down from his place of suffering, he saw that the twigs had formed themselves into patterns that became the sacred runes in which the stories of the gods could be written down. The power of the runes freed him from his suffering. He fell to the ground and gathered them up, rejuvenated by their strength. In a song to the power of the runes, which is really a song in praise of the power of myth, he said,

> Then began I to grow and gain in insight,
> To wax great in wisdom;
> One verse led on to another verse,
> One poem led on to another poem.[22]

In myth, story leads to story, and the story is never finished, for it is the story of human life itself, constantly unfolding. Clearly, mythology is a profound way of knowing the world, a way that is, in a word, "religious." And it is to the loaded word *religion* that we must next turn.

6 : Religion

W E OFTEN use the word *religion* indiscriminately and without thinking to refer to a body of dogma (the Catholic *religion*), an organization ("What *religion* do you belong to?"), or a way of being in the world ("What's your *religion*?"). And, of course, *religion* means all three of those things and more. But like many words that we overuse, its meaning has become dulled. In this time when the word *religion* is being used by some extremists as a bludgeon to get others to vote their way, it might be good to reexamine just what religion can and perhaps ought to be and do. This is a hugely complicated subject, of course, and to keep it somewhat manageable we'll start with what the word *religion* might mean to us as individuals, then as individuals living in a world filled with others who may or may not share our religion (chapter 7), and finally, in chapter 8, we will have to take on the question of what *religion* means in relation to that most loaded word of all, *God*.

We can begin with a simple question. What does it mean to live religiously?

The spring 2005 advertising campaign for Apple's new iPod Shuffle, a smaller version of its popular iPod, summed up perfectly what many people feel today. The new device is not programmable like its older brother but rather shuffles through the user's hundreds of uploaded songs randomly. The product's slogan was "Life is random," and its ad on Apple's Web page proudly states, "Random is the new order."[1] Exactly. Randomness in some ways has been the hallmark of life in the late twentieth and early twenty-first century. From the random mutations of genes that provide the mechanism for evolution to the random selectivity of hypertext on the Web, to the randomness of much postmodern art and philosophy, we have grown used to the idea that things in life happen without a reason.

Randomness, however, is the exact opposite of a religious view of life. A religion, if it is a good one, tells us life does have meaning, that events do happen for a reason, or at least in an orderly way, even if we don't fully understand the order behind them. A religion tells us that the universe didn't just happen.

When we look at the etymology of the word *religion*, we find justification for that belief. Philologists disagree about the word's ultimate root, but all three of its possible derivations suggest just how opposite the "Life is random" philosophy is from an authentic religious worldview. The first etymology given by the *OED* suggests that *religion* comes from the Latin root *religare*, "to tie or bind together," and thus *religion* shares its origin with the English words *ligature* and *ligament.*[2] Augustine recognized this usage. This derivation suggests that religion somehow binds our lives together in a meaningful way, just as our ligaments hold our bones together and allow them to function. Without our ligaments, our bones would be rather randomly organized. With them, our bones work together effectively. In this sense, religion should "re-ligament" us.

This meaning of the word is reinforced by the Sanskrit word *yoga*, which most of us know in its hatha yoga form as a series of postures and exercises designed to stretch the muscles and keep the joints flexible while also enhancing feelings of calm, peace, and connectedness. In the Hindu tradition, the word *yoga* is used generally to refer to a spiritual discipline, and there are several kinds, including bhakti and karma yoga. The word *yoga* itself is from an old Indo-European root meaning "to join together," which is also the root of our English word *yoke*, as in "a yoke of oxen." In effect, then, yoga has as its goal the same thing as *religion*. Whether we speak of *yoga* or of *religion*, we begin with an assumption that some sort of yoking together of elements that once were connected but that have come apart is both necessary and possible. Religions are based on myths, which as we saw in the last chapter, are narrative ways of knowing the world. One of the prime characteristics of narrative knowledge is its synthetic power, that is, its ability to draw together what previously seemed separate. So as we cluster words like *religion, myth,* and *yoga* together, we see a common concern with integration and wholeness, the opposite of the "life is random" philosophy.

In an alternate, but really complementary, etymology, Cicero suggested that the Latin *religionem* came from *relegere,* "to reread something."[3] Religious texts are the writings we return to and read over again when searching for the meaning and connectedness of life. The two etymologies nicely complement each other, for one of the purposes of a religious tradition is to expose us to beliefs over the course of our lifetimes and to reinforce those beliefs through the repetition of familiar texts and rituals, thus "re-ligamenting" us to our past (tradition), our community, and ourselves.

A third possible etymological sidelight on the word suggests that in Latin *religens* is the opposite of *negligens,* sometimes spelled *necligens,* meaning "to neglect."[4] From the Latin prefix *neg* or *nec* ("not") + *legere* ("to pick up"), to neglect is to not pick things up. Those "things" could be one's belongings or one's life. To live *neglectfully* is to live without paying attention to things, to live carelessly, unconsciously even. Those who live *religiously,* on the other hand, are not negligent about their lives. They do "pick things up," and live their lives with care, order, and consciousness. The philologist Walter Skeat connects this with yet another Latin word, *diligens,* from which we get our English *diligent.*[5] To live religiously is to live diligently, that is, to live with a steady, honest effort to move forward. In the Middle Ages, the opposite of this way of life was called *acedia,* one of the deadly sins, which we could translate as "spiritual laziness." A person with *acedia* was too lazy to undertake the hard job of spiritual life, or, as we might say in modern psychological terms, too lazy to take on the task of personal growth and would rather wallow about in random, purposeless behavior. To live religiously is to shoulder the burden of personal development, to live life in a forward, not a random, direction.

The first thing the varied etymology of the word should show us is that we should think of *religion* as more of an action word than a noun denoting a body of beliefs or a particular creed to which we subscribe. That is, even though we don't have a verb "to religion" in English, the origin of the word seems to indicate that "to religion" is a way of life, a way of being and acting in the world that we express as "to live religiously," that is, to live in such a way that our lives are bound together by rereading religious texts (or rehearing our tribe's myths) and participating in rituals that teach us how to live in a more or less connected way.

There has been a tendency in recent years for people to shy away from using the word *religious* to describe themselves. Perhaps it is due to the word's misuse or the way it seems inevitably linked in current discourse with the word *right,* as in the "the religious right." Or perhaps the word has been too often associated with a kind of piety that modern people feel somewhat squeamish about, a holding to the party line of this or that religion, which seems limiting. Or again perhaps enough people have been burned by the frequent hypocrisy of organized religion that they have grown wary of the word. It is very common for people to say today that they are "*spiritual* but not *religious,*" by which they frequently mean they have a private interior life. The problem with the word *spiritual,* as Lionel Corbett points out, is that it suggests a kind of disembodied and solitary stance, cut off from the physical and social aspects of our human existence. We'll have more to say about *spirit* later, but perhaps it's time to rehabilitate *religion* and its derivatives, for it really is a useful word that names a way of being and acting in the world that is distinct from other ways.

Let's begin the process of rehabilitation by putting forward a tentative definition. Let's say that one's religion is whatever binds one's life together in a meaningful way. But just what is the peculiarly religious way of binding a life together? And how does it differ from other ways of understanding our existence? And what role do traditional religions, including Christianity, play in that?

Lionel Corbett, a psychoanalyst, in a fascinating book entitled *The Religious Function of the Psyche,* suggests that in each of us there is a religious function, that is, a potential or capacity for living in a religious way. A Jungian, Corbett identifies this religious function with the archetype Jung called the Self, that is, a transcendent function in the unconscious that enables us to grow toward our fullest potential as human beings. To use an odd analogy, we might think of ourselves as hermit crabs, and the personality we have at the moment—our characteristic way of being and behaving in the world—is our shell. As we grow, we put pressure on that outer shell, creating strains and stress. If we remain trapped inside that shell—that is, refuse to leave its safety to undertake the risk of finding a new, larger shell—we will eventually die. In psychological terms, we might say that just as the body has its inner impulse to grow and pass through the various stages of development from infancy through adulthood and into old age and death, so, too, does the mind (or psyche or soul). If the process of growth gets stuck at any point, then, like the hermit crab trapped in a too-small shell, we die, which in psychological terms we could say is stagnation. Like the person who suffers from *acedia,* we are either too lazy or, more often, too afraid, to undertake the task of growth. But where is the new "shell" or new iteration of the self to come from? What form shall it take?

This is where religions, and the myths on which religions are based, come in, for if, as we suggested in the last chapter, the myth provides a narrative way of knowing, a sort of *savoir* regarding life itself, then inherent in the myth is an archetype or model for ongoing human life that will lead us to, and finally through, death.

Perhaps the easiest way to illustrate this is to start where Buddhism begins. The First Noble Truth revealed to the Buddha in his long, youthful quest for enlightenment was that all life is suffering. This is a profound religious insight. Note that the First Noble Truth of Buddhism does not say "There is suffering *in* life." It says all life *is* suffering. Some of us may find this a rather repugnant idea on which to base a religious approach to life, but it is no more repugnant than to believe that all human beings are born in a state of sin and degradation; in fact, it may be another way of saying approximately the same thing, at least from a psychological point of view.

At least part of what religion, or living religiously, should do for us is to resolve our psychological suffering by providing us a model for a way to live that enables us to heal or at least to make sense of the inner conflicts, the sense of futility, meaninglessness, and loneliness that seem to go with being human. In addition, and more positively, one's religion should give one something to live for. Without some sort of religion, some way of binding together the otherwise fragmented pieces of our lives and of healing the inner conflicts and suffering we inevitably have as humans, we may take our suffering out on others. Perhaps this is what *sin* is: in confusion, in pain, out of fear, or boredom, we impulsively lash out at others, committing violence, physical or otherwise, on them, if only for the perverse pleasure of seeing someone else suffer as I am suffering. These are the sorts of evils from which we need to be saved, and it is precisely from these that religion and the religious function of the psyche can deliver us, if we understand them correctly and learn to discern good uses of religion from the bad.

To be delivered from these darker manifestations of our own suffering is to be, in a word, *holy*. Like *religion*, the word *holy* has become somewhat debased through misuse. Suggesting either a milksop piety or a "holy Joe" kind of righteousness, *holy* and *holiness* have become separated from their original meanings. They really are useful words, deserving of better understanding. They come from the old Anglo-Saxon root *hal*, which was an amazingly comprehensive word. Over the past thousand years, *hal*'s various meanings have differentiated into other words that seem unrelated at first, but if we put the modern descendants of *hal* together, we get some idea of what this old word originally meant. They include *whole, healthy, hale* (as in "hale and hearty"), *heal*, the neologism *holistic*, and, as mentioned, *holy*, and *holiness*. To say "Hello" to someone, therefore, is to wish them health, wholeness, and holiness all together. Our holidays were originally "holy days," days when we suspended our usual workaday activities and celebrated all those aspects of life that transcended the getting of our daily bread and made us whole. So, the pursuit of holiness is nothing less than the pursuit of wholeness, and our religion, the thing that binds us together, should lead us in that direction or it is worth very little at all.

The pursuit of wholeness or holiness often comes from a personal encounter with what Rudolph Otto called the "tremendous and fascinating mystery." Of what? Of life itself, or of the human experience of it in all its dimensions. We see such encounters in scripture when

Moses comes upon the burning bush, when Jacob dreams of the ladder and wrestles with the angel of God, when Job faces God in the theophany of the whirlwind. Christians encounter it in the entire life of Jesus, who through his incarnation combines both the human being that we recognize as ourselves with the ultimate mystery to which we give the name *God*. We could say the Buddha had a similar encounter with ultimate mystery in what are known as the Four Great Signs, when he wandered out into the roadways at night and encountered, for the first time in his sheltered life, disease, old age, death, and, finally, a monk whose eyes shone with such a calm light in the midst of all the world's suffering that the young Siddhartha felt called to leave his comfortable home and set out to find enlightenment. Like these mythic heroes, we, too, have our encounters with divinity and mystery. Ours may come in the form of the death of a loved one, or in being suddenly taken over by the sheer beauty of a sunset on a lake shore or the immensity of the cosmos on a starry night, or in a terminal diagnosis from our doctor; one way or another, the existential condition of being human confronts us with our limited place in the whole scheme of existence and challenges us to make sense of it. This "sense" must be more than simply an intellectual comprehension; it must be "holy," that is, it must take into account all of our experience, not just one part of it. It must encompass our whole self, not just our intellect. And this is precisely the role that religion, at its best, can fulfill.

Modern psychology has given us a good template by which to judge the effectiveness of a person's religion. If religion calls us to become "holy," that is, whole, then an authentically religious person should at least have all, or most of, the characteristics of someone who has achieved the highest levels of human development. Different developmental psychologists call this highest level of development by different names, but the general characteristics are similar in each scheme. A full, self-actualized person is flexible, not brittle; has a tolerance for the ambiguity of life rather than seeing things in strictly black-and-white terms; accepts life's inevitable limitations, including death; and lives in a way that is not narcissistic, that is, that does not have the person's own ego needs at the center. At their best, mature individuals have a sense of what Eric Erikson called "generativity," a desire to pass on values and meaning to others, including the next generation, and to create a better world, not just for themselves but for all. In the final stages of growth they may even achieve wisdom, a word that is ultimately from the Indo-European word *wid,* meaning "to see." (It is related to the word *vision.*) The wise, in other words, have learned to see things in a broader perspective, free from the limits of their own egos.

Religion at its best calls us to live in such a way that, as we age, we continue to grow in our humanity, becoming our "whole self." The twentieth-century theologian Henry Wieman put the essential religious question quite succinctly in this way, "What ultimate commitment will deliver me from the false and superficial level of life and enable me to live myself out to the full with whatever struggle and suffering and courage and ecstasy this may involve?"[6]

Perhaps, in the end, this is what *salvation* means. Many picture salvation as the Rapture, when the saved will be taken up to their heavenly reward. As such, salvation is out there, yet to happen, but the root of the word suggests it is something that may be had here and now. While it is directly derived from the Latin *salvare,* "to save," it is certainly also related to the Latin *salvere,* "to heal," the same word from which we get the word *salve.* As we saw earlier, to *heal* and to be *whole* come from the same word that *holy* does, so the complex of these words suggests that one is "saved" by choosing to live in such a way that one becomes whole. The transformation that comes with an authentic experience of being "born again" is another way of saying that a person faced with the ultimate religious question of how to live his or her life finally sees a way, a model, if you will, of self-transformation in the story of Jesus or the Buddha or Muhammad or any of the other mythic culture heroes who have left their mark on the human psyche. The mythic narrative provides a template for human self-transformation. The world's mythologies and the religions that are based on them are time-tested patterns whose ultimate goal is to help their adherents live their lives to their fullest, through growth, suffering, joy, and sorrow, even into and beyond death.

To put it more concretely, and in Christian terms, the story of the incarnation, life, teachings, suffering, death, and resurrection of Jesus, told in the narratives of the Gospels, provides the mythic exemplar of how to live a whole and holy life. The disciples asked, "How then shall we live?" and Jesus responded, "Follow me," "I am the way, the truth and the life," or, as he said to the rich young man, "Sell all you own and distribute the money to the poor and you shall have treasure in heaven; then come follow me" (Luke 18:22).

This kind of shocking challenge, and the even more difficult challenge Jesus gives his followers to love their enemies and to turn the other cheek, as well as the ultimate challenge of the example of his death undergone for the sake of others have the cumulative effect of rattling us out of our everyday complacency with our lives. Religious language has a way of turning all our normal life expectations inside out. Blessed are the poor, blessed are the peacemakers, blessed are the merciful—this language flies in the face of ordinary human assumptions about life that say the rich, the warmakers, and the stern and self-righteous are the ones to emulate. In fact, Jesus goes on to castigate the rich and powerful in Luke's account, saying, "Alas for you who are rich; you are having your consolation now" (Luke 6:25). Religious language shifts our gestalt, as it were, and makes the world we thought we knew suddenly seem strange. Perhaps this is why we find religious language so appropriate and useful when events such as the death of a loved one or a natural disaster such as Hurricane Katrina turn our lives upside down. Religious language is already, in a sense, a topsy-turvy language, bending our usual use of words, reminding us of what is and isn't really important in this life. The message of religion is that we should *always* live in the way we live when we see a natural disaster or the grief of a friend; that is, the sort of compassion we show in extraordinary times we should also show in ordinary times, and those values that bring out the best in us should be operating, not just in times of obvious need but all the time.

The story of the Buddha, leaving behind his life of royal luxury and setting out on the path to enlightenment, challenges us in a similar way because it, too, is an affront to common sense. The Buddhist scriptures call us from our natural self-centeredness to live a life of other-centered compassion, even to having sympathy for the suffering of all sentient beings, not just other humans, and not just in this lifetime but in lifetime after lifetime, as in the case of bodhisattvas who choose to incarnate again and again until the whole world is brought to enlightenment. This certainly seems to counter the motive of self-interest, which many modernists believe to be the prime or only motive of human existence. But, on reflection, we come to see the wisdom of this way of life.

The stories we read in the world's scriptures and the tales we hear told in our myths call us to see life in a way that at first does not seem normal. In the end, however, they lead us to a fullness of being, for they show us how to turn the common wisdom of the world inside out and to live a life that is not self-centered and materialistic but that has at its core compassion and concern for others. The world's religions teach us that only this way of living will creatively transform individuals and make them "whole." This is because removing the ego from the center of the universe actually expands the self. This is the essential paradox of religion, expressed by Jesus in the following way: "For anyone who wants to save his life will lose it; but anyone who loses his life for my sake will find it" (Matthew 16:25). Living "religiously" in this way connects one to a larger community and, finally, to the universe itself. Compassion breaks down the barriers of the self and allows it to expand the way the hermit crab expands when it abandons its old shell and seeks a more capacious one.

Using these criteria, can we judge the value of the religious path we may be on without subjecting it either to the rigid standards of extreme fundamentalism ("Our way is the only way") or descending into postmodern relativism ("Any way is okay")? Applying what we know of human psychology, can we better understand the human experience of the divine?

The liberal theologian Henry Wieman identified three types of religion, and these may help us to judge when a path is a good one. The first kind of religion showed itself as mental illness. A schizophrenic, for example, might identify himself with Jesus, have delusions of grandeur, and feel called directly by God to commit various acts, as we see in the occasional news stories of mothers who feel ordered by God to kill their children, or assassins who say they are called by the voice of God to kill public figures. These people feel they are genuinely religious, but clearly these destructive and self-destructive uses of religion are an aberration from what religion, in the sense of "binding together," should be. The self in mental illness is fragmented and unstable, not "ligamented," and we need to reject this kind of religion.

The second kind of religion identified by Wieman is that of social conformity. People following this path do so because it is "the thing to do." To be a good citizen one should belong to a church, so I choose this one or that one and go, but never let the oddity of the religious calling bother me too much, not enough to significantly change my life. These people may do wonderful work in the world, helping out in church-sponsored missions, volunteering in soup kitchens, and so on, and this should not be ridiculed or put down. As we'll see in a moment, the social dimension of religion is a vitally important one, and part of the binding together that religion accomplishes is to bind us to other people in our religious community and in the larger communities in which we live. But this social form of religion is essentially an outer-directed thing and not religion at its most profound.

For Wieman, the deepest and most valuable form of religion for the individual is what he calls the religion of creativity, that is, living a life committed to whatever it is that brings about the transformation of the authentic self.[7] This is what we call a life of faith and belief. Faith, says Wieman, is "the act by which the individual commits himself in the wholeness of his being so far as he can to what he believes will transform man as he cannot transform himself to save him from evil and endow him with the greatest good, provided that he meet the required conditions."[8] The key notion here is that one commits one's whole self. Faith calls forth action, not just an intellectual assent, and anything less than a commitment of one's whole life leaves parts of the self fragmented and broken off.

Faith, trust, and *belief* are slippery words. We tend not to use them because we don't understand them or we want them to be something other than they are. We want proof, like the agnostic Thomas Huxley, but no proof is possible. Rather, we find we must take the Kierkegaardian "leap of faith." The narratives of religion, the stories and the language of the stories, may help us. If we are lucky, if we really understand the topsy-turvy language of religion and mythology, then we may have an "aha" moment, a flash of intuition about life, existence itself. We may see a pattern with some depth of understanding and inner sight. Then we may become "enlightened," or at least begin to see where the light comes from, and at that point we make an irrational commitment to live in the way our myth shows us. Whether that way is "true" in a scientific sense or not, we will find out its "truth," in the older, deeper sense of its reliability, trustworthiness, honorableness, and loyalty, when we are "true" to it in the way we live. As the Anglican bishop Ian Ramsey put it many years ago, this commitment, if it is going to be truly religious—that is, if it truly is going to bind us together—must be "a commitment suited to the whole job of living . . . not just to the pursuit of one's vocation or of knowledge or of personal relations but to all of those things (and more) together."[9]

This is scary territory for a modern person to enter. Conditioned by a hundred years or more of secularism, we distrust religious language and the religious impulse. In becoming religious, we are being asked to exchange our modernist lens, which seems so sure, for something that feels quite older and less reliable. Yet, in many ways, the religious way of looking at the world has been better tested, over a longer period of time, than any of the modern hard or social sciences in which we now place our faith. That is, long before there were pills for depression, mythology and religion—the narrative ways of knowing our existence—were helping people pass through the stages of life and all its travails. There is something deeply powerful in this narrative way of knowing, which, at its best, helps us to understand our lives, to function in the world, to accomplish works in the world that are perceived as meaningful, to relate to others in the world, to make commitments, and to get through life's vicissitudes, successfully leading what we call "a good life." *Belief,* that word that grows from the ancient word *lubh,* "love," underlies all these things. Belief is an action, a choice, not a body of dogmas. We don't *have* it, we *live* it. It is a way of comporting ourselves toward the world. When we put on the lens of belief, we see the world in a different way and we behave in the world in a different way. We may become "large-souled." That is the term used in India for Mohandas Gandhi, who was given the honorific title *mahatma,* from the Sanskrit *maha* ("great") + *atman* ("soul"). The word's synonym in

English is *magnanimity*. With a religious view of the world, one may become magnanimous, which comes from the Latin *magna* ("great") + *anima* ("soul"). The opposite of *magnanimity* is *pusillanimity*, which we could define as "small-souled," though its literal meaning is more interesting, for it comes from a Latin word, *pusus*, which means "small boy." Pusillanimous people are selfish, self-centered, temperamental, childlike in the worst sense, while magnanimous people have the largeness of soul to live in a way not centered on the self but on others.

So, why do we hesitate? Since the potential rewards are so great, why don't more of us become "religious"? Perhaps one reason is that many of us feel we lack an acceptable model of how to be religious in the contemporary world. That is, the most visible models of religious behavior today are the fundamentalists of the far religious right, who have been publicly flexing their muscular brand of Christianity for the past twenty years. Many people, even many Christians, find that model inadequate, if not repulsive. In fact, many people would say that form of religion is diametrically opposite to the real aims of religion.

But those of us who are uncomfortable with fundamentalism have let ourselves be put in a defensive position. We have grown unsure about our own religious principles and so have allowed fundamentalists to set the terms of the discussion about religion in America today. When we hear fundamentalists declare, with apparent utter confidence, that they have the real old-time religion, many of us back down from argument because we are not confident in our own beliefs. Or, if we don't back off, we find ourselves only able to offer the usual relativism and in reply say, weakly, that if fundamentalists believe fundamentalism is true for them, then it is true for them, but it doesn't have to be true for me, an argument that, after all, amounts to backing away. Those who object to hard-core funamentalism must come up with a better response, and after our discussion of what a religious way of life can do for the individual, I think we are ready to begin.

The first step might be to ask whether a particular approach to living religiously in the world seems to stunt people's genuine religious growth or to foster it. This is difficult to determine, because so many people who turn to religion feel, in the words of the song "Amazing Grace," that they once were lost but now are found, were blind but now they see. That may be subjectively true, but from an outside perspective, we need to ask whether they have simply traded one kind of blindness for another and have, as a result, only achieved the opposite of what an authentic religious vision ought to be. Whether they are born again into a conservative style of Christianity, or take up Zen practice, or become Wiccan or Episcopalian, the criteria should be the same.

Lionel Corbett, looking at religion from a psychoanalytic perspective, shows us how to judge whether a person's turn to religion is genuinely fostering growth or whether it is really symptomatic of incomplete psychological development. He writes that a healthy religious attitude leads to genuine "strengthening of the self . . . increased self-esteem, the discovery of a new direction in life, [and] increases the capacity for self-soothing and increased vitality"[10] that integrates the self and increases a person's tolerance for life's ambiguities. A bad turn to religion brings about just the opposite characteristics. True, many people who find religion feel stronger, but we should ask whether it is true strength—which includes flexibility and the wisdom of knowing when to apply it—or whether it is only a bully's strength, wielded indiscriminately on anyone who appears weaker. Is it a strength that relies on pointing out and ridiculing others' weaknesses? Is it mere stiffening of resolve, which is also not real strength? There is a brittle quality to the belief of many people who "get religion," a brittleness, Corbett notes, "in which palpable, often thinly veiled terror is partially bound by rigid adherence to a belief that is obviously necessary to hold things together."[11] This desperate rigidity "has the value of protecting individuals who need defensive containment to deal with an emotional difficulty," and associating with other like-minded believers reinforces this defensive attitude and provides support for what otherwise might be a delusional belief.[12] This, however, does not make it a good or even healthy path for them or for the world they live in. In fact, it describes the mentality of many people who join cults, seeking to boost their own self-esteem by retreating into compounds of like-minded believers cut off from the world.

The grandiose certainty of extreme fundamentalists when they say that they, and they alone, know what God wants for America or what

Allah wants for the world is, from a psychological point of view, an unhealthy reaction motivated by what must be an underlying and profound uncertainty that cannot be admitted without the brittle boundaries of the self collapsing. They, like us, live in the anxiety-provoking and fragmented modern world, and their coping mechanism is to withdraw into a righteous shell from which they lash out at the world. Even from a theological point of view, such certitude about the intentions of God suggests an overweening pride and a kind of spiritual arrogance that is the opposite of Christian humility or Islamic submission.

Other symptoms of a bad religious adjustment manifest themselves in symptoms such as "increased hatred, envy, rage, bitterness, and instransigence in relation to other people, cynicism about human [versus 'divine'] values, and increased self-absorption."[13] This self-absorption and cynicism may show themselves in the Christian fundamentalist theology of the Rapture, which, instead of connecting believers with the rest of humanity, separates them into camps of "we the saved" and "you the damned" and can propose for humanity's future nothing more optimistic than that it must end in a global conflagration from which they, and they alone, will be spared. Quasi-Christian cults such as Heaven's Gate, whose members committed suicide together in 1997, also divide themselves from "the world" and fear its contamination, withdrawing into enclaves where they feed one another's often-paranoid delusions. This is the ultimate in narcissism, to believe that all of human history is about themselves and that the divine, however it is imaged, has nothing else to worry about except their small world. The proud strutting of the self-righteous of all religions is the absolute opposite of the prophet Micah's injunction to "walk humbly with your God."

So there must be another way to be religious in the contemporary world, a way that leads to the ability to be responsive to modern life's complexities and ambiguities without bellicosity, that fosters genuine, not illusory, growth of the self, that can lead us to a larger sense of connectedness to and creative engagement in the world than we get from the shrill and divisive voices of the extreme right.

As we've seen, there is great need for a genuine religious way of being in the world today. The modern secular view of the world, which has dominated society for so long, is as limited, in its own way, as the fundamentalist one, and may even constitute another form of fundamentalism. That is, the modernist point of view, like the fundamentalist, views the world through only one lens. Like fundamentalism, it insists on literal truth, even though its means of arriving at it are through human reason and logic rather than through scripture. The strict modernist keeps demanding proof for things for which there may be no "proof" available, at least not in the sense that they demand it. And in the end, modernism, too, may be a dead end, exhausted as a way of being in the world. One sign of its exhaustion may be, ironically, the rise of religious fundamentalism as an alternative to it.

So what should contemporary religion look like? Why should we try to salvage religion in any form? Aren't all traditional religions just outmoded creeds with nothing to teach the modern world? The modernist cynic may ask whether they aren't all just hypocritical ways of making money from the innocent, or may join with the Marxists who regarded religion as an opiate that dulled the masses to the oppression of their lives and allowed the powers that be to maintain their hegemony by keeping the downtrodden in their place by citing divine authority.

It is certainly true that there has been and is much evil done in the name of religion, but religion itself, or the religious impulse, is worth cultivating, because when understood and practiced correctly, in accordance with the best of its traditions, religion can do a superb job of ordering our inner and outer worlds. There is a psychic function that religion performs for us in ways that nothing else does. It can open us up to the world and open the world to us in a complete way. It is capable of transforming us from top to bottom, making us more, not less, compassionate; more, not less, tolerant of other views; more, not less, bound up with the fates of others on the planet. At its fullest, religion calls us out of ourselves and gives us a way to be and to behave in the world. It should help us to make the whole world "holy," in the fullest sense of that word—whole, healthy, healed. Authentic religion is expansive, not restrictive. On the individual level, it breaks down the barriers of the self; it does not build them.

In the ethical monotheism of Judaism as well as in the teachings of the compassionate Buddha, and certainly in the Christian Gospels, we are called upon to live not just for ourselves but for others. The same is suggested in Islam, where one of its five "pillars" is giving alms to aid others. When an individual finds a religious path, any religious path that opens him or her to the world, that expands the soul in the way we have been talking about, and that enables him or her to live more compassionately in the world, then the path is good one. This is what it means to live in a religious way, to take this sort of stance toward life—one's own life, the lives of others, and life on the planet generally. Only thus is one made whole within oneself, and only thus does one get connected both to the world and to the divine. This is religion in its sense of *religare,* "to be bound together." Living religiously, one returns again and again to the narratives that reinforce this way of living, whether those narratives are from one tradition such as Judaism, Islam, or Christianity, or whether they belong to all the world's traditions. This is living religiously in the sense of *relegere,* "to reread." And finally, living religiously means we do not neglect our lives and sleepwalk through them, paying no attention to our own inner life, to the lives of others, or the divine. It means, rather, that we live consciously, and intentionally and diligently, and that we freely undertake the necessary work of spiritual growth. This is to live religiously in the sense of *religens,* to "pick things up."

The hard-core fundamentalists say there is only one path, ours. The strict modernist says the same. However, there is no one path that will do this for everyone. At the same time, everyone is called upon to find some path, for without one, life remains directionless and random.

But how can anyone know which of the many paths available in the world is the best one to follow? Perhaps that is the role of our next loaded word, *tradition.*

7 : Tradition

IN THE past thirty years or so, perhaps as an offshoot of the self-absorbed 1960s and '70s, the emphasis of much religious activity in America has been on the solitary journey, each person finding her or his own path through the world. This process was marked by a lot of experimentation, and movements came and went like fads in fashions, from the transcendental meditation of the Beatles' Maharishi days through the shamanistic writings of Carlos Castaneda and into the celebrity-studded development of Scientology. Easy for secular modernists to satirize, these movements nonetheless revealed an intense spiritual seeking and longing in people who were not having their spiritual hunger fed by traditional churches. Given all that cross-cultural ferment, however, who could have predicted the surprising growth of the evangelical Christian mega-church as we have it in the exurbs of America at the beginning of the twenty-first century? Clearly a great many people were dissatisfied with the sort of individualized salad-bar approach that had become popular, and wanted to share their journey somehow. They wanted that "old-time religion," even if it was something new delivered in a state-of-the-art worship center that looked like a large multiscreen movie theater.

In a rapidly changing and centerless world, they were looking for some kind of tradition, or at least something that seemed traditional. And they were right to do so. Religion should not be a solitary path, but should be a collective activity, shared generously with a group. At the very least, most of us need help finding and following a path through life, and most of us want a path that is rooted in some tradition that has the feel of eternity about it. The great religions of the world come to us as inheritances, handed down from our ancestors as something valuable. The word *tradition* comes from the Latin *tradere,* "to hand over or deliver" (*trans,* "across" + *dare,* "to give"). As if in a generational relay, the texts, stories, rites, and customary ways of doing things and thinking about things are given across the generations as gifts with the idea that they will be treasured and revered enough to be passed down, in turn, in the future.

Certain texts, certain stories, certain gestures and ceremonies are retained and sustained from generation to generation because they have been found to be true, in the old sense of reliable, steadfast, and time-tested. These are wisdom traditions, honed over centuries by those who pass them on. Most people simply receive their religious tradition unquestioningly; it is presented to them as something that existed before they did, as part of their fate and identity. Your tradition tells you, "This is who you are." As such, in most societies, religion forms a key part of one's personal and cultural identity; it is the border at which the "I-self" meets the "we-self." It enables one to say, "I am a member of this group, this tribe, this clan, this religion. We are the people who worship this god. We initiate our children into this worship through infant baptism, circumcision, Sunday school, or other forms of instruction."

Tradition of this sort, of course, is a great buttress to individual identity and leads to group solidarity, but it can also lead, as we know, to divisiveness, even war. As with religion at the individual level, religion at the collective level can be either good or bad, and it is at its most divisive and destructive when believers say their way is the best way or, most dangerous of all, the only way. Defining *truth* literally, they conclude that they alone possess it and that all others are infidels, a word that literally means "unbelievers" but that has negative connotations, suggesting that the other is something less than fully human or certainly less human than *we* are.

Clearly, there are drawbacks to this exclusive way of thinking, but if our personal religion is to be complete, it should not be a solitary journey. We are not isolated creatures; human beings exist in a world with others. However, here things get complicated, for once we move from a solitary spiritual journey to a collective one, we enter the complex crossing ground of religion and society. Once we join the collective journey of a particular tradition, we must deal with that religion's relationship to politics and government, and this is what seems to be causing so much turmoil in the world today. In the twentieth century, works such as Peter Berger's seminal *The Sacred Canopy,* as well as cross-cultural studies by anthropologists, exposed the deep sociological dimensions of religion. As we enter the twenty-first century, it is time to revisit some of those findings and apply them to our social and political landscape, for one thing is clear as we look at the world's troubled hot spots today and that is that much of the world's hostility is fueled by religion. It may be religion poorly applied and poorly understood, but unless we comprehend why the psychological and social dynamics of religion are so powerful, and so divisive, we may never get a grip on why religion seems to be tearing the world apart instead of bringing it together.

We can begin with language. What is it that religious language does for societies? How does it differ from our day-to-day use of language? What does it do for us to share a religious vocabulary with others, and what are the limits of that language? What does it mean to have a *tradition*? And what do we do when we are forced to encounter and live with people of other traditions? How do we begin to speak with them?

We are born into a world of others. Though we are the center of our own consciousness, we could not even have entered this world without others, and as children we quickly accept the world of our intimate others—our parents, family, clan, culture—as normal, as part and parcel of what it means to be "I." I am, to a large extent, who "we" are, and I do not make my identity so much as I receive it. That is, as a child, before I begin to mature and differentiate into a unique "I" later in life, I am largely given who I am. People call me by a name I did not pick, I find myself at a certain place in the birth order of my siblings, I discover that I have been born at a particular time and in a particular place not of my choosing, and when I begin to speak, I speak the language of the world in which I find myself. All this is simply given to me. If my people are very isolated, I may not even know that there are other ways of being human. Some Inuit, for example, simply had no word for human beings who were not like them, and so were left speechless when the first non-Inuit arrived in their part of the world.

Religion, especially, involves us in a complex and profound web of cultural language and symbols, and much of learning to be part of a religion involves learning the vocabulary of that religion. If we are raised in a particular tradition, we learn this language the way we learn our everyday language, acquiring it naturally as our "mother tongue" and not even imagining there are other ways to say things. In this way, religious language serves an important phatic function. Linguists use the word *phatic* to describe language that is primarily emotive and whose main purpose is social bonding. Phatic language enables the "I" to become part of a "we" by learning and using a certain vocabulary and recognizing others by it. The most familiar example of phatic language is the slang used by teenagers to indicate whether they belong to a particular "in" group that uses this slang, but phatic language also includes learning the stories, myths, proverbs, and rituals of any group. Fundamentalist and evangelical Christians, for example, recognize a bond with each other by using certain key terms, such as *born again, saved,* or the frequent interjection of *Praise the Lord* whenever something good happens in their lives. Catholics may have leftover Latin terms, and Jews who may have forgotten whatever Hebrew they learned for their bar or bat mitzvah still wish each other *Shabbat shalom.* But religious language is not simply *phatic.* If it were, it would be as superficial and fleeting as slang. Religious language, if it is really to be re-ligious, that is, a means of binding together the self, one's society, and one's God, must reach deeper.

Like law, religious tradition can be understood as a linguistic construct. Where the law is composed of words that constitute what a society thinks is legal and illegal, a religion can be regarded as a linguistic system (broadly expanded to include such means of expression as gestures, music, and art) that is used both to express and to interact with whatever a group deems *holy.* It is really not significant whether these words are the "right" or correct words or not, from a linguistic point of view. Rather, as Dallas High wrote, "the meaning and licitness of religious uses of language as speech-acts consist in the fact that people do use language this way to carry out various linguistic tasks or execute various religious performances—pray, worship, name a god or gods or God," and so on.[1] The meaning of religious language, therefore, may lie more in the way it is used than in what, specifically, it refers to. We might even say that religion constitutes both a "domain" and a "register" of language. A domain is a particular broad subject area in which certain specialized vocabulary is used. *Pot, pan, stove, kitchen* all belong to the domain of cooking, while *belt, blouse, pants,* and *shirt* belong to the domain of fashion. A register is a unique tone and specialized vocabulary that indicates we are engaged in one kind of discourse as opposed to another within a domain. For example, if I say, "I have a subdermal hematoma," I am speaking in the register of professional medicine. If I say, "I have an owie," I might mean essentially the same thing, but while still in the domain of medicine, I am in the register of childhood. Are there specific religious domains and registers? It seems pretty clear there are, but they are difficult to define exactly, though we may describe them and know them when we experience them.

People use religious language in particular ways, and in particular kinds of speech acts, to refer to a special category of experiences, and that means that the same word, say *holy,* can mean something quite different in the religious register than it means in everyday speech. Compare the usage of *holy* and *father* in the phrases "Holy God, we praise thy name" and "Holy Toledo!" or "Our Father who art in heaven" and "This is my father, Mr. Eberle." One utterance is in the domain of religion, one not. So, how do we know when we are speaking religiously?

For starters, we can say that there are certain sorts of words and topics that, when we speak them or about them, put us in the religious domain and register. These would include the names of various physical objects used in worship or ritual. In Christianity, these might include *pulpit, altar, sanctuary;* in Judaism *Tabernacle,* or *Torah;* in Islam *mosque, mihrab,* and so on. These words have precise meanings in a religious context and are rarely used outside the religious register. We also have certain language that is used to express or describe various experiences or attitudes that we think of as religious. Words such as *faith, sin, grace, good, evil,* and *blessed* fall into this category. And we also may use religious language to describe entities and qualities that are not literally visible but that we can conceive of: *God, angels, omnipotence, omniscience, immortality, heaven, hell.*

Religious language is also used in particular forms of discourse. It is used in kinds of conversations and speech acts that are unique, such as praying and myth-telling, and that engage us in an often-symbolic discourse that uses imagery, extended similes, analogies, and metaphors to get at meanings that are not expressible in other ways. Religious discourse is also used to talk about a particular way of being in the world, a way that is *holy* in all the senses of that complex word, which means "whole, healthy, and connected." In this vein, religious language can include ethical language about behavior toward others as well as proscriptions on certain kinds of behavior that are *taboo,* or forbidden. The religious register of language is also supremely fitted to describe ontology, that is, ultimate reality, or Being itself, as opposed to nothingness. How the universe is put together and how we human beings fit in the grand scheme of it are supremely religious questions, for they ask how everything, the entire experience of the cosmos, is "ligamented," but the way it approaches answering these big questions is quite different from that of science. The religious domain of language is also effective at enabling a particularly authoritative kind of discourse, providing ultimate authority for ethical injunctions (for example, the Ten Commandments) and, in many cultures, for the political legitimacy of a god-king or government. By invoking religion, one provides a more than human authority for the way things are.[2] The religious linguistic domain is comprehensive and powerful.

If the foregoing uses of religious language describe its possible subject matter, or domain, its register is often strange and paradoxical, as befits language that would broach such ultimate subjects. The oddness of religious language is something we will explore in detail in the next chapter, when we discuss the most paradoxical word of all, *God.* For now, however, let's just note that it does not work in the more or less straightforward way of most of our other registers of language.

One of the most important characteristics of religious language is that it is uniquely "performative." That is, unlike scientific language, which uses words primarily as a neutral medium by which to transmit information or data, much religious language actually effects change by the saying of the religious words themselves. The telling and hearing of the myths, the saying of the prayers and blessings, the words (and actions) of the rituals are not intended to convey information; rather they are intended to effect actions and bring about changes. Much religious language "performs" rather than "informs." As such, it is particularly powerful and resonates in deeply emotional ways. There are certain words, such as *God, holy, sacred, sanctify,* and so on, that allow us to do things that other words don't. The formula "In the name of God . . ." allows us to perform actions, such as marrying two people together, that the formula "In the name of Bill . . ." doesn't.

The idea of performative language was introduced by the British linguist J. L. Austin in the 1960s after a half century or more of attempts by logical positivists to pin down just what language was and how it worked. The more twentieth-century philosophers such as Wittgenstein and Russell tried to complete the eighteenth-century project of refining and ascertaining the meanings of words, attempting to make them mean one thing and one thing only, the less success they had. They realized that the scientific model of language was not a one-size-fits-all approach to how human beings used language. Linguists discovered that language, which we all take for granted until we begin to study it, turned out to be much more complex than anyone had thought. Words, especially words as used in talking about emotional topics such as religion, were multivalent or polysemous—that is, they conveyed many meanings or levels of meaning at once—and were capable of many functions beyond mere transmission of information. It turns out that language has social, emotional, and expressive dimensions that have little or nothing to do with the transmission of facts, and nowhere is this more true than in religious language. If we try to make religious language operate as a means of transmitting information as other language does, then we end up tying ourselves in intellectual knots. If, however, we look at the language of religion in terms of its performative function, much of what seems obscure about it comes into clear relief, and we can see how unique it really is.[3]

Performative language is "a language not so much concerned with imparting information as with getting things done," says John Macquarrie.[4] According to Austin, performative language "indicates that the issuing of an utterance is the performance of an action—it is not normally thought of as just saying something."[5] A wedding is a perfect example of how the language of a religious tradition is performative and phatic. Words are said in such a context and with such an intention that the saying of them makes a man and woman, who previously had been separate, into a couple. "I, John, take you, Susan, to be my wife" and "I, Susan, take you, John, to be my husband." The words do the action. But it is not the words alone, for presumably the couple had said these words the night before in the rehearsal, but they were not then married. Neither would they be married if they were simply actors who said the words on stage in the role of a marrying couple. Rather, the words gain their performative power by being uttered in a carefully prepared ritual context of some sort. The context will vary from culture to culture and religion to religion, but the essentials remain pretty much the same. A man and a woman make a public pronouncement of some kind, accompanied by gestures or actions, such as a ring exchange, and words expressing intention to do this act, and then someone who has authority to say such things says something like, "I now pronounce you husband and wife," and it is done.[6]

Not all performative language is religious, of course. An umpire calling "Y'er outta here!" has the performative power of removing someone from a game; a head juror pronouncing the word "Guilty" is also using performative language. However, an extraordinarily large part of religious language is performative. Christening a child, pronouncing words of blessing, marrying, ordaining, absolving from sin, conducting a funeral, performing a coming-of-age ritual—all of these constitute language used performatively to effect both a change in someone's self-perception and their status in the community. The purpose of performative language is "to make certain subsequent conduct in order and other conduct out of order" in a social context, says

Austin.[7] Once you have said the words "I do," then being unfaithful to your spouse is "out of order," whereas before you said "I do," infidelity was literally impossible because you had not yet spoken the words that made the behavior taboo. In performative language, the word *hereby* is generally included, and is always at least implied. That is, it is understood that it is the language itself that performs the action at the very moment at which it is spoken. "I hereby declare you husband and wife."

Religious language is filled with such performative verbs as *bless, curse, pronounce, affirm, declare, believe, confess, forgive, vow, dedicate myself to, pledge, pray, covenant, bind, promise, thank,* and so on. While all of these can be used nonreligiously, too, when they are used in a religious context, they gain special force because their speakers are calling on the ultimate witness of Being itself to give force and authority to their utterance. The power of reciting a creed is that the very act of reciting it is performative of the belief that it articulates. "I hereby declare that the following are the truths by which I live my life: I believe in . . ." And we all know from experience that such words, once pronounced, are difficult to go back on. We can call back a simple mistake easily. If we make an error of fact, a simple correction will do—"I meant to say twelve, not thirteen." But to call back a curse or a blessing, much less a marriage vow, is a much more difficult undertaking, for the nature of the performance of a religious statement such as a vow has brought about a change in the person's very state of being.

So, what exactly is it that religious language performs? How does it differ from performative language in, say, a court of law, or on a ball field? The vital difference, I believe, lies in its context, for while a legal contract between business partners is performative, its context is only the world of commerce, and while a baseball umpire calling "Y'er out" is performative within the ball park in the context of the game, religious language involves the performance of a person's whole self and very existence. That is, religious language involves us in the largest context of all, beyond space, beyond time, so what it involves is nothing less than a thoroughgoing commitment of our entire self, performing actions that join our deepest self to another person, other persons, and ultimately to the source of all life. This is religion in its fundamental sense of *re-ligare,* to bind together. The peculiar performative power of religious language is to bind us, body and soul, both to others and to the very wellspring of our ultimate being.

This is why religious language, when it is performative, must take place in the context of liminal or ritual time. Ritual time allows us to enter a psychological realm or state where the oddness of religious language seems normal. It provides the appropriate context for the "magic" to happen, if you will. The works of twentieth-century scholars such as Victor Turner and Mircea Eliade have shown that the underlying structure of rituals is quite similar from culture to culture and tradition to tradition.

There is always some sort of rite of entry into the ritual that serves to separate what we are doing in the ritual from the rest of our lives. Entering ritual time, we become aware of the sacred in a way we are not in our everyday mode. Rites of entry usually consist of some form of decontamination, either by leaving one's shoes at the door, blessing oneself with holy water, listening to a prelude (literally "before the game"), putting on a special garment such as a mask, or performing some gestures, songs, or rite such as lighting a candle or ritual fire that indicates we have crossed a threshold from ordinary time into sacred time.

The word *sacred* actually means "set aside." The noun form comes from an old English verb *to sacre* from the Latin *sacer,* which meant "to set something apart from other things." Thus one could *sacre* an animal by taking it out of the herd for sacrificial purposes. This idea of separating out a special time or special objects for religious purposes is quite widespread. The Hebrew word *kadosh,* translated as *holy,* also means "separated." The gestures, words, and songs reserved for the ritual have the psychological effect of separating, or *sacering,* us from our everyday lives and our ordinary sense of time and allowing us to enter another modality of experience, one we call religious. The rite of entry serves as a buffer, just as the narthex of the church serves as an intermediate space between the world of the street and the sanctuary.

Once we enter into the sacred, or set-aside, time, we may use the performative words (and actions) of religion to effect change. Either we can change a child into an adult through a rite of passage, or we can make a layman a minister through ordination, or we can dedicate children or join a couple together in marriage. This is possible because sacred time is a time when we can "religion" people and things, that is, join together things that we normally think of as separate. Or, if we are not involved in an actual rite of passage, we may, in the sacred time, intensify things we already believe, recontact the spiritual sources of our life, and feel once again as if we are "religamented." In this bubble of set-aside time that we call sacred or religious, we experience once again the wholeness/holiness of being, and we share that experience with others.

During this intense period of sacred time, we *worship*. That is, going back to that word's etymology, we give things worth. The original English sense of *worship* combined the root *worth*, or "value," with the suffix-*ship*, which is related to the word *scape* or *shape*, so that in worship, we literally shape or create that which is worth something to us. To worship therefore is to actively shape those things we have set aside, or that we have "sacred," as "worthy" for us to value. The sacred, or set-aside, objects we use in our worship— the texts, vessels, masks, and vestments—therefore have value precisely because they connect us with that which we value most highly, the divine—under the names God, Allah, Vishnu, and so on—and the divine within creation.

As Lakoff and Johnson write in their groundbreaking study *Metaphors We Live By,* "religious rituals are typically metaphorical kinds of activities, which usually involve metonymies—real world objects standing for entities in the world as defined by the conceptual system of the religion. The coherent structure of the ritual is commonly taken as paralleling some aspect of reality as it is seen through the religion."[8] By entering ritual time, we suspend, for the duration of the ritual, our ordinary understanding of these things. The chalice is no longer just a cup, the vestment is no longer just a piece of colored cloth. Through the power of the ritual, it gains an added value and demands to be treated with *reverence,* a word whose Latin root (*re + vereri,* "to fear") recalls that religion exposes us to the tremendous and fascinating mystery of existence. The religious rite thus attains the power to perform, transform, and intensify our deepest values and sense of who we are.

Finally, after the rites of transformation or intensification, we are ready to leave sacred time and cross back over the threshold into our everyday reality. The rite of entry is often reversed. If there was a procession up the aisle, there is now a procession back down the aisle. If candles were lit, they are now blown out. If vestments were put on, they are now taken off. We leave the sacred, set-aside space, and reenter the world transformed or with a more intense conviction of our beliefs, which have been reinforced by the tremendous emotional power of ritual, which operates in such a way that we feel the deepest parts of our individual selves have been bound thereby to the deepest parts of those with whom we shared the ritual, and, in the end, with the workings of the universe itself. Not only that, but since the rites are by nature traditional, one is also united with all those of past generations who found that tradition worthy of being passed on and also with all those in the future to whom we will hand it on.

No wonder being raised in a tradition or being initiated into one later in life is such a powerful experience—and why breaking from one can be so painful!

The popular musical *Fiddler on the Roof* begins with the stirring song "Tradition" in which Tevye and the villagers of Anatevka extol the virtues of tradition. Their world is small, isolated, and patriarchal, but seems profound in a way that modern life is not. Part of the reason for the play's universal success, even outside the Jewish community, is that *Fiddler* and the stories of Sholom Aleichem invite us to participate in a kind of bittersweet nostalgia for a world that no longer exists, a world of order where everyone knew his or her place and God was a constant companion, a world that was, in a word, traditional. The play was first produced in 1964 as America itself was beginning to break with tradition in the general upheaval of values that we now call, in shorthand, "the sixties." The sixties were a conscious break from tradition, a youthful rebellion that quite deliberately cut itself free from such traditional ties as religion, family structure, gender roles, and other cultural values and entered on what many judge to be a forty-year cultural drift into anomie and relativity. In the play, this is mirrored in Tevye's struggles with his daughters, who, as daughters will, fall in love with the wrong men. As we see through the course of the play, the traditional world of Tevye is under siege from the forces of modernism in the form of the communist revolution of 1905, but we understand that the world described is also ours, one from which tradition has all but disappeared.

As we saw in our discussion of *fundamentalism,* the religious right in the United States used the cultural drift of the sixties as a springboard to power and influence. Offering what they called "traditional values" to a large population of people for whom the tectonic shift of postmodernism was unsatisfactory, their invocation of *tradition* offered clear, if somewhat rigid, guidelines for behavior in the world, and people responded in great numbers. Similarly, Islamists in the Muslim world, reacting violently to the effect that modernization and Westernization had on their tradition, have called for a return to Islamic values, and fundamentalist Jews in Israel also cling firmly to tradition. The results have been and continue to be tragic.

So, is the answer to adopt the secular modernist position and simply reject religious tradition altogether if this is what it brings us to? Absolutely not, because, first of all, it would not likely work to bring any more peace and understanding to the world than we already have, which is precious little; and second, because, as we have seen, religious traditions have the potential to work so well at binding people together and calling them to be their best selves, not their worst. Our religious traditions can provide us ways that could lead to greater peace—if we live the best of parts of them, not the worst. In addition, today's religious fundamentalism will not be answered by secularism, because, as we have seen, religious vocabulary reaches so much deeper into us than the mere logic of secular modernism. Only an equally passionate response from those who believe that their religion should be a bridge to others, not a wall from them, will adequately answer the dangerous misuse of religious tradition by the world's religious extremists.

This can only happen, however, if liberal and traditional religionists first understand and acknowledge the darker side of the religious impulse. Because religious traditions are so powerful and reach so deeply into the self, because their language is both phatic and uniquely performative and bonds believers together through a sense of tradition that marks them as a distinct "we," religions and religious practices can become flash points for culture clashes. The darker side of religious tradition's ability to create a distinct and unified "we" of believers is that it can also create an equally powerful hatred for a "they," which may include all others whom we deem infidels or unbelievers. They become "others," essentially not like us. The concept of "the other" runs deep in human beings; we might even say it is an archetype deep within the psyche. We define "others" as those not like us, and we force them to wear the mask of the other, projecting on to them all our shadowy dislikes and fears, as well as everything that we may find disgusting about being human. They smell; we don't. They wear funny clothes; we don't. They have odd customs; we don't. They are barbaric; we're not. They are infidels; we aren't.

In recent years, largely as a result of postmodernist and postcolonial theory, the word *other* has come to occupy a large role in contemporary discourse. Though it isn't a commonly used verb, it really should be. To "other" someone would be to make him or her into an alien creature, different in some essential way from the "I" who stands at the center of my existence, and the "we" with whom I am intimate or whom I regard as "like me." To make someone or a group of people into *others* is to rob them of subjectivity, that is, to treat them as objects by denying that they are as human as "we" are and that they possess all the rights and privileges we enjoy as free humans. Othering, of course, is a terribly dehumanizing process. It is what makes much of the world's evil possible. Slavery, colonialism, sexism, war, terrorism, and violence are all made possible when we take away the full humanity of others and think of them as barbarians.

Before we can liberate our religious traditions to become ways of healing the world, we must first admit that religion has been, and continues to be, one of the human race's most powerful and effective ways of dehumanizing other human beings by turning them into "others." Because religion is so thoroughgoing in terms of individual and cultural identity, it can become one of the most volatile catalysts of otherness. Not only individuals but entire cultures and peoples may become "others" for each other. Saying that your gods are not our god is another way of saying you are not worthy of our consideration as human beings.

The consequences of "othering" human beings are staggering. When Spanish explorers first came ashore on Caribbean islands in the sixteenth century, they did not know what to make of the indigenous peoples. In the early years of exploration, European scholars, theologians, and philosophers carried on extensive debate over the humanity of the peoples of these new worlds.[9] Did they have souls like us? The answers they arrived at are shocking to our modern consciousness. At best, the colonizers usually granted the natives the status of incompletely formed human beings, some degrees below the level of fully human, and thought of them as children who had to be brought into full adulthood through education, Christianization, and abandoning their native ways. At worst, they were judged to be soulless creatures, which, like animals, could be maltreated, exploited, and enslaved.[10]

This process of othering is precisely what is going on in the various brands of extreme fundamentalism that plague the world today. Their belief is that "we" have found a way that is true, in fact we believe it is the one and only true way for all. "We," therefore, are sacred, or set aside, by the divinity, while "you" are outside the pale. The proof of the truth of what these people believe is their powerful subjective experience of their religion, wherein they have felt themselves deeply connected to the absolute sources of being. This is a hard proof to refute. Those who have experienced through their religious tradition a profound sense of holiness find it hard to comprehend that others would not experience the same thing if they only accepted this way of connecting with the divine. And herein lies the rub. For it takes an especially evolved religious consciousness to see that the structural underpinnings of the various world religions are nearly identical, and most people are not capable of this insight. It is terribly hard for believers to understand or to admit that all religions, including theirs, are only incomplete expressions of the divine; that beneath the bewildering array of gods and goddesses in humanity's religious traditions there is a universal reaching out, an attempt to express in merely human language what is ultimately beyond words; and that all traditions ultimately fail to achieve fullness.

The fundamentalists are right, however, in their claim that we need religion, and we should acknowledge them for reawakening us to that fact. There is a widespread feeling even among religious liberals that the modernist project of viewing the world as purely secular has been given its day and has been found wanting. As we've seen, there are some things that religions do for individuals and for society that are not done by other human activities. But the world has changed from the ancient times when today's great world religions were founded.[11] In previous ages peoples of different faiths were by and large saved from each other simply by the difficulty of traveling over distance. For the most part, people of different traditions could avoid each other. But in the modern world we no longer have that option. The Holocaust in World War II showed us how modern technology could abet the slaughter of those whom we deem "others." Since then, the planet has grown even smaller and the methods of mass destruction even more potent. Modern communications media such as the worldwide Web give us unprecedented access to each other. Something that appears in a small newspaper in Denmark, such as the intentionally inflammatory cartoons of the prophet Muhammad that appeared in late 2005, can be transmitted around the world at the touch of a button and can set off riots in the Middle East. Islamist extremists use the Internet and cell phones to keep in touch, and every day millions of people fly from their own culture into another. In addition, patterns of migration have led to an unprecedented mixing of cultures, with a large percentage of Western European countries now having to deal, for the first time really, with the kind of multicultural society that we have known in America for a long time. Clearly we cannot simply continue to ignore one another and hope that the other will go away. We are in too deep.

The solution, at least to the religious element of the current strife, is to rethink what we mean by the "truth" of our religious traditions. If we accept the modernist scientific definition of *truth*, which holds that truth has to be precise, unique, and singular, then we will continue to wage war against one another, for each tradition will continue, based on its experience, to believe it has the one and only truth. If we cling to this literal level of our religious tradition, then we are condemned to die by the sword. However, if we can return to a sense of *truth* that is older and more profound, then we open the door to what I call a "deep ecumenism." The word *ecumenism* was used widely in the 1960s as the Roman Catholic Church, after the Second Vatican Council, reached out to other Christian denominations in an effort at some sort of reconciliation or at least acknowledgment that we should recognize similarities among our churches rather than continue to focus on the differences. There was much discussion of religious "tolerance" in those days.

Today, I believe, we need to move beyond mere tolerance of religious difference. Tolerance, to me, suggests that we grit our teeth, smile politely, and try to be in the same room together for brief periods of time before withdrawing into the safety of our own house. But deep ecumenism suggests that mere tolerance is an intolerable state. The word *ecumenism* comes from an old Greek word, *oikoumene*, which was used to refer to the inhabited world. But etymologically, and more poetically, it meant something like "living in the same house." (In Greek, *oikos* meant "house.") Being in the same house is the situation of the world today. Thanks to modern mass communications and travel, to cross-cultural interchange, to mass migration patterns and global business practices, we almost literally live in the same place now. Simple tolerance is not enough anymore. Suppose somebody asked you how you get along with the people you live with in your house and all you could say was, "We're tolerating each other." How's your wife? "She tolerates me, I tolerate her." Clearly this would not be an acceptable state of affairs. Tolerance of religious differences may be a good first step, but in the contemporary world, the time has come to move beyond religious tolerance and into an active celebration of all the traditions by which the divine has revealed itself to humanity. This is deep ecumenism, beyond tolerance of the other's "otherness" and into active appreciation of it. We should be happy that not everyone is Christian, or Hindu, or Jew, or Muslim, or animist, or Wiccan, or Buddhist. The rich vocabulary of the divine-human interaction needs to be explored, understood, and acted out in all its manifestations.

In the United States, some Christian fundamentalists are actively attempting to "take back America for Christ," seeing a fully Christian America as the only answer to the world's problems. I would agree with them that the American model is, in fact, a very good model for the world, but I'm also sure that my interpretation of the American model varies greatly from theirs.

Over two hundred years ago, in a quite different historical and cultural situation, the founders of the United States set forth on a bold experiment to try a new form of government and a new social experiment that, from the perch of history, is breathtaking in its boldness.

Part of what the founders of our country were rebelling against was established religion of the sort practiced in England. When a nation has an established religion, only those who sign on to that particular church have full civil rights. In eighteenth- and even nineteenth-century England, only members of the Church of England could vote, hold public office, and attend university. Catholics and dissenting Protestants, freethinkers, and the like need not apply. The system was pernicious for both the church and the state, and the American colonists apparently envisioned this new country as a place where the civil rights of its citizens would not be connected to their participation in one particular, or even any, church.

Thomas Jefferson, that deeply flawed man who is, nonetheless, the fountainhead of so much that is still good about the *idea* of America, was explicit about this in his "Act for establishing Religious Freedom," which was made into law in Virginia in 1786, before the ratification of the U.S. Constitution. He wrote, "our civil rights have no dependence on our religious opinions, more than on our opinions in physics or geometry; . . . the proscribing any citizen as unworthy of the public confidence . . . unless he profess or renounce this or that religious opinion, is depriving him injuriously of those privileges and advantages to which in common with his fellow citizens he has a natural right."[12] Established religion, he argued, is bad for the country and even for religion itself, for it may lead to hypocrisy and cronyism. Instead he argued for freedom of conscience and separating religious profession from one's civic rights and duties.

Less than two hundred years before the American Revolution, King James I of England had put into words the philosophy of most rulers of most times in history: the divine right of kings, the notion that rulers governed over others by reason of their having been given sovereignty by God, or the gods. It was based on a top-down model of sovereignty in which the Almighty, by whatever name, delegated power to the king or queen, who then passed it downward to the people.

The seventeenth- and eighteenth-century philosophers Locke and Rousseau turned this notion on its head and suggested that, in fact, rulers do *not* get their power from the gods but from the people whom they govern, and it was out of this new idea that the founders of our country got the notion to begin their Declaration of Independence with the words "In the course of *human* events . . . ," and the Constitution with the words "*We, the people* of the United States."

But even in the revolutionary ferment of the late 1700s, they must have had a sense that the will of the people alone was not an adequate foundation for a stable governmental system. They must have asked, "Is there anything *beyond* collective human consent on which the power of government rests?" That is, are we to understand civil government as purely civil? Or do we also need to believe that human government rests upon a larger foundation—call it God, or Natural Law, or even Nature—than simply the collective will of human beings? And if so, then by what name do we call that larger, universal principle that human governments invoke as the foundation of their power?

The founders wanted to avoid both the inequities of an established religion and the chaos of a violent religious free-for-all (as they had seen in the European religious wars of the seventeenth century and in the religious persecutions of the early American colonies.) So they hit on a practical American solution. They looked for the broadest, most general word they could find, and they settled on "God" and synonyms such as "Nature's God," "the Creator," "Providence," "Supreme Judge of the World," and so on, and pointedly did *not* use "Jesus," or "Christ," or "Jehovah," or "Yahweh."

In place of an established religion, we developed what Forrest Church, in his recent book of the same name, called the American Creed, and it is a liberal, not a conservative creed.[13] Having suffered under the effects of an established church, the founders understood rightly the dangers of established religion, but they could not let go of religion altogether. The unique American solution—the American model—has been what Robert Bellah called "American Civil Religion": having done away with establishing a particular religion as the official religion of the United States, we nonetheless evolved a language and belief uniquely American in which the words *God* and *Creator* took on a distinctly generic, not sectarian, sense. It is this meaning of *God* that we are currently arguing over, from James Kennedy's prophecy that a fully Christian era of godliness is about to descend on America, to Judge Roy Moore's effort to get a huge granite sculpture of the Ten Commandments in the Alabama Supreme Court building, to controversial attempts to get the words "under God" removed from the Pledge of Allegiance. It has been a rocky road in America, especially in recent years, but over time, and in broad historical terms, the American Solution has worked surprisingly well. Permitting freedom of conscience and keeping a wall of separation between church and state has largely kept Americans from slaughtering one another in the name of our various gods for the past two centuries.

The reason the American model would work is that American Civil Religion, like any religion, has its sacred texts, key ideas, and unique rituals in which those who believe in that creed participate, but they are not specifically religious texts, ideas, and rituals. They do not belong to a particular religious tradition. In fact, what this uniquely American creed does *not* include is a requirement that anyone practice a particular religion, or, indeed, any religion at all. In his book, Church traces the lineage of this liberal, and uniquely American, approach to religion back through American history, even, interestingly enough, back to the Puritans of Massachusetts, whom we think of today as models of religious intolerance but who, in their time, represented the sort of freethinking Congregational approach to religion that, two hundred years later, gave birth to the patriots who came to Philadelphia from Boston to speak their minds.

Of course, times change. In colonial times, the vast majority of Americans were Christians of some kind or another (even Catholics could grudgingly be counted), and virtually all the rest were Jews (so they at least were biblical). The question of what we mean when we say *God* in our public life was less of an issue. One could use the word and suppose a fairly common understanding. However, in an America that is increasingly populated by those who call their gods by other names, or who believe in no god at all, or who worship a vaguely specified "higher power," or Spirit, or Presence, or Nature, we are running into a linguistic and semantic problem that the founders clearly couldn't have anticipated.[14]

But what is clear, it seems to me, is that the founders did *not* intend this to be a specifically Christian nation, in the narrow constructionist sense that some people who call themselves "real Americans" want, nor that they believed that the solution to America's problems would be found in the nation's collective turn to Jesus. And even if they did, the world today has grown too small, and human consciousness has come too far, to retreat to such a tribal notion.

We can only achieve peace, in religion at least, if we can get beyond thinking that those "others," whom we call *infidels,* worship "other" gods than ours. In order to do this, we must radically redefine *monotheism,* to reflect the fact that all the religious traditions of the world are but attempts to express in merely human language something in our universal human experience that will always remain essentially unnameable. As we outlined above, from a purely sociological perspective the performative nature of religious language, the traditional rituals, and the texts or stories that we hold as sacred are all alike in that they are attempts to express in imperfect human language ideas, experiences, and realities that, by definition, lie beyond the competence of human language to express. That is, each tradition inevitably ends up being an incomplete expression of an infinite reality. It really cannot be otherwise, for even if the truths of a religion seem to be revealed by a divinity, the expression of those truths, as we'll explore more in the next chapter, comes in the frail human language of a particular time, place, and culture. We must humbly admit that human religious language, even if divinely inspired, is only human, after all.

What that means is that instead of merely tolerating one another and living with a sort of mutual nonaggression pact, we should start actively reaching out to the "other" as a way of completing ourselves. This does not mean abandoning our own religious traditions, much less creating a new religion that is an amalgam of many religions. Each religious path, tested and proven by time, is sufficient unto itself. But, as the Iranian-born scholar Seyyed Hossein Nasr, now professor of Islamic studies at George Washington University, put it in a recent issue of *Parabola* magazine, since all the world's traditions "come from the Sacred, and they are there to lead us back to the Sacred, no tradition can be incomplete. . . . It is a path to God, although it is not the *only* path to God. There are other paths with their own characteristics. But if the goal is to reach God, each path must be sufficient unto itself."[15]

In the end, the importance of a particular religious language is not whether it is literally true but that we have one to begin with. That is, if we begin with the assumption that all religious language, being human language, is but a limited expression of an infinite reality, that does not mean that we can abandon that sort of language altogether, because it does serve a unique function. The importance of a religious language is not whether the names it uses for the divine are the correct names but whether it performs its function as a language that leads us to experience the sort of "re-ligamenting" we discussed in the last chapter. And as Nasr points out, each tradition is articulated and amplified enough to be sufficient to perform the unique human function that religion performs for us. Every one of the world's traditions, by definition, has been found to be valuable to its practitioners, or else they would not even have passed down the tradition. And because each tradition is grounded in a culture and language that is already a familiar part of its adherents' identity, most of us need not really go looking elsewhere to find an adequate pathway through life. In my own experiences in Zen temples, in various Christian churches, Jewish synagogues, and Hindu temples, I have been able to recognize the same religious impulse beneath the surface differences, and have come to the conclusion that these traditions both are and are not "mine." That is, as a Westerner who was raised in the Catholic Church and who teaches at a Catholic college, my cultural inheritance is Catholic. I see the world first in those terms. But I have also come to the conclusion that the other religious traditions of the world are "mine" as well insofar as they are part of the human legacy.

If we think of various religions as languages that express the divine dimension of human experience, then we might think of deep ecumenism in terms of learning another language. We are all born into a "mother tongue," the one we grow up speaking in our household and that comes loaded with emotional overtones, with ties of kinship and family, with an entire culture and civilization attached to it. But we may also learn other languages, and in learning those other languages we do not debase our mother tongue. Rather, we enrich our own ability to be expressive, and we may come back to our original language with an increased understanding and appreciation of it. As anyone who has learned a foreign language knows, you never become as proficient in it as in your first language. Unless you come by your second tongue at a very young age, you will always speak with an accent and you will feel most at home in your first tongue. Nonetheless, it is good for us to learn other languages.

Even as militant forms of fundamentalism seem to be on the rise in various parts of the world, movements are being made in the opposite and more hopeful direction. On the world stage, the late pope John Paul II made some extraordinary gestures of outreach in his visit to Israel, and the Dalai Lama has endured the tragedy of Tibet and, in exile, has become a beacon of spirituality and deep ecumenism in the world. Changes are happening on a smaller scale, too. I was in Evanston, Illinois, a couple of years ago and passed by a Baptist church that announced on its marquee that it was hosting a joint service with a Korean Zen temple that Sunday. It was an opportunity I could not miss, and, extraordinary as it sounds, I witnessed a service that was half Buddhist and half Baptist, with chants from the Sutras intermingled with traditional Christian hymns. There was no question of conversion, and neither was there an attempt to have a Buddhist-Baptist fusion sect. Instead, each minister spoke on the same topic, which that day was "refuge." The Baptist minister, using texts from the Bible, said that good Christians took refuge in God, the Bible, and their fellow religionists. The Buddhist preacher, taking as his text a particular Sutra, proclaimed that Buddhists took refuge in the Buddha, dharma, and sangha, that is, the Buddha, his teachings, and the community. Each tradition was allowed to be itself and, in being itself, showed itself not to be "other" but essentially the same.

Everything else—the incense, the statue of the Buddha, the Christian cross, the vestments, the bells and organ—was secondary to that.

As Phillip Ravenhill wrote, the important thing about religion may be that "in the context of a religious ritual, a speaker . . . may intend to address the gods, request favors, promise actions, or assert divine authority, and also intend the congregation to know that such actions have been performed and that the overhearers are now permitted or prohibited certain undertakings in consequence."[16] From this performative point of view, the hearers don't even have to understand the language in order for the rite to be efficacious. In the case of a hieratic language—such as Hebrew for the Jews, or classical Arabic for Muslims, or archaic Korean for Korean Buddhists—the importance "may not lie in the propositional content of the priest's words but rather in the fact that the community witnesses a particular illocution which counts as a specific action, say of cleansing or creating order."[17] We recognize the domain and register of our religious tradition as our mother tongue.

Naturally the implications of these ideas are dangerous and frightening to those who think their tradition has an absolute lock on literal truth. It is perhaps only natural that when the integrity of a group's identity is threatened by competing beliefs, other gods, and other ways of being human, there will be a defensive reaction. But unless we let go of our fear of others and embrace deep ecumenism, we condemn ourselves to be stifled in our own hard shells of intolerance and we will continue to slaughter one another in the names of our various gods of mercy.

We can only make progress in this, however, if we can get beyond thinking that other people worship "other" gods than ours. In order to do that, we must come to a new kind of radical monotheism based on an understanding that all human religious language is an imperfect and incomplete attempt to name something that is essentially unnameable—and that brings us, as it must, to discussing the most loaded word of all, *God.*

8 : God

THE WORD *God* has become a problem. What exactly do we mean when we say it? What or whom does it name?

In the 1200s, Thomas Aquinas constructed a series of thought experiments, based on Aristotle, that tried to answer these questions. They are sometimes called the five "proofs" of God, but they are actually five "ways" that lead one toward the idea of God. They serve as good warm-up exercises for our minds as we approach the difficult task of speaking about that which may be, in the end, unnameable.

Thomas begins with what we see. We see that things in the world move. In order for them to move, they must be put into motion by a mover. If I move my pencil across the page in writing, I am the pencil's mover. So far, so good. But what moves me? If I answer, "the earth," or "the principle of life," then I am led to the question "What moves them?" We can go on and on. What moves the earth? The solar system. Then what moves that? The universe. Okay, but what moves that? By this regression, we must come, finally, to the idea of some "unmoved mover," that is, something that is the source of all the movement in the universe but which itself does not move. And this, Thomas says, "is what we call God."[1]

His second way was to consider causality. Everything we observe has a cause. I am the cause of many of the things that happen in my environment, but who or what caused me? My parents? But what caused them? Their parents who, in turn, were made possible, ultimately, by the earth, whose "cause" was the material universe, and so on, until we stretch our questioning to the utmost limit, at which point, we arrive at something that simply has no cause, what Aristotle called the "uncaused cause," from which all other effects proceed. Thomas says this is what we call God.

His third way is to think of different things that exist. They all take their existence from other things, which also exist and which have come to be. But where did they come from? By following an infinite line of questions, we finally come to something that cannot *not* be—that is, something whose being is necessary in order for all that to come into existence in the first place. And this "necessary being," says Aquinas, is what people understand as God.

His fourth way is based on our mental categories of "more" and "less." We understand the concept of "more," so we can imagine "more" of everything—of goodness, of beauty, of truth, of wisdom, and so on. At the farthest limits of our imagination of "more," we must come to some absolute maximum beyond which there can be no more "more," where all attributes have reached perfection. And this plenitude, says Thomas, is what we call God.

And finally, using Aristotle's notion of *enteleche,* that everything in the universe has an inborn *telos,* or direction and purpose to become what it is, Thomas works from purpose to purpose and arrives at the conclusion that the whole universe must have something that directs it and everything in it to its proper end. And this we call God.[2]

Thomas's logic would seem to lead us to the inexorable conclusion that there must be something out there that gave rise to all that exists, but, when all is said and done, Thomas's thought experiment is really only capable of delivering up a grand abstraction, what we call the "Philosopher's God." While one can appreciate the intellectual grandeur of Thomas's approach, in the end it can only take us to a personality-less, feelingless, grand concept, a remote something too large for definition. The five ways do lead us to conceive of the ultimate cause of all beings, to Being itself, but that Being has no distinct personality, shape, or character. In the end, the five ways lead us to, at most, an emotionless abstraction that dwells apart at an infinite distance from our daily lives.

Even if we can dimly grasp the Philosopher's God, what has such an abstraction to do with the sometimes irascible, sometimes loving, sometimes terrifying, sometimes consoling character called God whom we meet in the Hebrew scriptures? Or with the Jesus whom we meet as the incarnation of this God in the New Testament, or the Holy Spirit, which manifests itself as fire, wind, and a dove? Or with the plethora of divine characters in the rest of the world's pantheons whom we also call God or gods?

Fundamentalists say *God* means *our* God, end of conversation. His workings and personality are revealed between the covers of one book, the Bible or Koran, and within that book his revelation is complete. All other "gods" are idols and false. Modernist rationalists, on the other hand, say the abstract Philosopher's God is all we can hope to have, that if we want to talk about the divine at all we can only speak of absolute Being, dwelling apart, like Shelley's Mont Blanc, "remote, serene and inaccessible." Any other view is merely misguided anthropomorphism. Both these points of view, though implacably opposed to each other, equally impoverish the divine and fail to account for the richness of the world's religious traditions. The fundamentalist would confine the divine within the binding of a single book, and the rationalist would remove the divine from the day-to-day world in which we live. Neither viewpoint is satisfactory.

Will examining the peculiar nature of God-language enable us to close the gap between the abstract philosopher's God and the dazzling array of gods and goddesses whom we meet in our, and the world's, scriptures and religious traditions?

Let's go back again to the five ways of Thomas. Thomas concludes each of his ways with the formula "this is what men call God" or "this is what all understand to be God." By a simple device of typography, we can change the emphasis of Thomas's formula and point toward a way of reopening religious dialogue that could lead us to the "deep ecumenism" discussed in the last chapter.

Suppose we wrote Thomas's formula this way: "this is what human beings call *God*," using italics to call attention to the fact that *God* here is a word rather than a being. Even better would be to invert the word order a bit for emphasis and say, "*God* is what human beings call this." This phrasing emphasizes that *God* is simply a convenient word that provides a name for all that toward which the five ways point. That is, rather than recapitulate and capitalize *Unmoved Mover, Uncaused Cause,* and so on, every time we want to refer to the Ultimate Source of all existence, we will simply use the word *God* to stand for all that. That—*all* that—is what we mean when we utter the name *God.* This reading of Thomas, though unconventional, can lead us safely between the Scylla of fundamentalism and the Charybdis of secular modernism, for it rests on the humble acknowledgment that human language can never fully name the divine, and that the word *God,* grand as it may be, is finally inadequate to express the full nature of the divine as we experience it in our lives.

Obviously this gestalt shift is tricky, but it is worth the effort. Human beings are linguistic creatures, through and through, and we say things in order to understand them, even if we must admit that any words we utter are in the end provisional and inconclusive. Putting things into words is the way we bring them into the light of consciousness. John Macquarrie, in his book *God-talk,* points out that the etymologies of the term "to say" in various languages are often derived from words that mean "to see." The English word *say* is clearly related to the word *see;* and in Greek, *phemi* ("to say"), is related to *phaino,* which means "to show," and thus is related to the religious word *epiphany,* or "showing forth the divine." The Latin *dicere,* "to say," is related to the Greek *deiknumi* and the later German *zeigen,* all meaning "to show," and the first syllable of all three words seems to be traceable "to an old Indo-European root, *di,* signifying 'bright' or 'shining.'" This connection between speech and bringing things to light seems to hold true even in non–Indo-European languages. In the Semitic languages, the Hebrew word *'amar* ("to say") "is likewise connected with the idea of 'showing.'"[3] It seems a common idea that by saying things we see them.

Language is the means we use to call things forth out of the darkness and make them shine. In using human language to talk about God, we are like explorers shining a flashlight in an immense dark cave, now illuminating this part of the cave, now that. The limited scope of our light is not capable of lighting up the whole cave, but nonetheless it provides a tool by which we can negotiate our way.

And so we come back to the troublesome word *God*. According to the *OED*, *God* is a very old Germanic word derived from an even older Indo-European word. It has many cognates in the Germanic languages, coming ultimately from one of two pre-Teutonic Indo-European words: *g,heu,* which probably meant "to invoke," or another word, pronounced the same way, that meant "to pour, or to offer sacrifice." The Germanic *God* is related to the Sanskrit word *huta,* meaning "what is worshipped in sacrifice." The use of *god* thus considerably predates the Christianization of the Teutonic peoples. As actually used in the pre-Christian era, it had the distinctly generic sense of any object of worship. Whatever one poured out sacrifice to was considered one's god.[4] The philosopher John Macquarrie was not far from this meaning when he wrote that to find one's god is "to set one's heart on something as the highest good and to orient one's life by it."[5]

After the Christianization of the Germanic peoples, however, the word *God* changed its meaning. In effect, the lowercase usage of *god* became uppercase *God*. The common noun got transformed into a proper noun, a particular god whose name was God. Not surprisingly, perhaps, the word also underwent a gender shift. In the Germanic languages nouns are gendered, as they are not in modern English, and they are assigned a grammatical gender as masculine, feminine, or neuter, with corresponding articles and case endings. After Christianization, the word *god,* which was originally grammatically neuter, became the distinctly masculine *God,* reflecting the patriarchal nature of the new Christian religion.[6] These two minor shifts radically changed the understanding of the ancient word *god* from a generic to a very particular one. In polytheistic pagan northern Europe, there were many gods and goddesses, each with his or her proper name. From conversion on, however, the ancient word *God* would be reserved only for the Christian God described in the Bible, a God who allowed for no other god to be named God.

But, of course, it's not nearly that simple.

In the very scriptures from which we get the concept of this monotheistic God, there are actually many names by which he is known. In Hebrew, the proper name El Shaddai (Genesis 17:1ff) originally meant "the mountain god."[7] God was also known as Elohim, Adonai, and, of course, as Yahweh. All these proper names served to emphasize different aspects of the God who revealed himself to Moses in the burning bush. That story is very useful to us as we continue to explore the meaning of *God*.

Exodus tells us that Moses was looking after the flocks of his father-in-law, Jethro, and led them out into the wilderness to a mountain called Horeb, where he came upon a bush that was burning but that was not consumed by the fire blazing in it. This event has all the characteristics of an archetypal religious experience, a human encounter with a tremendous and yet fascinating mystery. Being a brave spirit, Moses did not turn away in fear but said to himself that he had to go take a closer look. As he approached the bush, the voice of God spoke to him and commanded him to take off his sandals, for he was on holy ground. The voice then revealed that he was the God of Moses's ancestors, Abraham, Isaac, and Jacob, and then Moses grew afraid and covered his face. God spoke from the fire and commissioned Moses to lead the Jews out of Egypt, and after some resistance, Moses agreed. He then asked the name of the one who was sending him, whereupon God replied, *"Ehyeh asher ehyeh"* (Exodus 3:14). Variously translated as "I am who I am" or "I am who am," the words derive ultimately from an archaic form of the Hebrew word meaning "to be."[8] It is by this name that he wishes to be known forever afterward—Being, he who is, I AM.

There is a powerful reality expressed in this Hebrew story. This name, "I am who I am" or "I am who am," supersedes the other names of God and suggests Being itself, as it would later be understood. In modern philosophical terms, we might say that God replies, "I am the ground of Being itself," and we find ourselves back to Aristotle's and Thomas's God who is the cause of all causes, the unmoved mover of all movers, the infinite expression of all values, pure Being. But the God whom we encounter in the Bible is not the philosopher's God; he addresses Moses directly, and he manifests himself in manifold ways throughout the Hebrew scriptures as a recognizable literary character who is, by turns, an angry father, a loving shepherd, a pillar of fire. He afflicts Job with boils, he guides armies to victory, and he calls on prophets to correct his people when they stray from worship of him. He has a distinct personality; he does not dwell off in abstraction but is actively engaged in the history of the people whose story the Bible recounts.

The situation is the same in other world religions when it comes time to name the ultimate ground of reality. In a fashion similar to what happened to the word *god* in the Germanic languages, Islam took a generic Arabic word, *Allah,* and made it particular. *Allah* was a word that was originally the name of the high god of the pre-Islamic pantheon of gods, and was later used by Arabs to name the God of the Jews and Christians even before Muhammad appropriated it for Islam. Linguistically, *Allah* simply means "the God," being a contraction of the Arabic *al-ilah,* but like *Yahweh,* the word *Allah* takes on characteristics of gender and he interacts with humankind.[9]

We find parallel linguistic attempts to name the unnameable in Hinduism, where the word *Brahman* names what we have been calling the Philosopher's God. In its earliest usage, in the Vedas, the word meant "prayer," "holy knowledge," or "magic formula." Then by extension it became the name for the power that is being invoked in prayer, that is, the "one source of all existence," a formula that recalls Thomas and Aristotle again.[10] Etymologically, according to scholar Heinrich Zimmer, the first syllable, *brah,* comes from a Sanskrit verb, *brh,* meaning "to grow or increase," or, if referring to a sound, "to roar." (An elephant's roar is *brmhita.*) As a root, *brh* can form words to mean "to fatten" or "to heal," or "to increase, strengthen, fortify, intensify," and, abstractly, it can form nouns meaning "energy, force, power, potency." *Brahman,* in other words, names the ground of all being, the source from which all else comes. This force is inside and outside of human beings and all beings, "like the butter is hidden in the milk" or the salt in salt water, and out of its substance are formed all the lesser gods and the universe itself.[11]

This concordance of words and underlying concepts should give us hope, for all of these names satisfy Thomas's criteria for what we call "God," and in this sense all name the same thing. All of these words from various linguistic traditions point toward the same ultimate reality, so it is a puzzle why we continue to kill one another over them. This is especially troublesome when we consider that virtually all of the traditions that use these names admit that the word they use cannot, in the end, denote God truly. This is acknowledged in the orthodox Jewish tradition of pausing silently when coming across the tetragrammaton in reading scripture, and it is in the Hindu formula *neti, neti,* ("not that, not that"), which is used after religious affirmations to remind us that our human language is inadequate to express the divine. Similarly, in Islam, Allah may not be depicted visually because to form an image of Allah is to limit him. Whatever we say about God may be true, but it is still "not that." Even Thomas Aquinas admits this. In question thirteen, article eleven, of the first section of the *Summa Theologiae*, Thomas informs us that, in the end, the substance of God is "incommunicable and . . . singular."[12] Some cultures even hesitate to name the ultimate god at all. The Igbo of Nigeria, for example, refer to their god only indirectly as "the-One-whose-name-is-not-spoken," for if the god hears his name, he may think he has been summoned, and this could be offensive to him, since being summoned by a mere mortal would be beneath him.[13] To call the god's name has the power of activating it, so it is best to leave it silent and unnamed. Even the apostle Paul, that man of words, acknowledges the ultimate futility of trying to express the divine reality. In 2 Corinthians, he writes of a man, presumed to be himself, who fourteen years before had been fetched up into the third heaven where he "heard things which must not and cannot be put into human language."[14] It is reminiscent of the first chapter of the *Tao te Ching,* which tells us that the "nameless" is the beginning of the myriad creatures, and that the Tao that can be named is not the true Tao.[15]

As we've noted many times, the ultimate ineffability of God is why our God-language gets odd around the edges. God-talk only seems to operate according to the rules of regular language, but when we try to treat it like other language, then we find ourselves running up against insuperable obstacles. As Paul Van Buren noted, "The word 'God' marks the point at which the religious man has come up against the final limit of what he can say about the object of his concern."[16] The word *God* might even be said to be a failure of language, because in using it we acknowledge that the object of our ultimate concern is too large to be limited by words. Ironically, the fundamentalist and the atheist both make the same linguistic mistake; they both assume that the word *God,* like the word *bicycle,* has a specific referent. The fundamentalist uses the word *God* to refer solely to the character who appears between the covers of the Bible, and the atheist, finding no single entity resembling that *God,* denies the existence of God. Both assume *God* is a concrete noun referring to a concrete thing. They want the word to name something and then to be able to say "this" or "that" to it or about it, but in God-language the answer is most often "this *and* that," or in Sanskrit *neti, neti,* "not that."

One response to the problem of human language's inability to name the unnameable is to take the *via negationis,* the way of negation, defining the divine by what it is not. This is a tempting path to take: simply to remain silent about that which, in the end, we cannot express fully. In attempting to articulate the inarticulable, the Heart Sutra of Buddhism speaks of a state of being where there are no eyes, no ears, no mouth, no consciousness, no life, no death, and no absence of them either. In that ultimate realm, nothing starts, nothing stops, there is no old age and death, and no extinction of them either, and so on until, finally, there is no mind or consciousness. Everything is, as it were, dissolved in the great salt ocean of Being. This paradoxical language tells us that the enlightened mind understands that all the categories we use to see and understand our reality are false and that from the perspective of ultimate reality there are no distinctions.

If, in the end, nothing we say about God can be complete, yet it still seems we must talk about it. Except in the hands of gifted mystics, the *via negationis* may lead us to silence and vacuum. We human beings find ourselves compelled to name the unnameable. As that brilliant modernist Samuel Beckett put it, "There is nothing to express, nothing with which to express, nothing from which to express, no desire to express, together with the obligation to express."[17] But how? What form should the language take if it hopes to point to matters of ultimate concern? The cynic says that religious language simply creates God in our own image, that our God-language fabricates a God whom we then turn around and worship as if he, she, or it created us. From this point of view, any god is simply an illusion, a nonexistent Rorschach blot on to which we project our own human desires, fears, and hopes. God language then becomes mere fiction, "myth" in the popular sense of something completely made up and having no relation to reality. So which view is correct? Does *God* refer to anything or doesn't it? Does the word *God* name something or not? The answer, as always, lies in the middle, not in the either/or language of fundamentalism or modernism but in the "yes *and* no" language of metaphor, to which we turn next.

Religious language is thoroughly metaphorical. Without even leaving Genesis we find God, the ultimate source of all being, compared to a wind, breath, a bird. He walks, talks, sees, speaks, works, and blesses like a human (a prime metaphor). He is a sculptor in making Adam from clay, a gardener in forming Eden, a tailor (Genesis 3:21), and he manifests himself as the sound of someone walking in the garden in the cool of day. He acts like a judge, he repents and grieves, he smells burned offerings wafting up to heaven, he establishes covenants like a lawyer. To Avram, he says he is a shield (Genesis 15:1) and he appears as a smoking furnace and a firebrand. He is El Shaddai, the god of the mountain and, like Zeus, he rains down fire from the sky (Genesis 19:23–24). There is no end to the things he is like and in which he is seen. All these are, must be, metaphors for the source of all toward which Thomas's five ways point.

Like *myth,* the word *metaphor* has become a synonym for falsehood, or at least is often connected with the adjective *mere* by which we relegate it to a kind of second-class status as a way of talking about the world we live in. Paul Ricoeur in *The Rule of Metaphor* traces the decline of this once-important word from ancient Greek times to the present.[18] In his *Poetics,* Aristotle noted that those who thought in terms of metaphors were the most intelligent people, because they could see similarities between things that others regarded as different. The ability to look at one thing and see something else is a hallmark of creative people in all times and places. Aristotle felt that, in its poetic function, metaphor seeks to "compose an essential representation of human actions [mimesis]; its appropriate method is to speak the truth by means of fiction, fable and tragic *mythos.*"[19] Here he links together the loaded word *truth* with *myth,* as we have done in previous chapters. He went even further in the *Poetics* and said that the ability to metaphorize was a mark of genius, since it seemed to be innate and intuitive and could not be learned from others.[20]

However, after this promising beginning, Aristotle went on, in his *Rhetoric,* to turn metaphor into a mere tool of persuasion, just one more weapon in an orator's arsenal. Following the rhetorical line of Aristotle, for the next two thousand years metaphor increasingly came to be regarded as mere decoration on the way we say things, a clever device perhaps, but not really necessary for clear expression. After the scientific revolution ushered in a new way of thinking about language, metaphor became the property of poets only, and, as poets became more marginalized, the importance of metaphor shrank even further. Even twentieth-century literary critics forgot the way that metaphor reveals truths not expressible in other terms.

Now, however, since we are in an age when fundamentalism and modernism seem stuck in literalism, the time is ripe to restore metaphor to its central position in God-language, for properly understood, metaphoric language is the best language with which to express the divine. In fact, it may be the only kind of language adequate to the task, but only if we allow it to function as metaphors should and do not attempt to judge it by the rules of normal referential speech. John Macquarrie wrote that in speaking of the unspeakable we must "stretch language beyond its normal usage."[21] This is precisely what metaphor does. It increases the elasticity of language by taking what philosophers call the *via eminentiae,* using that which is eminent, or visible, to describe that which is beyond visibility. Similar to the medieval *analogia entis,* or analogy of being, this method uses the things that we do know from our human experience of existence to address those aspects of being that we do not know and that, perhaps, are beyond our full knowing. Aquinas addressed this very idea in the *Summa* when he questioned whether scripture used metaphors to convey its truths. This is a crucial question for us in the modern age, too, for upon the answer hinges the only adequate response to fundamentalism's claims that scripture is literally true and extreme modernism's that it is literally false. If the divine speaks literally, then we must either accept the fundamentalists' interpretation of scripture or join the modern secularists and reject it. If we can admit that the divine speaks metaphorically, however, we may build bridges instead of walls between us.

But first we must get over the idea that there is anything "mere" about metaphor.

Interestingly, in discussing the metaphoric nature of scriptural truth, Aquinas himself first raises some objections we might hear today from both scientific rationalists and religious literalists. He notes that some may say metaphors are low forms of communication more proper to (mere) poetry than truth, and that they obscure rather than reveal things. Others say that talk of God and religious matters should be in a language more befitting the lofty subject matter than comparisons to earthly things. Aquinas replies to all these objections thus:

> It is befitting Holy Writ to put forward divine and spiritual truths by means of comparison with material things. For God provides for everything according to the capacity of nature. Now it is natural to man to attain to intellectual truths through sensible objects because all our knowledge originates from sense. Hence in Holy Writ spiritual truths are fittingly taught under the likeness of material things.[22]

Thomas's point is that since we are the sorts of creatures we are, revelation of the infinite will inevitably be understood by us in human terms, based on our capacity to understand. The only way we humans can truly know anything is through our sensorium, that is, through the five senses of seeing, hearing, smelling, tasting, and touching, which connect our inner world with the outer world in which we live and move. Out of that bodily experience we articulate our thoughts, talking about them in terms of concrete experiences. When we encounter something that we do not yet know or understand—the tremendous and fascinating mystery, for example—we inevitably refer back to our experience and try to cast the unknown in terms of what is already known. Aquinas goes on to build a case for a multilevel understanding of religious language, harking back to the traditional fourfold method of interpretation popular since the earliest days of the church, in which it is understood that below the literal level of the text, there are additional levels of meaning, namely the spiritual, allegorical, and anagogical senses, all of which are based on the literal. In other words, to stop at the literal level, for Thomas and for the long line of scriptural exegetes who preceded and followed him, was to give only the most superficial reading to religious texts.[23] One had to read them not just across the surface of the page but also down into the text's depths, *through* the page as it were, in order to discover the many dimensions and levels hidden below the surface. This can happen only if we have an adequate appreciation of how metaphor works in religious discourse, because metaphor, far from being a mere ornament to religious language, is its very foundation and, without it, God-talk might not even be possible.

We need, therefore, to take a short digression and look more closely at how metaphor operates.

There are essentially three traditional views of what metaphors are and how they work.[24] The first and most common understanding of metaphor is what is called the "substitution view." In this way of looking at metaphor, some literal expression can be used instead of the metaphor with no great loss of meaning. If I refer to King Richard I of England as "Richard the Lion-Hearted," for example, I might substitute for the metaphor by saying, "Richard, who is brave, courageous, and kingly, and who possesses great inner resources." In the substitution view, the second way of saying this is the equivalent of the first, and the metaphor "lion-hearted" is simply a fanciful way of saying what is said more directly (and plainly) in the second. Only a fully concrete thinker would read the name literally, thinking that, for example, Richard had had a weird cross-species heart transplant and now has the literal heart of a lion beating in his chest. The substitution view, though popular, actually reduces the metaphor to mere ornament, taking the scientific view that this metaphorical way of speaking is simply a way of gussying up something that could be said more simply. In this understanding, the concrete image (lion) simply serves as the vehicle for the meaning, called the "tenor" by literary critics, which can be expressed as well in other language. Metaphor is superficial and merely adds color to our expressions. This is the common view of literalists and concrete thinkers.[25] In terms of religious use of metaphor, the stories, symbols, and imagery of myth simply serve to encode religious messages that are then "decoded" by exegesis.

The second way of thinking about metaphor is the "comparison" view. In this view, a metaphor sets up a sort of equation that says something is *like* something else. Robert Burns's "My love is like a red, red rose" is a prime example. Setting a woman and a rose side by side in our mind, the image challenges us to see similarities. So, in terms of religious language, if I read the Twenty-third Psalm and find that God is like a shepherd who protects and guides me and also like a host who spreads a banquet before me, I am challenged to see the similarities between the ultimate source of my being and those two known quantities from human experience, shepherds and hosts. This certainly adds a dimension to our understanding of metaphor that the substitution view does not, for it admits at least that the poetic metaphor stands on its own as an explanation of something that perhaps cannot be expressed exactly the same way in prose. The psalm, after all, does not say that the Lord is "like" my shepherd and host, it says he *is* my shepherd and host. Still, the comparison view has a weakness in that it implies that there was a preexisting similarity between a woman and a rose and the Lord and a shepherd to begin with, whereas, before the poems were written, no one had explicitly noticed the similarity. The metaphor, in other words, may not simply reveal a similarity; it may actually create one. And it is this idea that gives rise to the third view of metaphor, the interactive view, which will be the most valuable one for our discussion of religious language.

In the interactive view, the two terms of the comparison (woman/rose, Lord/shepherd) serve to illumine each other. It's not simply that the image carries a paraphraseable meaning. Rather, both terms are active at once, and a tension is created between them. After all, a woman is most obviously *not* a rose, and how could we say that the source of all Being is a shepherd? On the literal face of it, both expressions are absurd. But once we put the comparison forward, we may not ever look at women, roses, God, or shepherds in quite the same way. The comparison implied in the metaphor organizes the way we look at a subject, highlighting some aspects of it (God's personal care for us, his bounty, and so on) and obscuring others. Like looking through a lens, the metaphor focuses our attention and allows us to see certain things clearly. The tension created in the image takes us into a deeper understanding of both terms, what may be called the "frame" and the "focus" of the metaphor, but the identity of the two can only be taken so far. Clearly we are not meant to think of the thorns that come with roses when we think of Burns's love, and the psalm does not encourage us to remember that shepherds eventually either shear or slaughter their sheep. The metaphor defines itself and its limits as it is elaborated in the context of the poem (and remember that most scripture is poetic in form and approach). So to think of God as a heavenly father highlights ways in which the ultimate source of Being is like the father(s) we have known, and we contemplate the similarities. But there is always the "not that" in the equation, too. For starters, thinking of the fatherly qualities of God prevents us from thinking of God's motherly qualities at the same time. The metaphor simultaneously reveals and conceals aspects of what it refers to. The necessary and enlightening tension arises from the metaphor's incompleteness, not only from the similarity between the image and what it refers to but also, and more importantly, from the difference.

This model of metaphor was elaborated at length by French critic Paul Ricoeur. The most striking thing about metaphor, says Ricoeur, is that it is, on the surface, literally wrong. It involves an apparent mistaken perception, that, for example, the creator of the universe is a shepherd. It is, however, not just an error of attribution. It is a "calculated error," and it is "discursive" in the root sense of that word, which means to "run around" something, that is, we may not talk about it directly.[26] The result of the happy error, however, is not confusion. Instead, it makes a kind of sense and offers an insight into something, because it forces us to see it from a new angle, one we wouldn't have thought of if we had looked at it in a conventional way. In fact, a fresh metaphor helps us see things in a way we couldn't otherwise. It is what epistemologists call "heuristic," a way of exploring and discovering reality. Thus, good metaphors are, to use a postmodernist buzz word, "transgressive." They break our old categories of thinking and establish new ones. They break the rules, and in breaking them open up new ways of understanding.

This is especially important in religious language, because the resulting effect is what Ricoeur calls a "semantic collision." Like hydrogen and oxygen coming together to form water, the two terms of the metaphor (woman/rose, Lord/shepherd) combine to form a mental image that is simultaneously both and neither of the elements that make it up. There is, as it were, a gap between the image and what is being talked about with the image, something like the gap between the anode and the cathode on a battery. The semantic spark jumps across the gap like an electrical charge, and a new meaning is created. Ricoeur identifies three distinct steps that we go through when we encounter a metaphor that is fresh. First there is an element of surprise. (The creator of the universe is like a shepherd?) Then bewilderment as we ponder the image that has caught us up short. (The source of all Being is a *shepherd?*) Then, finally, something clicks, a new understanding is born, we see that behind the paradox lies a previously unnoted relationship. (Oh, yes! He leadeth me to green pastures, and when I pass through the valley of the shadow of death, I fear no harm. I get it!) The flash of insight is intuitive and sudden. In Zen, this is the method of the koan, which sets up a seemingly senseless paradox ("What is the sound of one hand clapping?") and then challenges the novice to beat his or her head against it until, like a nut, the shell cracks and it opens up with meaning. Ricoeur says, "metaphor astonishes and instructs rapidly. Here surprise, in conjunction with hiddenness, plays the decisive role."[27]

This idea of metaphor rescues it from being mere ornamentation to speech. It also rescues it from the substitution model of metaphor, which assumes that what we say metaphorically can be said just as adequately in a more prosaic way. It also liberates us from literalistic fundamentalism, which would remove the difference between the terms and insist on their identity, robbing the image of its electrical charge. The value of this interactive model, especially in considering religious language, is that the meaning of the metaphor cannot be put in any other way than in the metaphor itself. The metaphor does not need to be explained, because it is, in a real way, already an explanation of something. "The Lord is my shepherd" is, in fact, an explanation of what God is and therefore should not need further elaboration. We are to rest in the image itself, in the tension between the two terms, in the electric space between the positive and the negative pole. If the tension is resolved, then the energy goes out of the metaphor and it dies. (An example of a dead metaphor is the use of "table leg," which no longer strikes anyone as odd. Similarly, we can lose touch with the surprising nature of metaphors when, like "The Lord is my shepherd," we hear them so often that their really shocking nature is no longer noticed.) The actual meaning of a metaphor takes place between the two terms of the metaphor and is not in either of them. In Ricoeur's words, metaphor "holds two thoughts of different things together in simultaneous performance upon the stage of a single word or expression, whose meaning is the result of their interaction."[28]

When we return to examine religious language, we see then why it simply cannot be taken literally. Because the object of our attention in religious discourse is nothing less than the source of all Being—existence itself—and the relationship between the infinite and the finite, anything we say about it will end up being, in one sense, wrong or at least incomplete and imprecise. Our statements about our relationship to the ultimate reality inevitably end up being catachrestic, which is a fancy literary term for the "improper use of words, [the] application of a term to a thing which it does not properly denote."[29] Religious language must take the form of catachresis because, by definition, human language simply cannot adequately or accurately express what remains ultimately ineffable and unnameable. To the chagrin of literalists, then, religious language cannot be literal.[30] It has to be metaphoric, because only metaphor can allow us to express the ambiguous, the indeterminate, and the infinite, using terms from the known to express the as-yet-unknown. In the end, even though we may talk about its "meaning," the metaphor remains unparaphraseable in terms other than itself. Like God, it remains mysterious, and to dwell in its mystery is the proper way to understand it.

As the Koran says, "God does not disdain to make comparison with a gnat or with a larger creature. The faithful know that it is the truth from their Lord, but the unbelievers ask: 'What could God mean by this comparison?' By such comparisons God confounds many and enlightens many."[31]

Just one or two more comments need to be made before we leave the thin air of theory and move into the earthy atmosphere of the actual metaphors we use to describe God. Our goal here is to unjoin the adjective *mere* from the noun *metaphor*. By now, of course, it should be clear there is nothing "mere" about it, but in case the idea needs further elaboration, we should remember that the Greek roots of the word *metaphor* (*meta,* "with, among" + *pherein,* "to carry") indicate that it is a vehicle of sorts that carries us somewhere. I have seen a picture of a Greek moving van, in fact, on whose side is written "*Metaphora.*" This is the notion we must bring to the religious use of metaphors. They are designed to carry us somewhere, to move us and our mental furniture somewhere new. That new place is toward a further discovery and understanding of the divine, a destination we will never fully reach, but one toward which we are irresistibly drawn.

But the universe is not a Rorschach blot. Our metaphors are not simply our human imagination rather randomly assigning images to a void. Rather, the divine, in a real sense, calls out to us to articulate it. In the view of those who lean toward fundamentalism, the actual words of scripture were revealed by God to Moses or by Allah through Gabriel to Muhammad. In that understanding, the Creator spoke ancient Hebrew and Arabic and used just these words in just these ways. From the secularist point of view, there is no such thing as this sort of revelation. Rather, they would say that purely human authors wrote purely human poetry. The gods described in the world's myths are figments of their authors' imaginations only and there was no such thing as divine inspiration or revelation at all. As usual, these points of view, the fundamentalist and the modernist, seem irreconcilable. But a third possibility exists, which is that we human beings, as part of our human consciousness, hear a call from Being itself—call it God, Allah, Brahman, Gitchee-Manitou, the ground of Being, or any other name—which we feel compelled to answer. This call comes from outside us, prompted by moments of cosmic awe, and something deep inside of us responds, and we fill the gap between the infinite call and our finite being with metaphor, the language of middle places.

Rather than conceiving of religious language simplistically as either divine word-for-word revelation or as mere human fabrication, to understand it as metaphor is to understand it as something in between. Metaphorical god-language is, as MacCormac said years ago, the "human response to the divine."[32] To give the name *God* to that which calls us to name it is merely to give a local habitation to the infinite so that we may say anything about it at all. To say we name it and describe it does not deny the existence of something infinite, nor does it reduce our cosmic awe. It simply gives us a provisional vocabulary for approaching and articulating our human experience of the divine. The transcendent is calling us to a fuller consciousness of itself and of ourselves, and, ultimately, the word we use to name the ineffable does not stand alone. It stands at the heart of a complex of metaphors that are the scriptures, myths, rituals, and traditions that surround it. The names we give to the source of Being are like seed crystals, which, when put into saturated solutions, cause solid forms to materialize from the liquid medium. God is not any one of the metaphors or languages we use to talk about the divine; rather, God is all of them taken together, and even that totality of the world's metaphors and the sum of all our species' God-talk does not come near to expressing the reality. But, like good moving vehicles, the metaphors of God may take us and our mental and spiritual furniture to the place we wish to be.

But where exactly is that place?

The Kena Upanishad begins with a series of startling questions that point us in the right direction:

> Who sends the mind to wander afar?
> Who drives life to start on its journey?
> Who impels us to utter these words?
> Who is the spirit behind the eye and the ear?[33]

These are the fundamental religious questions of human life, and in these words we hear the voice of a consciousness awakening to its own existence in a universe it did not create. Rather than seeming to come from the natural curiosity of the speaker, the words evoke a sense of being called to think upon these impossible things by another sort of intelligence, perhaps by the universe itself. In the same way, we find characters in the Hebrew and Christian scriptures suddenly and unexpectedly called by God. Whether the call comes in the form of a burning bush, as with Moses, or after being thrown from a horse, like Paul, or when one is awakened in the middle of the night by the voice of the Creator calling one's name, as happens to the prophets, we get the sense that human beings experience their awakening to the divine as a kind of "called" thinking. We feel we are being summoned by something simultaneously inside and outside of ourselves. It beckons us to name its name and to understand it. The act of naming the caller, or finding the name of God, is the first act of religion; all else seems to follow from it.

The "called" nature of the religious impulse is what sets it apart from human curiosity about other things. The German theologian Eberhard Jüngel, whose works are not widely available in English, devoted quite a bit of attention to the language of belief. According to John Webster, Jüngel sees "an intrinsic connection between faith and language" in which "faith is itself identified and characterized primarily by the traditions of language which it brings into being."[34] While the language we use to talk about God is and remains human language, Jüngel insists that we are called to use this language by something outside us. We do not simply make it up, nor are we projecting our words out onto nothing. Some experience—cosmic awe, awareness of our own finitude, a catastrophic irruption of nature—summons us, as it were, to ask questions like those posed by the opening of the Kena Upanishad, questions of ultimate meaning. Because of the nature of the subject and of this sense of being called to respond by something external to and larger than ourselves, religious language puts "heavy demands" on our linguistic abilities. Any attempt to articulate our experience of the divine involves stretching human language to its limit, even to the extent of apparently misusing words. The Kena Upanishad, as it answers the questions it poses, shows us that religious language can become almost like a Möbius strip, turning back on itself and creating an impossible topography that is nonetheless real. The Upanishad tells us that the force that gives rise to its initial questions "is the ear of the ear, the eye of the eye, and the word of words, the mind of mind, and the life of life."[35] That is, it is not the physical organ of hearing, speech, or thinking itself; rather, it is that which it enables ears, eyes, hearing, vision, and thinking to exist in the first place. Brahman is the name given to it.

As we saw above, this level of experience resists expression in everyday language and lends itself best to metaphor, the "as if" language of comparison. As Sallie McFague pointed out in *Metaphorical Theology*, we resort to metaphor because "in a sense, we feel more than we can express, we know more than we can interpret."[36] Only an in-between language such as metaphor can capture the numinous quality of authentic religious experience.

Derek Bickerton, in his book *Language and Species,* speculates on the origins of human language and on how it functions in human life as what he calls a "Secondary Reference System." Bickerton contends that human language works in a qualitatively different way than other animal communication. Where animal language, such as territorial bird song, is a closed reference system, human language forms a kind of open-ended reference system that allows us tremendous flexibility of expression and understanding. Thanks to the evolution of our large brain, our immediate experience of the world that comes through our senses "gets mapped onto a conceptual representation, and then this conceptual representation is mapped onto a linguistic representation."[37] The unique feature of the human capacity for language is that it is arranged to operate hierarchically, sorting external sense impressions into categories and creating, as it were, a map to which we then refer when we interact with the world. Bickerton says, "at least three distinguishable mapping processes are going on: from reality to sensory perception, from sensory perception to categorization, from categorization to language."[38]

We human beings use language to organize and reorganize endlessly the elements of the world with which we interact. Depending on which category of experience we select, we call different figures out from the undifferentiated ground in front of us. Language can thus be regarded as "an enormously efficient filing system, organizing . . . our entire knowledge of the world, [and it] forms one of the major factors in our success as a species."[39]

The open-ended nature of human language allows us to talk not just about our immediate environment but about anything at all, physically present or not, and if we follow the analogy of language as a map, we can find our way back to the unique nature of religious language.

Cartography is a process of increasing refinement as the mapmakers move from a rough understanding of a territory to a more precise one. If we look at antique maps, we are struck by their inaccuracy compared with modern maps. For example, seventeenth- and eighteenth-century maps of the Great Lakes region show only a very rough comprehension of the shapes of the lakes and the land masses touching them. Michigan's lower peninsula, which modern maps show as a mitten shape, appears as a kind of squashed muffin with water only on its east side in early French maps of the territory. Lake Michigan is nonexistent, and the state is connected to the land mass of the upper Midwest, curiously blank. But mapmaking is an always-evolving process, and generations of maps later, the shapes of the lakes and the land correspond more closely to the actual shape of the land, verified by the experience of air flight and satellite imagery.

Like a map, language, says Bickerton, is a "way of representing to ourselves ourselves and the world around us."[40] As we encounter new phenomena in the world, our language attempts to incorporate them into the conceptual map we have created by relating them to known things that already have names. This is possible because "any word in any language is intertranslatable, that is to say, capable of being converted into a string of other words in the same language, [and it] falls into place in an intricately patterned structure of words that forms, as it were, a universal filing system allowing for rapid retrieval and comprehension of any concept."[41] Language thus enables us to push knowledge forward and to invent things that previously did not exist because of its ability to cross-reference categories. It is "as if nature has provided us with a black box containing a machine that enables us to orient ourselves in the semi-simulacrum of the real world that language-as-representation creates."[42] The conceptual maps we create with language enable us to comprehend the world around us, to plan itineraries through it, and to imagine places we have never been.

From a purely biological perspective, it is easy to see how the evolution of language in humans enabled, and continues to enable us to survive, but following this line of reasoning leads us to an intriguing question. What is the particular evolutionary advantage to the human species of God-language? That is, accepting the Darwinian assumption that successful evolutionary adaptations serve the interests of a species' continuance and even thriving, then there must be some evolutionary advantage to the universal existence of something we can call religious language in human societies. And if the conceptual map that language allows us to create is organized in hierarchical categories, then what exactly are the hallmarks of the category into which God-language falls?

To begin to answer these questions, we need to look at what we use God-language for. We first of all express in God-language those things that we experience as uncanny, things otherwise unexplainable, experiences that defy or contradict the way we normally think of how the world works. Perhaps one purpose of God-language is to serve as a means of expressing what is not known, what is new territory not yet on our conceptual map. That is certainly one function of God-language. To say that this is all that religious language does, however, is to agree with the modernists, who would say that religion is simply primitive science and that we may dispense with religious language once we understand through modern science what the phenomenon "really" is. For example, in the Middle Ages, it was widely thought that the Black Death was God's punishment on sinful humans for our transgressions. It would be several hundred years before we discovered that the disease was actually caused by the bacterium *Yersinia pestis* and was spread by fleas that went from rodents to humans. Similarly, once we understood the nature of biological evolution, many felt we could dispense with the archaic God-language of Genesis. Modern scientific language, in this view, supersedes religious language as a reliable conceptual map for life, and in fact, as witnessed by science's success in the treatment of disease and in understanding the underlying processes of species' evolution, it is a good thing this is so.

But does that mean we can jettison religious language altogether in the contemporary world or that we reserve it only for those parts of the world we don't yet understand scientifically? Not at all. If we think of religious language in light of Bickerton's notion of linguistic categories, of what he calls "semantic space," then we see that religious language is not in competition with scientific language at all. Rather, where scientific language might give us a vocabulary and syntax to successfully map the physical world, it can function well only within that category. True, science provides a conceptual map with an extremely large horizon that includes the material universe, from the tiniest atomic particle to the boundaries of the farthest galaxies. But it is incompetent to navigate us to the answers of the ultimate questions posed by the Kena Upanishad. What happened before the Big Bang? What lies outside the universe? How can we even think of these things? And it is severely limited in its ability to address the ethical questions posed by the fact that we live our individual human lives among others.

We might even say that the "God category" we're trying to address here is the category of categories, forming the utmost possible horizon of any conceptual map we can have of life itself. The domain of God-language contains all the other categories and universes of discourse, and provides the largest possible context for the other categories into which we sort our existence. Though it sounds odd to say, religious language puts the universe in perspective. It also provides, as it were, a map of the border territory between the inner and the outer worlds of our experience, and thus gives us an invaluable and indispensable tool for navigating that strange realm by providing itineraries, destinations, and valuable navigation tools.

The conceptual map of religious language only works, however, if we know or can remember how to read it. And it is on this point that we seem stuck today. The scientific modernist looks at the religious conceptual map as an antiquated chart of a world that doesn't exist. The strict fundamentalists, stuck in their literalism, confuse the map with the terrain it describes. Losing touch with the metaphorical nature of religious language, we have temporarily lost our bearings, but we can get them back by exploring further how religious language uses metaphor to map the largest terrain of all, the terrain of meaning in life.

Our religious language has its roots in experience, but authentic religious experience, as we have said repeatedly, resists clear articulation in words because it is rooted in our encounters with the numinous ground, limits, and horizons of our human experience. In that territory, we feel ourselves in the presence of things we did not create, as when we experience the action of Fate in the sudden death of a loved one or in a natural disaster, or in times when we find within ourselves a void or emptiness, or, conversely, an unaccountable fullness of being, or when we encounter human evil. In times like those, we feel compelled to fit the experiences into the conceptual map we have of the world we live in by putting them into words. But this is difficult. These threshold experiences often have an uncanny feeling about them. They may shock us out of our normal everyday minds and put us in a state of mind that evokes something holy or unholy, awakes a sense of awe or adoration, and then we feel called to try to map an understanding of the experience in words. The experience is undeniable, but the articulation of what it is and what it means is difficult, so we turn to metaphor, explaining the unknown (and perhaps unknowable) in terms of the known. "Well," we say, "It was like this . . ." and we tell a story. And, not surprisingly, the language of the story gets odd.

Not least among its odd characteristics is religious language's ability to open up, in those who hear it, something like the actual experience of the divine that gave birth to the language in the first place. That is, certain religious geniuses—Moses, the Buddha, Muhammad, Jesus, Zarathustra—used words to talk about their experience, and those words in turn served as bridges for generations of others to cross to something very like the original experience. This works because, as Walter Ong says, "There is a primordial attunement of one human existent to another out of which all language comes," including God-language.[43] The human realities of birth, coming of age in the universe, suffering, joy, and death provide the raw materials out of which we construct ultimate meanings that, in turn, become our religious traditions, passed down from generation to generation as reliable maps and itineraries through life. Not surprisingly we find the divine described in images drawn from life but referencing something that is both within and beyond everydayness. We use religious language to help us deal with such perennial human situations as birth and death as well as with everyday events in our contemporary world, testing the adequacy of our conceptual map against our lived experience, modifying it and clarifying it, using it to navigate life's passages.

We may use many different kinds of maps to map the same territory. Each map shows only one aspect of the terrain. A subway map of Manhattan shows only a stylized diagram of the world below the streets, while a street map of the same island shows the grid of crosstown streets and uptown avenues on the surface. A topographical or relief map of the same territory would show elevations and natural features, while a cultural geographer interested in ethnography might draw a quite different map. The same territory is represented by all the maps, but they look quite different and yield quite different perspectives. All are valuable for certain kinds of information, and all are symbolic, but none is perfect. The only perfect map, as Jorge Luis Borges pointed out, would be a map as large and detailed as the territory it described, and such a map would be utterly useless.

So our linguistic maps of the territory between the human and the divine, the sacred and the profane, being metaphorical, are necessarily schematic and limited as well.

This is not because they are purely subjective. The metaphors of God-language map a real area of human experience, and the test of their validity is whether they can successfully guide us through life along a path that is "holy," that is, whole, healthy, and meaningful to us and beneficial to others. George Lakoff and Mark Johnson, in their influential book *Metaphors We Live By*, speak of an "experientialist" test of a metaphor's truth.[44] Human beings, in their subjectivity encounter the outer world in all its complexity, but they function in the world by means of metaphors, which allow them to make sense of the otherwise disparate experiences they encounter. Such metaphors as "life is a journey" or "love is an intricate dance" enable meaningful action in the world, that is, help us to conceptualize an otherwise overwhelming and apparently chaotic experience. Of course, life is not literally a journey, and though love may involve dancing, there is more to it than that. Still, the metaphors help pull things together. The metaphor, as a conceptual map, forms a middle ground, as it were, between our subjective, inner experience and the objective world through which we move.

Like the various maps of the same terrain, however, no metaphor completely describes the experience it is addressing. There is, in that sense, no absolute truth or one way or even any "universally valid point of view," Lakoff and Johnson say.[45] On the other hand, metaphors are not simply imposed on reality by the imagination, for they are based on experience. There is a dynamic interaction between subjectivity and objectivity, tested and verified by the metaphor's ability to illuminate aspects of the experience it is addressing in a way that allows meaningful action. The perceived similarities between the image and the referent of the metaphor "provide a partial understanding of one kind of experience in terms of another kind of experience. This may involve pre-existing isolated similarities, the creation of new similarities, and more."[46] Metaphors form a kind of "glue" of meaning that holds unlike things together in an illuminating way.

The word *God,* then, is an attempt to name what is, and must remain, unnameable. The name forms a focus around which metaphors tend to constellate in the form of myths as we attempt to articulate further what the name means. As Earl MacCormac said, "The term 'God' forms an integral part of a series of relationships and beliefs that finds confirmation or disconfirmation in human experience."[47] The territory of *God* is mapped in our consciousness by certain root metaphors, none of which is perfect, but all of which point toward the experience of the divine. To get a complete sense of God, just as to get a complete sense of any territory, it is best to have a number of maps. As John Macquarrie put it, "What must be done is to have a number of images [of the divine], each correcting and supplementing each other."[48] Multiple images must be called upon because the territory we are mapping is infinite and because all metaphors are limited.

So, we come away from this with two ideas. First, the religious traditions of the world provide reliable maps of the experience of whole and holy living. Second, all these maps are limited and imperfect. Our metaphorical God-language uses analogies and comparisons to attempt to articulate the tremendous mystery that is existence. It then elaborates on the words, constantly approximating the truth but never quite achieving it. At some point, of course, we must act upon the approximation of truth we have arrived at, but it is an act of faith more than of knowledge. Metaphor, like a stylized map, highlights only certain aspects of what we are trying to describe and, in doing that, it inevitably obscures others.

The words of the world's scriptures and mythic traditions, including the writings of mystics, are the history of the human race's encounters with the infinite. They form the record of a deeply poetic colloquy between the human and the divine, expressing divinity in the only language that could adequately convey it. The result is a profusion of metaphors, of which we can sample only a few in the remaining pages of this book. Taken singly, they provide insight into an aspect of the divine; taken together, they may form a pattern that will cause a light to go on in our souls, a light that illumines that which is dark, a light that enables us to see the unseen, to hear the unhearable, using what the Upanishad called the eye of the eye and the ear of the ear. They provide an indispensable map to the middle world, between the finite and the infinite, a mesocosm revealing the deep links between the large universe around us and the small universe within.

As we have seen, it is strange linguistic territory. The *Tao te Ching* warns us that the way that can be named is not the true way and that the nameless is the source of all beings. Thomas Aquinas, too, admits the inadequacy of all names and attempts at description. This is in the apophatic tradition, that is, the tradition that says the divine can only be defined by what it is not. (The word is from the Greek *apo,* "away," and *phatikos,* "speech.") And yet, we feel called to try, to speak about it like explorers setting out to map a country that can never be fully explored.

We should begin humbly, like the Persian Sufi poet Sana'i (d. 1150 C.E.), whose parable of the blind men and the elephant is really a parable about finding the name of God. Like them, one of us may grab the leg of the divine and proclaim it to be like a tree, another may feel its trunk and declare it to be like a rope, while yet another, feeling its side, will proclaim it to be like a wall. While we usually focus on the blind men's blindness and inability to see the whole elephant, it is important to remember that, metaphorically speaking, they all are correct, even while they are wrong. As the blind men discover, an elephant, in fact, *is* like a tree, a rope, and a wall, yet also, as a Hindu might say, "not that, not that."

Like them, we may touch and feel the enormity of the divine, but in the end, we will finally, humbly be brought to *silence*.

9 : Silence

WHEN WE begin to pray, we often say, "Let us bow our heads and lift up our hearts to God." This prelude to prayer seems to acknowledge that the head, that place of words, must be silenced to allow the wordless heart to arise. There is something about approaching the divine that confounds language. Indeed, the divine is most often shrouded in unspeakable mystery. We can approach it only at an angle.

When Moses ascends Mount Sinai in the book of Exodus, God waits for him shrouded by clouds and engulfed in storm. God warns Moses that the people are to come only so far up the mountain, and they are not to look on him directly or they will die. Moses himself, being a great religious hero, can ascend into the cloud and storm and commune with God, but only in the darkness. When he emerges, he carries the Decalogue, whose first commandments forbid us from depicting God or invoking his sacred name for irreverent or trivial purposes. These taboos hark back to the episode earlier in Exodus when Moses first met God in the burning bush. At that time, Moses asked to know the name of God, and God replied, "I Am Who Am." As we discussed above, this name that is not a name is tantamount to God's saying, "Do not attempt to label me, to pin me down to a name. I am that which I am." In orthodox practice, the proper name of God is so sacred that readers pause in silence when they come to it in scripture.

This is a very strange God, who both reveals and conceals himself. He tells us his name, but we may not pronounce it. He manifests himself, but we are not to look at him. Even Moses, a great holy man, is only permitted a view of his back side, for the full view of God in all his godhood would be more than Moses's mortal frame could bear. It seems we can only meet this God in the obscurity of cloud or hear his voice amid the thunder's roll. He is smoke and fire, seen and unseen. As Paul Van Buren wrote of this God, "We are given . . . a largely absent presence, an unmentionable name of what is neither to be imaged, nor pictured, nor otherwise represented."[1] Implicit in all this, of course, is the idea that we cannot fully describe the divine in human terms. And yet, being the linguistic creatures that we are, we continue to seek a name for that which is nameless, a face for that which is faceless.

As we have seen, religious language, by the very nature of what it is talking about, is inevitably paradoxical. That which we seek to describe with words is, we admit, indescribable, but, throughout history, the very indescribability of the divine compelled us to try to say more and more about it. Perversely, we continue to speak about God even though the more we speak, the more we call attention to the incapacity of our language to capture fully the essence of what we are talking about.

Even the great preacher and letter writer Paul, in Romans 8:26, admits the failure of language to scale the heights of divinity. Sometimes, he says, language gives out, and then "the Spirit himself intercedes for us with signs too deep for words." This tension between naming God and remaining silent, between God's self-manifestation and his obscurity, is the necessary paradox of religious language. If our God-language is too sure, too particular, too confident, or too definitive, then we can be certain we have descended into superficiality and have made an idol of the divine. If the God of whom we speak has no shadows, then we have missed the mark somehow.

The conundrum of trying to name the nameless is acknowledged in the Western tradition in the idea of the *deus absconditus,* or the hidden God, but historically it has been more fully elaborated in the Eastern traditions, in both Hinduism and Buddhism, and most especially in Taoism and the Zen tradition, which explicitly point to the nameless as the source of all things. However, the *Bhagavad Gita,* buried in the heart of the Hindu epic the *Mahabharata*, may be the most dramatic narrative depiction of both the problem of naming God and of the proper understanding of the relationship between the names of God and the divine reality. Following its richly detailed narrative will enable us to trace the paradoxical journey through language to silence.

The *Bhagavad Gita* was composed orally over a long time, beginning perhaps three thousand years ago in its earliest forms. It was transmitted by storytellers for hundreds of years and finally written down sometime around 300 C.E. It forms the middle of the *Mahabharata*, which is, on the one hand, a long religious poem and, on the other, an epic adventure on the order of the *Iliad* or the *Odyssey*. Like its Greek counterparts, it concerns the interaction of gods and men, and there is much in it about how to live appropriately in this often-confusing world. Properly understood, it is a profound religious poem about the workings of dharma, a Sanskrit word that includes both our Western notion of duty and also something like natural law. It forms the setting in which the *Bhagavad Gita* is mounted like a jewel.

While it is impossible to summarize the *Mahabharata* briefly, its narrative spine concerns a civil war among two sets of brothers. One set, the Pandavas, are from two wives of King Pandu. Their actual fathers are various Hindu gods, because Pandu himself was prevented by a curse from having intercourse with his wives, but he could acknowledge any sons begotten by gods on his wives. These five brothers were headed by Yudisthira, the eldest, and they ruled half the kingdom of their uncle, the blind old king Dhritarashtra. Meanwhile, the other half of the kingdom was given to the hundred sons of Dhritarashtra and his wife, Gandhari. Their head was Duryodhana, the eldest of the sons.

Duryodhana, jealous of Yudisthira's prosperity, tricked Yudisthira into a game of dice. Yudisthira lost roll after roll, eventually gambling away everything he owned—all his possessions, his kingdom, even the liberty of his brothers, himself, and, finally, his wife. Through the intervention of the old king Dhritarashtra, Yudisthira and the Pandavas were given one final chance for redemption. The old king declared there would be one more roll of the dice, and the losing side would have to spend twelve years in exile as forest dwellers. In the thirteenth year, they would have to live among the common people in disguise, but if they were then able to escape being recognized, they would inherit the entire kingdom.

Yudisthira's bad luck continued, and the Pandavas were forced to spend twelve years wandering in the forest. Then, in the thirteenth year, through a number of stratagems, they successfully avoided detection and so ultimately won the wager. However, when they went to claim the kingdom that was now rightfully theirs, Duryodhana refused to give it to them, and civil war erupted between the clans.[2] It is in this context that the *Bhagavad Gita,* also known as *The Song of God,* is set.

The story of the *Gita* takes place on the night before the climactic battle. Arjuna, one of the Pandavas and the world's greatest bowman, sits brooding over what is to occur the following morning. He is understandably upset that things have come to this, and that at dawn a battle will begin in which he may have to kill his relatives and perhaps even confront his old and revered bowmaster and slay him. Arjuna may be slain himself. Unable to sleep, he summons his charioteer, Krishna, and orders him to drive him to the no-man's-land between the encamped troops, where Arjuna will try to puzzle out the meaning of it all. Unbeknownst to him, his charioteer Krishna is actually the incarnation of the great god Vishnu, the Sustainer, whose dream is all of creation. In the course of the long conversation that makes up the *Bhagavad Gita* section of the *Mahabharata,* Krishna-Vishnu brilliantly expounds the doctrine of dharma, and soon Arjuna realizes that this humble, charming charioteer whom he has known all his life is more than he appears to be.

Arjuna finally asks Krishna, the incarnated god, to reveal himself as he really is, in all his manifestations, and the *Gita* reaches its philosophical climax as, one after the other, Krishna, glowing brighter than a thousand suns, names the names of the gods, great and small, and all the natural phenomena in the world in which his divinity may be found. In poetry of breathtaking scope, the great god says he is the beginning, middle, and end of all things, he is the wind, he is the moon, and the sun and the stars, and he catalogs the exhaustive names of the thousands of Hindu deities, male and female, as well as the divine characteristics of human beings that are also him, and he concludes the episode by reminding Arjuna that he has only revealed to him the most prominent of his manifestations, and that, truth be told, "I support this entire universe constantly/With a single fraction of Myself."[3] And with that, Arjuna sees that all his previous thoughts about the gods and the universe have been delusions. He understands things as they are and understands himself and his own life in a universal context. He is ready to follow his dharma.

The thousands of manifestations of Vishnu revealed in the *Gita* make up what Joseph Campbell, in his great four-volume analysis of world mythology, called "the masks of God." The world is populated with a near-infinite number of gods and goddesses that form the religious heritage of the human race. For tens of thousands of years, the world's myths have carried on a poetic dialogue with the divine, seeking its name and shape and always falling short. Today, we are embroiled in a world conflict over which of those masks is the true mask of God, and it is time to avail ourselves of the wisdom expressed in the *Bhagavad Gita* two thousand years ago. The masks of God are endless, but all are manifestations of the same power. All reveal, and at the same time conceal, divinity.

It is impossible even to begin a complete recounting of the ways in which the divine has revealed itself to humanity, but by now we should be able to understand that any one way, even a way as comprehensive as those presented in the *Bhagavad Gita,* the Bible, or the Koran, limits the divine reality we strive to depict, a reality that in the end remains nameless. And yet, we still feel called to find a way to speak of it, and the best way is through the poetic language of metaphor, stretching human language as far as it can be stretched to approximate the experience of the divine.

It is impossible for modern people to approach religious language with the same naïveté as those who created the myths in the first place, for theirs was a lived experience of the myth, while ours must be filtered through our modern consciousness of history, world cultures, and the knowledge brought to us by modern science. But today, modern people are being challenged by both fundamentalists and modernists to rethink what religion can mean in the contemporary world. For many fundamentalists, who interpret religious language in a literal way, the worship of the written word has become idolatrous. It is as though they are unable to see beyond the mask of God to the Godhead itself. Clearly this is causing much strife in the world, strife that contradicts the compassionate teachings of the spiritual founders of most world religions. On the other hand, for most modernists, the alternative to the idolatry of the word has been to regard religious language as irrelevant. Seeing its divisive tendencies, they either ignore or ridicule the religious impulse. Both extremes—idolatry and irrelevance—rob the religious dimension of its tremendous power to lead us to a sense of healing, wholeness, compassion, and goodness. As we approach the end of this essay on religious language, it's time to look forward and begin to come to a new understanding of the masks of God by creating a foundation on which a deep ecumenism may be built, one that will allow us to live with and even esteem our differences rather than war over them.

One way to begin is to recapture the poetry of the divine as it is expressed in the divine metaphors of all the world's traditions. John's Gospel says "In the beginning was the Word." By that he did not mean the words he was writing, but something far more deeply interfused in the cosmos, the divine Logos, a spirit or principle of order, to which the various names of God are given. The religious traditions of the world are the record of how human beings have used words, images, songs, and rites to try to tease out the nature and meaning of that principle and to express their relationship to it. Being raised in a particular sacred tradition, or coming to one later in life, means committing oneself to a particular way of expressing that religious experience, entering a particular universe of religious discourse, as it were. One becomes competent in the language of that tradition. But it is a mistake to think that our own language is the only language in which the experience of the divine can be expressed.

The world's religious traditions can be thought of as distinct dialects or varieties of one great language that expresses sacred human realities, and each dialect is sufficient to point us toward the whole, but each, taken by itself, is incomplete. All languages will have words for common human experiences. Every language, for example, has a word for mother and father, for life and death, for food, and for the divinity that calls us to name its name. Around that name, or those names, cluster stories, poems, and songs that speak of ultimate realities in language that uses different images to get at the same ultimate truth. As Krishna-Vishnu showed Arjuna, there is no end to the manifestations of the divine in the world, and our adherence to one or another or several of these manifestations can lead us into our fullest humanity, but only if we can remember not to idolize our image. The idolatry of one's own tradition, of course, stems largely from fear of change, a fear that is natural enough in our speeded-up contemporary world, and from fear of the "otherness" of the other. If we cling rigidly to our own set of metaphors for the divine as the only way in which the divine can be expressed, then we may feel secure within our own group, but we condemn ourselves to alienation and bloodshed when we encounter others. If, however, we can learn to appreciate the beauty and richness of all the world's traditions, then not only can we deepen our own belief but we may also be able to open the door to lasting peace.

This will not be an easy task. Anyone who has ever set out to learn a foreign language knows how hard it is to transcend the limits of one's own language. Not only is there new vocabulary to learn, there is new grammar and new syntax. Learning a foreign language involves learning foreign attitudes, shaped by long cultural histories. It also calls us to learn of our own foreignness because we come to see ourselves through the eyes of the other. As difficult as it is to learn a new language, however, doing so enriches our lives. Of course, it is even more difficult to learn to appreciate another's religion than to learn a new language, for the embrace of religion is total. Moreover, in the case of the contemporary situation, our attitudes toward other faiths have been hardened by hundreds of years of prejudice, misunderstanding, warfare, and tragedy. But we must try to understand.

Appreciating religious diversity is a noble and necessary goal, but it is easier said than done. There is no reason it cannot eventually happen, however. In fact, in spite of the headlines, it has already begun. Interfaith dialogue is occurring. It is being forced by the changing world in which we live. Responsible Muslims, Christians, and Jews are beginning to speak to each other, trying to understand, and as the world shrinks, it will become ever more necessary for us to reach out and learn about each other, to attempt to appreciate one another's traditions, perhaps to enrich our own by borrowings or to enlighten our own by helpful metaphors that will deepen our own understanding of the divine. To do this is to move beyond a kind of wary tolerance of one another's traditions into an active appreciation of diversity.

In the twentieth century, modernism envisioned a unified world culture, embodied in the international style of architecture, where buildings would look the same from country to country and people would one day dress alike and perhaps even speak one language. More than that, the modernist worldview, based on reason and science, and manifesting itself in technology, would provide a unified world culture. Today, we can see how misguided that vision was. People will not and should not let go of their local cultures, their long traditions, or the language in which they express their deepest hopes and desires for life, but a necessary part of growth is to value one's own cultural tradition while learning to appreciate the richness and integrity of the traditions of others. Today, we have come to realize the advantages of diversity in everything from the ecosystem to the human genome. We know that for the health of the planet, there must be diversity in genetic strains of plants and animals so that they are not so susceptible to disease or blight. The same must be true for the various religious traditions of the world by which human beings have found meaning in existence for thousands of years. A rich variety of religious perspectives enhances everyone's appreciation of God.

Learning to navigate our way through a diverse world that is changing every instant is the peculiar challenge of contemporary life. As of yet, we are still beginners at it, and have barely learned the ABCs of one another's alphabet, much less come to full understanding. But, as the *Tao Te Ching* says, the journey of a thousand miles begins with the ground beneath our feet. The goal may be far off, but that is no reason not to hold it in our minds as worth getting to, or for not taking the first steps.

As Frithjof Schuon pointed out, there is "a transcendent unity to world religions" if we are able to see beyond the surface differences.[4] To do that, however, we must get over our literalism and learn again to hear the poetry of God-language. We must learn to unlink *truth* from literalism, to get over the idolatry of the word and see that to which the word points. The truth of God does not lie in any one tradition. It resides, paradoxically, in the sum total of all the wild metaphors used in all the world's spiritual traditions.

When we turn to the world's various mystical traditions, we find striking similarities among them, especially when we focus on the imagery used to express the actual experience of the divine mystery. These poetic images, these metaphors, give us hope, for they point the way toward the deep ecumenism we so badly need.

Back in the second and third century C.E., Origen was quite comfortable reading scripture as metaphor. He interpreted the Song of Songs as a Solomonic epithalamium, or wedding song, and understood the bride as anyone who was on fire with love for a bridegroom, which was the Word of God. He said of the metaphorical nature of God-language, "The holy prophets discovered this divine faculty of sensing and seeing and hearing in a divine manner, and of tasting and of smelling in the same way. They touched the Word with faith in a way that was, so to speak, simultaneously sensing and non-sensing so that it poured over them like a healing rain."[5] And Gregory of Nyssa in the fourth century C.E. also sought the mystical sense (*theoria*) of the scriptures, not their literal sense (*historia*).[6] Gregory himself, in writing of his own experience of God, used striking metaphors and paradoxical language, referring to his encounters with the divine as "sober intoxication," "watchful sleep," "passionless passion," "dazzling darkness," and "satisfied dissatisfaction."[7]

Surprisingly for poetry coming from a culture in which drinking alcohol is banned, many Sufi poems also describe the experience of God as a divine drunkenness, a reeling and giddiness and inability to find one's bearings. The seeker wanders the streets with a raging thirst for the divine liquor that will intoxicate him.[8] A Christian mystic, Jacopone da Todi (ca. 1230–1306 C.E.) also uses images of divine intoxication, and writes of a soul drowning like a drop of wine that has been spilled into the sea.[9]

God is like that, yes, and like other things as well.

Augustine of Hippo spoke of God as light, song, perfume, beauty, and wisdom. Life in the house of God, he wrote, is like a "never-ending festival" and "eternal holiday," and "from that everlasting perpetual festivity there sounds in *the ears of the heart* a mysterious strain, melodious and sweet, provided only the world does not drown out the sounds."[10] That paradoxical phrase, "the ears of the heart," recalls to our minds the Kena Upanishad, which said that the mind is sent to wander far by the "eye of the eye, the ear of the ear, the mind of the mind." Augustine also said that the desire for God was like a thirst, hearkening back to imagery from the Psalms and from John that described God's love as a fountain of living water. We drink that water, Augustine said, with "the mouth of our heart."[11] It is hard to literalize that image, but, properly read, the image itself suffices.

There is no end to the metaphors used by spiritual writers of all traditions for the experience of the divine. Bernard of Clairvaux (1090–1153 C.E.) used the metaphor of honey. "Jesus is to me honey in the mouth, music in the ear, a song in the heart," and he wrote that the presence of God in the heart is like the fire beneath a boiling pot. Catherine of Sienna (1347–80 C.E.) wrote of Christ as a bridge and a doorway, and of God as a peaceful sea in which one may be immersed and even drown.[12] Hildegard of Bingen wrote that when she was in her mystical ecstasy, she was a feather on the breath of God. God is like that, and more.

The Sufi poet Ahmad Ghazali (b. 1061 C.E.), compared the soul searching for God to a moth circling a candle flame. The doomed moth's whole attention is focused on the globe of yellow light in which the flame exists, and it circles the dangerous flame until finally it flies into it and is immolated by that which has attracted it. The moth becomes the flame as the flame possesses and overpowers it. So the soul finds its final release in the divine consummation of Allah's fiery love.[13]

All of these metaphors do what good metaphors should. They shock us with their impropriety, they force us to think about the divine in a new way, but they hardly exhaust the topic. They are catachrestic—they misuse language, applying mundane imagery to an experience that eludes words, stretching language and comprehension to the limit—yet to those who can see with the eye of the eye and hear with the ear of the ear, they ring true.

One of the most elaborated strains of imagery for how humans interact with the divine is based on human love, which stands as a metaphor for divine love. Sufi poets exploited this imagery, and perhaps it was their half-erotic, half-religious poetry that influenced the evolution of the troubadours of courtly love in Europe in the twelfth century. Rabbi'ah bent Ka'b (tenth century C.E.) compared this divine love to a great ocean with invisible shores, and to sweet poison. Rumi's evocations of divine love are well known. In Hinduism, the erotic metaphor is greatly elaborated, both in the intercourse of Shiva and Parvati, which symbolizes the union of male and female principles of life, and in the *Kama Sutra,* or the *Scripture of Pleasure,* which Westerners read as a manual of sexual technique, but which proclaims itself as a guide to deep wisdom, for it understands that learning to make love well—that is, learning to obliterate one's self in the arms of the other—is a prefiguring or emblem of our union with the divine and the loss of our particular self in Brahman.

The imagery of love is also found in the poetic language of medieval Christian mystics. Ramon Lull (1232–1316 C.E.), a Spanish mystic who had once been a troubadour at the Majorcan court, used his skill as a poet and the body of imagery of courtly love to speak about his relationship to God. For Lull, love of God, like the love of a woman in medieval romantic lyrics, is both bondage and freedom. The lover wanders through the streets like a madman or fool, and the Beloved, God, is high above him. Lull begins from the scripture passage that says "God is love and he who abides in love abides in God and God in him" and he takes it to the limit, exploring the metaphor in all its dimensions. The human lover announces that he has come from Love, was born in Love, lives in Love, and returns to Love. He seeks his Beloved's dwelling place and courts the Beloved. He rises on wings of Love to the Beloved, and in the end surrenders his entire will to the Beloved.

The idea of imaging the divine in terms of an earthly lover is not unique to Lull, of course. The use of courtly-love imagery in medieval mystical writings is common, calling upon a well-tested and elaborated body of imagery and symbols to express the experience of the divine in a new way. Andre of Reivaulx (ca. 1110–67 C.E.) takes the courtly-love metaphor to an erotic extreme, sighing and pining for the kiss of Christ, saying, "Let him kiss me with the kiss of his mouth," and exclaiming, like a lover possessed, "His left hand is under my head and his right hand shall embrace me."[14] Mecthild of Magdeberg (ca. 1210–97 C.E.) used the conventions of the Minnesingers to describe her intoxication with God, speaking of "our twofold intercourse" in which "He gives Himself to her/And she to Him."[15] Anyone who has seen the Bernini sculpture of Saint Teresa in ecstasy knows that the image of being ravished by God can still be shocking and enlightening, but it cannot be literal.

We need to recapture the liveliness and poetry of religious language to rescue it from the dull literalism of fundamentalism on the one hand, and the equally dull concrete thinking of literalist materialists on the other. We need to rescue the *spirit* of the sacred word from those who would reduce it to the letter. The word *spirit* has a plethora of meanings in English. It can mean the vital principle in humans and animals, the principle that gives life to the mere material part of creatures. It also refers to things incorporeal, including the human soul, as well as any nonphysical being. When capitalized, it refers to the Holy Spirit; and when not capitalized, it can refer to a spirit of any kind. It also means a kind of attitude or energy as in "school spirit" or a "spirited" personality. When it refers to one's personality, as someone's "guiding spirit," for example, it can mean an outstanding or dominant characteristic. Thus, the Spirit of the Times (or, in German, the *Zeitgeist*) can refer to the peculiar or distinctive qualities of a particular period of history. But first and foremost, *spirit* means *breath*.

When we talk of reviving the spirit of sacred language, we mean to breathe new breath into it. Derived from the Latin *spiritus,* the word *spirit* originally meant "breath" and its verb form, *spirare,* "to breathe." Other English words related to or descended from *spiritus* indicate some of the richness in the original metaphor. We need to free the spirit of sacred language again, to release it from the tight, constricting bonds of literalism and let it breathe. Breathing, enspiriting, is a creative and liberating act. In Hebrew, the word *ruah,* or "breath," at the very beginning of Genesis is used to indicate the spirit of God, which hovered over the formless waters at the beginning of creation. We need that breath again to bring order and form to the chaos of contemporary life.

In Asian traditions, breath and breathing as images of life and pathways to wisdom figure prominently. We can live without food for several weeks, without water for about one week, but without breathing only for a few minutes. The sense of this near-universal metaphor is clear: breathing is the essence of life. Whatever the animating principle of the universe is, it must be very like breath, and we take it into us each time we inhale, and part of us goes back to it when we exhale. In both yoga and Zen, the connection between literal breathing and spiritual growth is made explicit, and great amounts of practice are undergone to learn to breathe properly. We are reminded again that the word *yoga* means "to yoke or couple together." There is, in these traditions, explicit acknowledgment that to breathe, just to live, is to be coupled with the source of all life. The better one breathes, the better the connection. When one expires, one's spirit is breathed out into the atmosphere, becoming one with the air all around. This is the essential meaning of the word *nirvana*. When one achieves ultimate enlightenment, one is "breathed out" into Brahman.

And so we speak of people who are filled with the spirit, who seem to breathe forth a life spirit or contain more of this breath of life than others. This is, really, what we mean by a spiritual person, and by spiritual practice. It may not be about professing a particular creed or following certain orthodoxies except insofar as they help us to breathe with the life-giving spirit of the universe. In Christianity, this is something of what is meant by the Holy Spirit and being baptized in the spirit. Just as Adam was breathed into by God and ceased being only a clay body, so too any of us can be breathed into by the spirit and can come alive, in a new and spirited sense.

Like the wind, which it is named after, the spirit cannot be seen, but its effects can be. Speaking of spirit in this metaphorical way grounds the mystical in the physical, and helps us understand the unknown through the known and familiar. It is *like* that.

We need to relearn the art of reading sacred metaphors so that we can use metaphors to correct mistaken interpretations of sacred language made by literalists. Here I am thinking in particular of those who wish to turn the United States into some kind of Christian kingdom, using the biblical metaphor of the "kingdom of God" as their proof text that this is what Jesus had in mind. Taking the word *kingdom* literally and in its modern sense is leading us into all sorts of mischief, and if we hope to counter it, we must understand what the word and the image originally might have meant.

If Jesus had wanted to describe the kingdom of God as an earthly kingdom, he had a metaphor ready to hand in the Roman Empire, which occupied Palestine and the rest of the Mediterranean world. When asked about the kingdom, all he had to do was point at the worldwide hegemony of Rome and say, "It's like that." The Roman Empire surrounded him from cradle to grave. It is the reason he was born in Bethlehem (thanks to Augustus's census), and when he died, he was tried and executed by the Romans. But he didn't use the ready-to-hand metaphor. Instead, he chose strikingly humble illustrations of the kingdom he was proclaiming. The kingdom he envisioned was like "a man which sowed good seed in his field" and like "a grain of mustard seed" and like "leaven which a woman took and hid in three measures of meal" and "a treasure hid in a field" and "a merchant seeking goodly pearls" and "a net that was cast into the sea."[16] The Greek word translated into English as *kingdom* was *basileia,* a word that indicated something more like a tribal or clan organization than a nation-state. Even the word *kingdom* in English did not originally mean what it means today. Originally, the Anglo-Saxon *cyning* was the leader of a small band of warriors and their families, akin to a tribal chieftain, someone in close relation to his small, intimate kingdom. The words that cluster around *kingdom* are similarly domestic. The Latin word *dominus,* which we translate as "lord," is related to the word *domus,* or "home." The *dominus* was a head of household, and the English word *lord* itself did not originally denote a high, mighty, and aloof feudal ruler. Rather, it was derived from the Anglo-Saxon *hlaf-weard, hlaf* meaning "loaf," and *weard* meaning "keeper" or "ward." Thus, prior to the late Middle Ages and Renaissance, when the nation-state notion of kingdom began to emerge, the "kingdom of

God" was conceived of us as a domestic arrangement, a personal-household type of relationship, in which the one who kept the daily ration of bread was the one to whom you owed personal loyalty. This meaning is reinforced by the use of the word *abba* in the Lord's Prayer, a familial term akin to "daddy," who "gave us our daily bread." To abstract from this metaphor the idea that Jesus intends Christians to mold America, the world's reigning superpower, into his militant kingdom on earth seems, in this context, downright blasphemous and clearly is far from the Lord's intent. By reading words literally and in their modern sense, and thus removing them from their metaphorical context, fundamentalists end up distorting the really useful and beautiful language and meaning of scripture.

It is surely ironic that many of those who proclaim to follow this man who spoke mainly in parables and metaphors are hobbled by an inability to appreciate and understand metaphors themselves. This is unfortunate because, in the end, we may even understand the entire story of Jesus itself as a grand parable. That is, if religious language and myths are metaphors that attempt to articulate the human relationship to the divine, then perhaps we could look at the entire life story of Jesus, or the entire story of the Bible, for that matter, as extended metaphors. The relationship between the human and the divine is like this: "In the Beginning . . . ." Read in this way, the story of the history of the Jews in the Bible becomes the tale of a people who engaged the divine in this way, who expressed their history of involvement with God in these images, and who saw the infinite manifested in these ways. Christians could read the story of Jesus as one extended parable of how to live a fully human life, following the model and the words "Go thou and do likewise" that Jesus himself laid down for his followers. If you wish to be fully human, live like this: give your life for others as Jesus did. Just as ancient Greeks used the heroes of the *Iliad* and the *Odyssey* as models for living, and the Hindus use Rama's life in the *Ramayana* as archetypes of good human life, we need to reclaim sacred stories and hold them in our hearts.

In the end, there is no one way of expressing this. Rather, there is a glorious mixing of metaphors by which human beings express their relationship to matters and realities of ultimate meaning. God is simultaneously light, lamb, shepherd, cloud, spirit, wind, dove, fire, smoke, lover and Beloved, rock, mighty fortress, cloud, ocean, fountain, living water, Jesus, Vishnu, and the ten thousand other names of the divine, darkness, blood, bread, wine, vine and vineyard, and more. Like white light passing through a prism, the deep unity of the Godhead passes through the human imagination and emerges split into a vast rainbow of colors, each of which, if followed, leads us back to the one light. That is the common quest of humankind, to reach the white light through the many colors of the world's traditions.

To do this, we must remember to treat the metaphors of God as metaphors. God remains "I am who I am," and we struggle to find the language to express that reality that lies beyond words. As Sallie McFague wrote, "A metaphorical theology will insist that many metaphors and models are necessary, that a piling up of images is essential, both to avoid idolatry and to attempt to express the richness and variety of the divine-human relationship."[17]

And that brings us, as it must, to the outer limits of language.

In Christian Pentecostal services, it is not unusual to hear people speaking in tongues. Known technically as glossolalia, it is considered in Christian tradition to be one of the gifts of the Holy Spirit. In Acts 2:4, where glossolalia first appears, many of the metaphors for God that we discussed above come together in one place. Forty days after Jesus left them, the apostles, gathered fearfully in an upper room, heard a mighty wind that came from heaven, and mysterious tongues of fire appeared and hovered in the air above their heads. The text tells us they were filled with the Holy Spirit and began to speak in many foreign tongues, so that all those from different nations who were in Jerusalem at the time could hear and understand them.

Regardless of the historicity of this event, or its literalism, on a metaphoric level it expresses perfectly what we have been talking about in this essay so far. The one spirit divides itself into many tongues, of fire and of flesh. The one language of the spirit of life becomes the many languages of Jews and Medes and Persians and Romans—and Arabs, Hindis, Africans, Polynesians, Native Americans, and all the world's races.

Modern scientists, of course, have studied glossolalia, tape-recording episodes of speaking in tongues at Pentecostal prayer meetings. They have then played these tapes for linguists and experts in various rare languages, but "it has never been possible to identify the language or discern any grammar or structure."[18] One might conclude that glossolalia is simply humbug, or that it indicates some kind of mental instability manifesting itself, as in cases of schizophrenia, in a kind of "word salad" that has no semantic content.[19] However, this modernist analysis really misses the point.

Perhaps glossolalia in the context of religious worship marks the moment when language runs out. The songs of American Shakers are filled with examples of glossolalia, which they called "Angel language." The lyrics handed down to us are what literary critics call "macaronic verse," mostly in English but at points switching to angelic language. In one song, entitled "Holy Angel," the singer proclaims he is the holy angel of the Lord whose name is "Sakanala Vinda," and a few lines later he proclaims, "I vas ka re, I vas ka re ne voo / I voo-le vo this power you know, this power you feel. / But levan nevan kaana voo."[20] Listening to the haunting melody, and knowing how these songs were "given" (the Shaker word for inspiration) to the singers, one can imagine that in the course of a long Shaker service, after hours of ecstatic dancing and singing, the singer's experience of the divine suddenly became too large for words that mean anything in the usual sense of the word *meaning*. God, so close in the moment, got expressed in pure sound, divorced from semantic content, divorced from metaphor, divorced from anything human at all, and language achieved for a moment an "angelic" quality, gaining the abstract immediacy of music notes, pure expression of the divine beyond ordinary words. The singer to whom the song was "given" had reached the point where language breaks down, disintegrates before the divine, and lapses into a "hieratic" language understood, really, by no one but the speaker and the gods. Such language transcends speech altogether and leaves ordinary talk far behind.

The principle behind this understanding of glosslalia is essentially the same as that behind the mantra in Oriental tradition or the ecstatic shout of "Alleluia!" That is, the uttering of "sacred sounds," syllables that really have no semantic content, expresses the experience of the divine in words that have no other meaning than their own utterance. Mircea Eliade writes, "Phonemes discovered during meditation probably expressed states of consciousness 'cosmic' in structure and hence difficult to formulate in secular terminology."[21] Since Vedic times, the method of repetition of a single sound has been found to deliver one up to an altered state of consciousness in which one experiences the presence of the divine. "These are experiences . . . that are in some measure bound up with the discovery of language and that, by this ecstatic return to a primordial situation, shatter diurnal consciousness."[22] Such language delivers the practitioner to a prelinguistic state and consciousness.

Reduced now to one word, *alleluia,* or to one syllable, *aum,* the mantra or the ecstatic shout brings religious language just one step from silence, and this brings us nearly to the end of this essay on religious language, for in many traditions it is only in silence that one finally and fully finds God. Gregory of Nyssa referred to it as the "discipline of silence."[23] This discipline has a long history in both the East and the West, and it rests on a humble acknowledgment that our words, in the end, are incapable of expressing the fullness of the divine. In the West, it is known as the apophatic, or "away-from-speech," tradition, which rests on an admission of "the radical failure of speech and thought in God's presence."[24]

It may seem odd to end a book on God-language with a discussion of silence, but in fact, that is where we have been headed all along. The words of our sacred traditions are mere conveyances. Like bridges and ferry boats, they are meant to take us over to another way of being, but we must remember that when we reach the other side, we need to step off onto the other shore.

The tension between speech and silence is difficult to maintain, but it is necessary. It is elaborated in the writings of many mystics, including Pseudo-Dionysius (fifth or sixth century C.E.), who speaks of it also as the "Divine Dark," which is beyond all categories of divinity, goodness, light, limits, even beyond unknowing. God is found "in the dazzling dark of the welcoming silence," he says.[25] Striking in their similarity to the Prajna Paramita Sutra of Buddhism, the writings of

Pseudo-Dionysius proclaim a God beyond all that we can sense, know, see, One who is all Being as well as all Nonbeing. Admitting the paradox of a theology that is both large and small, broad yet narrow, Pseudo-Dionysius uses an extraodinary metaphor to develop this idea of meeting the presence of the divine along the *via negationis*. Just as the sculptor removes marble bit by bit from a block, and in the process takes away all that hinders us from seeing the form beneath the stone, so too we may strip away layer after layer of that which hinders us from seeing God until at last the hidden form is displayed from what seemed to be solid rock. Divine beauty is revealed not by adding but by taking away. Finally, beyond words, beyond images, we "are on the point of entering the Dark that is beyond intelligence, [where] rational discourse will not merely become more brief; it will disappear in the total cessation of word and thought."[26]

The discipline of silence is elaborated further in the anonymous medieval text called *The Cloud of Unknowing,* a profound guide to the spiritual life that begins with the assumption that a cloud of ignorance "is always between you and your God, no matter what you do."[27] The author, addressing a young novice just entering upon his spiritual journey, encourages few or no words, for words may clutter the direct experience of the divine. At most, the author says, use only the shortest word possible, *God,* for it expresses in its three letters all that needs to be expressed. "Fasten this word to your heart, so that whatever happens it will never go away."[28] Like the Eastern practitioner chanting her mantra, the Western monk, in silence, meditating on the single syllable, finds divinity revealed. This practice is enshrined in the West in the hesychastic tradition. *Hesychia* means "stillness" in Greek, and the hesychastic method involved repetition of the name of Jesus in a mantralike way until inner stillness and silence was reached.

The Zen tradition is filled with stories of the final failure of language to point directly at the inner experience of the divine. In one such tale, the Sutra master Dok Sahn, supposedly an expert on the Diamond Sutra, sets out to correct everyone's understanding of this key Buddhist text. Traveling from temple to temple, he lectures everyone he meets and impresses them with his ability to expound upon the words of the scripture. Then one day, he gets word of a group of monks far away who do not study the Sutras. They only eat, sleep, and sit *zazen* all day. He decides to go straighten them out, but on the way he stops for lunch at a small hut. The owner of the rest stop, a woman who practices *zazen* regularly, recognizes him and asks where he is going. He tells her, quite pompously, that he is going to set right a group of monks who do nothing but sit all day and do not know the Diamond Sutra. She, in turn, challenges him, if he is so smart, to use the Diamond Sutra's distinction between past mind, present mind, and future mind—all of which fade away and cannot be grasped—to drink his soup. "Which mind will you use to drink your soup, eh?" He is confounded and realizes that all his erudition counts for nothing. He goes to the monastery, burns his commentaries, and just sits silently, finally a free man, free from the idol of the word.

Thomas Aquinas, in a strikingly similar story, seems to have had some sort of mystical experience late in life, after which he proclaimed that all his great summas were as straw compared with the actual experience of the divine. And Tolstoy's short story "The Three Hermits" tells a similar tale, where a supposedly wise bishop tries to bring three hermits who live on an isolated island to orthodoxy by teaching them the "proper" way to pray, that is, the correct words. Shortly after he leaves their island, they, being holy fools, forget the right words, so, supported by God, they simply walk across the surface of the water to the bishop's ship and ask him to repeat the words for them once more. The bishop, humbled by their manifest closeness to God, falls to his knees before them, speechless.

The path that can be named, says the *Tao te Ching,* is not the true path. The Taoist writer Chuang-tzu (ca. 300 B.C.E.) with his usual wit, chides Lao-tzu for first saying that the Tao is beyond words and then proceeding to write a book of five thousand characters about it. Later, in his own writing, Chuang-tzu sets us straight on the relationship of the word to the way. The fishnet, he says, is only useful until the fish is caught, after which you can forget it. The rabbit trap is useful only until you catch the rabbit, after which you can forget it as well. He concludes, "Words exist because of meaning; once you've gotten the meaning, you can forget the words. Where can I find a man who has forgotten words so I can have a word with him?"[29]

Susan Sontag, in "The Aesthetics of Silence," points out that many modern artists, after mastering their art, turned away from it. It is a good analogy for those following a spiritual path, perhaps. She writes, "Now the highest good for the artist is to reach the point where those goals of excellence become insignificant to him, emotionally and ethically, and he is more satisfied by being silent than by finding a voice in art. . . . Silence is the artist's ultimate other-worldly gesture."[30]

We live in a world filled with words. Twenty-four hours a day they spill out of our radios and televisions. We read them in our books, magazines, newspapers, and on the Internet. We fill every possible moment with words, talking on our cell phones obsessively, never experiencing the silence in which the wordless word of the divine can be heard with the ears of the heart. As Walter Ong, priest and linguist, wrote many years ago, "Could it be that God is not silent but that man is relatively deaf . . . ?"[31] In a world of so many passionate talkers, so convinced of the literal truth of their words, a world of so many speakers and so few real listeners, perhaps it is time to let our religious language lead us into the profound silence of the divine.

Henri Le Saux, a twentieth-century French Benedictine who lived much of his life in India and gained the name Abishiktananda, wrote:

> Man is made not merely to work with his hands and to think with his mind, but also to *adore* in the deep silence of his heart. Even more than to adore, he is called to plunge into that silence and to lose himself there, unable to utter any word, not even a word of adoration or of praise; for no word can express the mystery of God, the mystery of man in the presence of God.[32]

In this essay on God-language in the age of fundamentalism, we have tried to lay a foundation on which we can open and continue religious dialogue. We live in a time of fierce and rigid orthodoxies, orthodoxies united in fear and distrust of the modern world in which we are all trying to live. It is a world of shrinking resources, burgeoning population, inequitable distribution of wealth and economic benefits; a world of war, disease, death, and strife. It is a world, in short, not much different from what the world has always been. The great religious traditions of the world still have the power to lead us through the confusion, but only if we live out the best of their teachings, not the worst. As this essay has tried to show, an adequate response to the fundamentalist threat in the contemporary world can only come from a religious, not a secular, point of view. We must use religion to save the world from both religion and secularism. Deep dialogue is crucial, and it must begin now. Words are our tools, but the profound shared silence of the divine is our goal.

Like the builders of the great medieval cathedrals, we may never live to see the end of the project we are working on, but that does not excuse us from trying, or from having faith that one day, in the future, the believers of the world will understand there really are no infidels. We must begin to speak. The rest is . . .

. . . silence.

Notes

Chapter 1

1. A note on the use of italics: Because this is a book about language, it sometimes talks about words as words and at other times uses words to name the concepts they are talking about. To distinguish between the two, this book follows the usage of the Modern Language Association and of *The Chicago Manual of Style,* 15th edition. That means it uses italics to indicate the word as the word itself, as in the following sentence: "*Truth* is derived from an old Anglo-Saxon word." However, when the concept itself is referred to, ordinary typeface is used, as in the following sentence: "Some people believe truth to be absolute." Every effort has been made to be consistent in this usage, though in a book on the subject of religious language, the concept and the word naming it are often difficult to distinguish.

Chapter 2

1. Richard Antoun, *Understanding Fundamentalism: Christian, Islamic and Jewish Movements* (Walnut Hills, Calif.: Alta Mira Press, 2001), 3.
2. Deborah Wickering, *Negotiating Intimacy: Life Among Tarabiin Bedouins in the South Sinai.* Unpublished manuscript.
3. Gary Eberle, *Sacred Time and the Search for Meaning* (Boston: Shambhala, 2003).
4. Judith Dupre, *Skyscrapers* (New York: Black Dog and Leventhal, 1996), 67.
5. The place name Babel means "gate of the god," but in its original language it suggested the Hebrew root *bil,* meaning "to confuse." *The*

Jerusalem Bible (New York: Doubleday and Co., 1966), 25n. Surprisingly, there is no etymological connection between the biblical story of Babel and the English word *babble,* which the *OED* says is onomatopoeic for either baby talk or the way foreign voices sound.

6. For more on this, see my *The Geography of Nowhere: Finding One's Self in the Postmodern World* (Kansas City, Mo.: Sheed and Ward, 1994).

7. Robert Bellah, "Civil Religion in America," *Daedelus* 96, no. 1 (Winter 1967): 1–21.

8. For a fuller discussion of the relationship of religion and government in American history, see Forrest Church, *The American Creed* (New York: St. Martin's Griffins, 2002), and Noah Feldman, *Divided by God* (New York: Farrar, Straus, Giroux, 2005).

9. Antoun. *Understanding Fundamentalism,* 11.

10. Karen Armstrong, *The Battle for God: A History of Fundamentalism* (New York: Ballantine, 2000), vii.

11. Not all evangelical Christians are fundamentalists, though many do favor a more literal interpretation of scripture than more liberal Christians. For an excellent short discussion of the distinctions between evangelicals and fundamentalists, see George S. Marsden, *Understanding Fundamentalism and Evangelicalism* (Grand Rapids, Mich.: Eerdmans, 1991).

12. Stephen Adams, "No Overt Discrimination," *Christianity Today* (August 2005). www.christianitytoday.com/2005/008/5.22.html (accessed July 13, 2005).

13. Patrick Henry College home page, www.phc.edu (accessed August 15, 2005).

14. For an excellent treatment of the rise of twentieth-century fundamentalism in Christianity, Islam, and Judaism, see Armstrong, *Battle.* An exhaustive account can be found in Martin Marty and R. Scott Appleby's six-volume *The Fundamentalism Project* (Chicago: University of Chicago Press, 1991).

15. Armstrong, *Battle,* 366.

16. This idea will be developed at greater length in chapter 6, in which we discuss the religious function of the psyche and the psychic function of religion.

Chapter 3

1. Recounted in Alberto Manguel, *A History of Reading* (New York: Viking, 1996), 42.

2. Ibid., 46.

3. Karen Armstrong, *Islam* (New York: Modern Library, 2000), 4.

4. Walter Ong, S.J., *The Presence of the Word: Some Prolegomena for Cultural and Religious History* (New Haven, Conn.: Yale University Press, 1967).

5. Ibid., 8.

6. Ibid., 30.

7. Private conversation, Aquinas College, September 10, 2003.

8. For more on how oral-aural cultures transmit their stories from generation to generation, see Frances Yates, *The Art of Memory* (Chicago: Univ. of Chicago Press, 1966); and Albert B. Lord, *The Singer of Tales* (Cambridge, Mass.: Harvard Univ. Press, 1960).

9. Michael Olmert, *The Smithsonian Book of Books* (New York: Wings Books, 1992), 113–14.

10. Elizabeth Eisenstein, *The Printing Revolution in Early Modern Europe* (Cambridge: Cambridge University Press, 1983), 148.

11. Ibid., 155.

12. Ibid., 156.

13. Ibid., 169.

14. Ibid., 177.

15. Quoted in Dennis Freeborn, *From Old to Standard English*, 2nd ed. (Ottawa: University of Ottawa Press, 1998), 343–44. Emphasis in Sprat's original.

16. In Albert C. Baugh and Thomas C. Cable, *A History of the English Language*, 3rd ed. (Englewood Cliffs, N.J.: Prentice-Hall, 1978), 262.

17. Samuel Johnson, "Preface" to *A Dictionary of the English Language* (New York: AMS Press, 1967), n.p.

18. Jonathan Swift, "A Proposal for Correcting, Improving and Ascertaining the English Tongue," http://etext.library.adelaide.edu.au/s/swift/jonathan/s97p/ (accessed January 11, 2006).

19. That this prescriptive impulse is still alive and well is clear from the enormous popularity of Lynne Truss's *Eats, Shoots and Leaves* (New York: Gotham Books, 2004), advertised as a "zero tolerance" guide to the misuse of English grammar and punctuation.

20. In Freeborn, *From Old to Standard English*, 386–88.

21. Ong, *Presence*, 189.

22. In Freeborn, *From Old to Standard English*, 391. (Italics Harwood's.)

23. Compare, for example, the following passage from Corinthians. The King James, or Authorized, Version reads, "And though I have the gift of prophecy, and understand all mysteries, and all knowledge; and though I have all faith, so that I could remove mountains and have not

charity, I am nothing." Harwood reads, "And I was endowed with the amplest prophetic powers: could I unravel all the mysteries of nature: had I accumulated all the knowledge of the sons of men: could I exert such stupendous powers as to remove mountains from their basis and transfer them at pleasure from place to place—and yet my heart a stranger to benevolence, I am nothing." (Quoted in Freeborn, *From Old to Standard English*, 392–93.) The Latinate vocabulary is approaching modern dissertations in its leaden deadening of metaphor. It is more precise, perhaps, but it certainly loses energy.

24. In Richard S. Westfall, *Science and Religion in Seventeenth-Century England* (Ann Arbor, Mich.: Ann Arbor Paperbacks, 1972), 42.

25. Another fascinating example of how the Western mind had shifted to primary textuality is found in Eisenstein, where she recounts the eighteenth-century story of Swedish scientists who discovered certain features of the Baltic shoreline that seemed to contradict scripture. When confronted by Stockholm theologians that their work, which did not conform to the Bible, ought to be condemned, the scientists replied that the book of nature, which they read, was the "original," while the Bible was merely a copy from the original and therefore necessarily in error. What is fascinating about this story is not the controversy, but that nature, too, is now seen as a book to be read, showing the triumph of primary textuality. The Bible thus comes into conflict with the equally persuasive book of nature. Eisenstein, *Printing Revolution*, 272.

26. Leonard Huxley, "The Huxley-Wilberforce Debate at the Oxford Union," in *The Norton Anthology of English Literature*, vol. 2, 7th ed., ed. M. H. Abrams (New York: W. W. Norton, 2000), 1690–93.

Chapter 4

1. See Jaroslav Pelikan, *Luther the Expositor: Introduction to the Reformer's Exegetical Writings* (St. Louis, Mo.: Concordia Publishing House, 1959), and Heiko A. Oberman, *Luther: Man Between God and the Devil* (New York: Doubleday Image Books, 1992), 168–74, 224–25.

2. Karen Armstrong, *The Battle for God* (New York: Ballantine, 2000), 90. Here Armstrong refers to Alistair McGrath's *A Life of John Calvin* (Cambridge, Mass.: Blackwell, 1990).

3. Emily Dickinson, "The Bible is an Antique Volume," www.bartleby.com/113/5104.html (accessed December 30, 2005).

4. Thomas Huxley, from "Agnosticism and Christianity," *The Norton Anthology of English Literature*, vol. 2, 7th ed., ed. Myer Abrams. (New York: Norton, 2000), 1565–66.

5. Charles Hodge, *Systematic Theology* (New York: Scribner & Armstrong, 1876), 1.

6. Ibid., 3.

7. Alexander Hodge, *Outlines of Theology* (Grand Rapids, Mich.: Eerdmans, 1929), 15–16.

8. *Oxford English Dictionary,* s.v. "science."

9. Karen Armstrong, *Battle,* 137–38.

10. Nancy Ammerman, "North American Protestant Fundamentalism," in *Fundamentalisms Observed,* ed. Martin Marty and R. Scott Appleby (Chicago: University of Chicago Press, 1991), 20.

11. Ibid., 20–21.

12. James Grey, "The Inspiration of the Bible: Definition, Extent and Proof," www.xmission.com/~fidelis/Volume2/Chapter1/gray.php (accessed January 11, 2006).

13. In Armstrong, *Battle,* 141.

14. Ammerman, "North American," 22.

15. Ibid.

16. See www.xmission.com/~fidelis.

17. David Heagle, "The Tabernacle in the Wilderness," www.xmission.com/~fidelis/ (accessed January 11, 2006). A large number of the original texts of *The Fundamentals* is available online at this Web address. The quotes that follow are all drawn from this Web site.

18. Rev. James M. Gray, D.D., "The Inspiration of the Bible—Definition, Extent and Proof." www.xmission.com/~fidelis/volume2/chapter1/gray.php (accessed January 11. 2006).

19. Henry Beach, "The Decadence of Darwinism," www.xmission.com/~fidelis/volume4/chapter5/beach.php (accessed January 11, 2006); and Phillip Mauro, "Modern Philosophy," www.xmission.com/~fidelis/volume4/chapter1/mauro_2.php (accessed January 11, 2006).

20. Rev. James M. Gray, D.D., "The Inspiration of the Bible—Definition, Extent and Proof," www.xmission.com/~fidelis/volume2/chapter1/gray.php (accessed January 5, 2006).

21. Summarized from Armstrong, *Battle,* 171.

22. Quoted ibid., 172.

23. Ibid., 173.

24. Ammerman, "North American," 2.

25. Ibid., 42.

26. Council for American Private Education (CAPE), www.capenet.org/facts.html.

27. www.wwnorton.com/nael/20thcentury/topic_3/crystal.htm (accessed December 20, 2005).

28. Ammerman, "North American," 43.

29. Ibid., 45.

30. FindLaw for Legal Professionals, "U.S. Supreme Court, Tarcaso v. Watkins," www.laws.findlaw.com/us/367/488.html (accessed January 6, 2006).

31. Quoted in Armstrong, *Battle,* 315; original source A. Weissman, "Building a Tower of Babel," *Texas Outlook* (Winter 1982): 13.

32. Frances Fitzgerald, "The American Millennium," *The New Yorker* (November 11, 1985): 88–113.

33. Ibid., 113.

34. Ammerman, "North American," 2.

35. Ibid., 41.

36. "The Chalcedon Foundation," www.chalcedon.edu (accessed January 11, 2006).

37. "CNN.com Election Results," www.cnn.com/ELECTION/2004/pages/results/status/US/P/00/epolls.0.html (accessed January 6, 2006).

38. Matt VandeBunte, "Evangelist Says Christianity Will Grow," *The Grand Rapids Press* (May 29, 2004): Sec. B. For more on Kennedy and his ministry, see www.coralridge.org/about_djk.htm.

39. See "The Center for Reclaiming America," www.reclaimamerica.org.

40. Bob Moser, "The Crusaders," www.rollingstone.com/politics/story/_/id/7235393 (accessed July 13, 2005).

41. See "Tim LaHaye Ministries," www.timlahaye.com.

42. Tim LaHaye, "The Prophetic Significance of Sept. 11, 2001," www.timlahaye.com/about_ministry/pdf/lahaye_Sept11.pdf (accessed July 13, 2005).

43. Ammerman, "North American," 55.

44. The complete text of the interview is available at www.commondreams.org/news2001/0917–03.htm.

45. "Many Have Asked If God Will Judge America," www.operationsaveamerica.org/articles/articles/judgments.html (accessed December 20, 2005). Also see the following Web site for links to the reactions of other religious-right groups to 9/11: www.publiceye.org/frontpage/911/christianright.html.

Chapter 5

1. There was limited early use of the related words *mythic, mythical,* and *mythological,* all adjectives, but (significantly) none of them dates earlier than the 1600s. A verb—*to myth*—does appear (with variants) in Mid-

dle English, meaning, variously, "to show" or "to measure," but it is un-related etymologically to the modern noun *myth*. *OED*, s.v. "myth."

2. For a summary of attempts to find the ultimate etymology of *myth*, cf. Wim van Binsbergen, "Rupture and Fusion in the Approach to Myth," www.shikanda.net/ancient_models/myth%2omineke%20 defdefdef.pdf, 2n.

3. In light of our discussion of *truth* in the chapter of that name, we should note that the ultimate derivation of *false* is from a Latin word meaning "to be deceived or mistaken." That is, falsehood, like truth, resided in persons who could deceive us, and in ourselves, who could be mistaken, but not in things.

4. *OED*, s.v. "myth."

5. Sir G. L. Gomme, quoted in *Funk and Wagnall's Standard Dictionary of Folklore, Mythology, and Legend* (San Francisco: Harper and Row, 1972), s.v. "myth."

6. Amadou Hampate Ba, "The Weaver and the Blacksmith," *Parabola* (Fall 1995): 29.

7. Bruce Chatwin, *The Songlines* (New York: Penguin, 1987).

8. An excellent summation of this position is given in Stephen Jay Gould, "Nonoverlapping Magisteria," *Natural History* (March 1997): 16–22ff.

9. Martha Beckwith, *Hawaiian Mythology* (Honolulu: University of Hawaii Press, 1970), 128–32.

10. Quoted in Mara Freeman, "Word of Skill," *Parabola* (Fall 1995): 67.

11. Ian Ramsey, *Religious Language: An Empirical Placing of Theological Phrases* (New York: Macmillan, 1957), 41.

12. These characteristics are developed at further length in John Macquarrie's *God-Talk: An Examination of the Language and Logic of Theology* (New York: Harper and Row, 1967), 171–76.

13. For further discussion of this, see Amos Wilder, *Theopoetics: Theology and the Religious Imagination* (Philadelphia: Fortress Press, 1976).

14. Macquarrie, *God-Talk*, 128.

15. Ibid., 169.

16. Walter Ong, *The Presence of the Word* (New Haven, Conn.: Yale University Press, 1967), 320.

17. *OED*, s.v. "believe."

18. Earl MacCormac, *Metaphor and Myth in Science and Religion* (Durham, N.C.: Duke University Press, 1976), 40.

19. A. S. Reber, "Implicit vs. Explicit Learning," *The Nature of Cognition*, ed. R. J. Steinberg (Cambridge, Mass.: MIT Press, 1999), quoted in

Theodore Brown, *Making Truth in Science* (Urbana: University of Illinois Press, 2003), 10.

20. MacCormac, *Metaphor*, 60.

21. These are adapted from Frederick Ferre, "Metaphors, Models and Religion," *Soundings* 51 (1968): 337–38.

22. Quoted in Tod Harris, "The Word Made Flesh," *Parabola* (Fall 1995): 17.

Chapter 6

1. "iPod Shuffle," www.apple.com/iPodshuffle.

2. *OED*, s.v. "religion."

3. The *OED* calls this etymology "doubtful" and prefers the derivation from *religare*, but it is still useful for our purposes.

4. Robert K. Barnhart, ed., *The Barnhart Dictionary of Etymology* (Bronx, N.Y.: H. W. Wilson, 1988), s.v. "religion." Skeat also makes this connection, though the *OED* does not.

5. Walter Skeat, *An Etymological Dictionary of the English Language* (Oxford, Eng.: Clarendon Press, 1924), s.v. "religion."

6. Henry Nelson Wieman, *Man's Ultimate Commitment* (Carbondale: Southern Illinois University Press, 1958), 11.

7. Ibid., 18–20.

8. Ibid., 20.

9. Ian Ramsey, *Religious Language: An Empirical Placing of Theological Phrases* (New York: Macmillan, 1957), 30.

10. Lionel Corbett, *The Religious Function of the Psyche* (New York: Brunner-Routledge, 1996), 168.

11. Ibid., 173.

12. Ibid., 163.

13. Ibid., 176–77.

Chapter 7

1. Dallas High, *Language, Persons and Belief* (New York: Oxford University Press, 1967), 135.

2. These ideas are summarized from John Macquarrie, *God-Talk: An Examination of the Language and Logic of Theology* (New York: Harper and Row, 1967), 123–46.

3. For more on the performative versus the "constative" function of language, see J. L. Austin, *How to Do Things with Words* (Cambridge: Cambridge University Press, 1962).

4. Macquarrie, *God-Talk,* 45.

5. Austin, *Words,* 7.

6. Ibid., 8.

7. Ibid., 44.

8. George Lakoff and Mark Johnson, *Metaphors We Live By* (Chicago: University of Chicago Press, 1980), 234.

9. For their part, the New World and African natives went the other way. The Arawak took the Europeans for beings who had descended from the sky. In Peru, the Inca took them for supernatural creatures and, with tragic results, did not at first resist them. On the coast of the Congo, the Portuguese arriving in their broad sailing ships were believed, at first, to be sea spirits. In all cases, both sides were unable to recognize the other as merely human like themselves.

10. Anthony Padgen, *The Fall of Natural Man: The American Indian and the Origins of Comparative Ethnology* (Cambridge: Cambridge University Press, 1986).

11. The world's major religions were founded or came to flower in a period known as the Axial Age, roughly between 1000 B.C.E. and 1000 C.E. During that time, Hinduism, Buddhism, Judaism, Christianity, Islam, and Zoroastrianism were established. Historically speaking, it was a remarkable flowering of religious genius in a brief time. Is it now time for another evolutionary step forward in human consciousness?

12. Thomas Jefferson, "An Act for Establishing Religious Freedom," in *The Life and Selected Writings of Thomas Jefferson,* ed. Adrienne Koch and William Peden (New York: The Modern Library, 1972), 312.

13. Forrest Church, *The American Creed* (New York: St. Martin's, 2002).

14. For an excellent historical review of the evolution of the separation of church and state in America, see Noah Feldman, *Divided by God: America's Church-State Problem and What We Should Do About It* (New York: Farrar, Straus, Giroux, 2005).

15. Lorraine Kisly, "The Sacred World of the Other: An Interview with Seyyed Hossein Nasr," *Parabola* (Winter 2005): 38.

16. Phillip Ravenhill, "Religious Utterances and the Theory of Speech Acts," in *Language in Religious Practice,* ed. William Samarin (Rawley, Mass.: Newbury House Publishers, 1976), 33.

17. Ibid., 37.

Chapter 8

1. In the original Latin, Thomas ends each "way" with slight variants on the formula, including *hoc omnes intelligunt Deus, quam omnes Deum*

nominant, quod omnes dicunt Deum, and *hoc dicimus Deum.* S. Thomae Aquino, *Summa Theologiae* (Ottawa: Studdii Generalis, 1946), 1, 2, Articulus III.

2. Summarized from Peter Kreft, *A Shorter Summa* (San Francisco: St. Ignatius Press, 1993), 55–65.

3. John Macquarrie, *God-Talk: An Examination of the Language and Logic of Theology* (New York: Harper & Row, 1967), 63.

4. *OED,* s.v. "God."

5. Macquarrie, *God-Talk,* 135.

6. *The Barnhart Dictionary of Etymology,* ed. Robert K. Barnhart (Bronx, N.Y.: H. W. Wilson, 1988), s.v. "God."

7. Jerusalem Bible, fn, 33.

8. Jerusalem Bible, fn, 81.

9. *OED,* s.v. "Allah."

10. Margaret Stutley, *Hinduism: The Eternal Law* (Wellingborough, Eng.: Crucible, 1985), 26.

11. Heinrich Zimmer, *Philosophies of India,* ed. Joseph Campbell (Princeton, N.J.: Princeton University Press, 1969), 77.

12. Thomas Aquinas, *Summa Theologica,* trans. Fathers of the English Dominican Province (New York: Benziger, 1947).

13. Austin J. Shelton, "Controlling Capricious Gods," in *Language in Religious Practice,* ed. William J. Samarin (Rawley, Mass.: Newbury House Publishers, 1976), 66.

14. 2 Corinthians 12: 2–4. (JB)

15. This business of the power of names and naming is widespread in world mythology. In Egyptian myth, the creator called out his own name to bring himself into existence, and in later stories Isis fools Ra into revealing his name and thus she gains power over him. In Native American cultures, children are named after others, living or dead, which is said to give the child the qualities of those who've borne that name before. Inuit are reported not to say their names out loud for fear of breaking the protective spell cast by the name itself.

16. Paul Van Buren, *The Edges of Language: An Essay in the Logic of a Religion* (New York: Macmillan, 1972), 135.

17. Quoted in Martin Esslin, *Samuel Beckett* (Englewood Cliffs, N.J.: Prentice-Hall, 1965), 17.

18. Paul Ricoeur, *The Rule of Metaphor,* trans. Robert Czerny with Kathleen McLaughlin and John Costello, S.J. (Toronto: University of Toronto Press, 1977).

19. Ibid., 13.

20. Ibid., 23.

21. Macquarrie, *God-Talk*, 27.

22. Thomas Aquinas, *Summa Theologica*, trans. Fathers of the English Dominican Province, vol. 1 (New York: Benziger, 1947), 6–7.

23. This understanding was not unique to Christian tradition. The Neo-Platonist Plotinus wrote, "Since we are powerless to find the terms with which it would be appropriate to speak of the Supreme Reality, we take inferior characteristics from inferior things and apply them metaphorically to Him. . . . Yet there is no way by which we can apply anything in the proper sense to Him . . . everything comes short of Him, all beauty, all majesty." In Edward Bevan, *Symbolism and Belief* (Port Washington, N.Y.: Kennikat Press, 1938), 18.

24. These are summarized from Max Black, "Metaphor," in *Models and Metaphors* (Ithaca, N.Y.: Cornell University Press, 1962), 25–47.

25. An interesting area of exploration into fundamentalism might be to follow up on a point made in passing by Karen Armstrong, Joseph Antoun, Nancy Ammerman, and others that an unusually high percentage of fundamentalists and believers who are flocking to the new evangelical mega-churches work in technical professions. The question to ask would be whether a technical training, with less emphasis on literature, the arts, and imagination than a humanistic training, predisposes people to a fundamentalist reading of scripture and to not understanding or being comfortable with metaphor.

26. Ricoeur, *Rule of Metaphor*, 21.

27 Ibid., 34.

28. Ibid., 80.

29. *OED*, s.v. "catachresis."

30. We can leave aside, for the moment, the argument that all forms of language are metaphorical, not literal. Our goal is to make a case for religious language as being especially metaphorical.

31. Koran 2:27, trans. N. J. Dawood (London: Penguin Classics, 2003).

32. Earl MacCormac, *Metaphor and Myth in Science and Religion* (Durham, N.C.: Duke University Press, 1976), 60.

33. "Kena Upanishad," in *The Upanishads*, trans. Juan Mascaro (London: Penguin, 1965), 51.

34. John Webster, "Eberhard Jüngel on the Language of Faith," *Modern Theology* 1:4 (July 1985).

35. "Kena Upanishad," 51.

36. Sallie McFague, *Metaphorical Theology: Models of God in Religious Language* (Philadelphia: Fortress Press, 1985), 36–37.

37. Derek Bickerton, *Language and Species* (Chicago: University of Chicago Press, 1990), 13.
38. Ibid., 30.
39. Ibid., 43.
40. Ibid., 24.
41. Ibid., 43.
42. Ibid., 57.
43. Walter Ong, *The Presence of the Word* (New Haven, Conn.: Yale University Press, 1967), 15.
44. George Lakoff and Mark Johnson, *Metaphors We Live By* (Chicago: University of Chicago Press, 1980).
45. Ibid., 227.
46. Ibid., 153–54.
47. Earl MacCormac, *Metaphor* (Durham, N.C.: Duke University Press, 1976), 48.
48. Macquarrie, *God-Talk,* 228.

Chapter 9

1. Paul Van Buren, *The Edges of Language: An Essay in the Logic of Religion* (New York: Macmillan, 1972), 75.
2. For an excellent, readable, and accessible telling of the *Mahabharata,* see William Buck, *Mahabharata* (New York: New American Library, 1973).
3. *The Bhagavad Gita,* trans. Winthrop Sargent (Albany: State University of New York Press, 1984), 452.
4. Frithjof Schuon, *The Transcendent Unity of Religions,* trans. Peter Townsend (New York: Harper Torchbooks, 1973).
5. Quoted in Harvey D. Egan, *An Anthology of Christian Mysticism* (Collegeville, Minn.: The Liturgical Press, 1991), 30.
6. Ibid., 32.
7. Ibid., 33.
8. Peter Lamborn Wilson and Nasrollah Pourjavady, trans. *The Drunken Universe: An Anthology of Persian Sufi Poetry* (Grand Rapids, Mich.: Phanes Press, 1987).
9. In Egan, *Anthology,* 265.
10. Ibid., 64. (My emphasis.)
11. Ibid., 65.
12. Ibid., 355.
13. Wilson and Pourjavady, *Drunken Universe,* 87.

14. In Egan, *Anthology,* 184.

15. Ibid., 256.

16. Cf. Matthew 13:24–47.

17. Sallie McFague, *Metaphorical Theology* (Philadelphia: Fortress Press, 1982), 20.

18. "Glossolalia," Oxford Reference Online, www.oxfordreference.com (accessed July 19, 2005), s.v. "glossolalia." Cf. also John Frederick Jansen, "Glossolalia, *The Oxford Companion to the Bible,* ed. Bruce M. Metzger and Michael D. Coogan (New York: Oxford University Press, 1993).

19. For more on this, see James T. Richardson, "Psychological Interpretations of Glossolalia: A Reexamination of the Research," *Journal for the Scientific Review of Religion,* 12:2 (June 1973): 199–207; and Daniel J. Smith and J. Roland Fleck, "Personality Correlates of Conventional and Unconventional Glossolalia," *The Journal of Social Psychology* 114 (1981): 209–17. The research is inconclusive on general patterns of mental stability among those who experience glossolalia, but generally they seem not statistically much different from the general population in terms of relative psychological health.

20. Joel Cohen, *Simple Gifts: Shaker Chants and Spirituals.* Performed by Shakers of the Sabbathday Lake, Schola Cantorum, the Boston Camerata (Erato 4509-98491-2).

21. Mircea Eliade, "Mantras," *Parabola* (Fall 1995): 39.

22. Ibid.

23. Ross Fuller, "On Listening and the Word," *Parabola* (Fall 1995): 34.

24. Egan, *Anthology,* 96.

25. Ibid., 101.

26. Ibid.

27. Anonymous, *The Cloud of Unknowing,* ed. James Walsh, S.J. (New York: Paulist Press, 1981), 120–21.

28. Ibid., 134.

29. Chuang-tzu, *Basic Writings,* trans. Burton Watson (New York: Columbia University Press, 1964), 140.

30. Susan Sontag, "The Aesthetics of Silence," *Styles of Radical Will,* www.susansontag.com/stylesofradicalwilexcrpt.htm (accessed September 19, 2005).

31. Walter Ong, *The Presence of the Word* (New Haven, Conn.: Yale University Press, 1967), 16.

32. Abishiktananda, *Prayer* (Philadelphia: Westminster Press, 1973), 29.

Selected Bibliography

Abishiktananda (Henri Le Saux, O.S.B.). *Prayer.* Philadelphia: Westminster Press, 1973.

Adams, Stephen. "No Overt Discrimination." *Christianity Today* (August 2005). www.christianitytoday.com/2005/0085.22.html (accessed July 13, 2005).

Ammerman, Nancy T. "Accounting for Christian Fundamentalisms: Social Dynamics and Rhetorical Strategies." In *Fundamentalisms Observed,* 4: 149–70. Edited by Martin Marty and R. Scott Appleby. Chicago: University of Chicago Press, 1991.

———. "North American Protestant Fundamentalism." In *Fundamentalisms Observed* 1:1–65. Edited by Martin Marty and R. Scott Appleby. Chicago: University of Chicago Press, 1991.

Anonymous. *The Cloud of Unknowing.* Edited by James Walsh, S.J. New York: Paulist Press, 1981.

Antoun, Richard T. *Understanding Fundamentalism: Christian, Islamic and Jewish Movements.* Walnut Creek, Calif.: Alta Mira Press, 2001.

Armstrong, Karen. *The Battle for God: A History of Fundamentalism.* New York: Ballantine, 2000.

———. *Islam.* New York: Modern Library, 2000.

Aquinas, Thomas. *Summa Theologiae.* Ottawa: Studdii Generalis, 1946.

———. *Summa Theologica.* Translated by Fathers of the English Dominican Province. New York: Benziger, 1947.

Austin, J. L. *How to Do Things with Words.* Cambridge, Mass.: Harvard University Press, 1962.

Ba, Amadou Hampate. "The Weaver and the Blacksmith." *Parabola* (Fall 1995): 29–31.

Barber, Charles. *The English Language: A Historical Introduction.* Cambridge: Cambridge University Press, 1993.

Barnhart, Robert K., ed. *The Barnhart Dictionary of Etymology.* Bronx, N.Y.: H. W. Wilson, 1988.

Baugh, Albert C., and Thomas Cable. *A History of the English Language,* 3rd ed. Englewood Cliffs, N.J.: Prentice-Hall, 1978.

Bellah, Robert. "Civil Religion in America." *Daedelus* 96, no.1 (Winter 1967): 1–21.

Berger, James. "Falling Towers and Postmodern Wild Children: Oliver Sachs, Don DeLillo, and Turns Against Language." *PMLA* 120, no. 2 (March 2005): 341–61.

Bevan, Edward. *Symbolism and Belief.* Port Washington, N.Y.: Kennikat Press, 1938.

Bickerton, Derek. *Language and Species.* Chicago: University of Chicago Press, 1990.

Black, Max. "Metaphor." In *Models and Metaphors.* Ithaca, N.Y.: Cornell University Press, 1962, pp. 25–47.

Brown, Theodore. *Making Truth in Science.* Urbana: University of Illinois Press, 2003.

Christian, Jane M. "Patterns of Telugu Religious Language." In *Language in Religious Practice,* edited by William J. Samarin, 114–30. Rawley, Mass.: Newbury House Publishers, 1976.

Chuang-tzu. *Basic Writings.* Translated by Burton Watson. New York: Columbia University Press, 1964.

Church, Forrest. *The American Creed.* New York: St. Martin's Griffin, 2002.

Cohen, Joel. *Simple Gifts: Shaker Chants and Spirituals.* Performed by the Shakers of the Sabbathday Lake Schola Cantorum and the Boston Camerata. Erato 4509-98491-2.

Corbett, Lionel. *The Religious Function of the Psyche.* New York: Brunner-Routledge, 1996.

Crystal, David. "Nonsequential Phonology in Religious Modalities." In *Language in Religious Practice,* edited by William J. Samarin, 17–25. Rawley, Mass,: Newbury House Publishers, 1976.

Danesi, Marcel. *Of Cigarettes, High Heels and Other Interesting Things: An Introduction to Semiotics.* New York: St. Martin's, 1999.

Davidson, J. A. "Some Fundamentals of Fundamentalism." *Verbatim: The Language Quarterly* 20, no. 2 (Autumn 1993): 1–3.

Dupre, Judith. *Skyscrapers.* New York: Black Dog and Leventhal, 1996.

Eberle, Gary. *The Geography of Nowhere.* Kansas City, Mo.: Sheed & Ward, 1994.

———. *Sacred Time and the Search for Meaning.* Boston: Shambhala, 2003.

Egan, Harvey. *An Anthology of Christian Mysticism.* Collegeville, Minn.: The Liturgical Press, 1991.

Eisenstein, Elizabeth L. *The Printing Revolution in Early Modern Europe.* Cambridge: Cambridge University Press, 1983.

Eliade, Mircea. "Mantras." *Parabola* (Fall 1995): 39–40.

Emerson, Ralph Waldo. "An Address to the Senior Class in Divinity College, Cambridge, July 15, 1838." In *Essays and Lectures,* ed. Joel Porte, 73–92. New York: Library of America, 1983.

Feldman, Noah. *Divided by God: America's Church-State Problem and What We Should Do About it.* New York: Farrar, Straus, Giroux, 2005.

Ferguson, Charles. "The Collect as a Form of Discourse." In *Language in Religious Practice,* edited by William J. Samarin, 101–109. Rawley, Mass.: Newbury House Publishers, 1976.

Ferre, Frederick. "Metaphors, Models and Religion." *Soundings* 51 (1968): 327–45.

Fitzgerald, Frances. "The American Millennium." *The New Yorker* (November 11, 1985): 88–113.

Freeborn, Dennis. *From Old to Standard English,* 2nd ed. Ottawa: University of Ottawa Press, 1998.

Freeman, Mara. "Word of Skill." *Parabola* (Fall 1995): 63–67.

Fuller, Ross. "On Listening and the Word." *Parabola* (Fall 1995): 39.

Gilkey, Langdon. *Naming the Whirlwind: The Renewal of God-language.* Indianapolis: Bobbs-Merrill, 1969.

Gould, Stephen Jay. "Nonoverlapping Magisteria." *Natural History* (March 1997): 16–22ff.

Harding, Susan. "Imagining the Last Days: The Politics of Apocalyptic Language." In *Fundamentalisms Observed,* vol. 4, edited by Martin Marty and R. Scott Appleby. Chicago: University of Chicago Press, 1991.

Harris, Tod. "The Word Made Flesh." *Parabola* (Fall 1995): 17.

Hicks, John. *Philosophy and Religion.* Englewood Cliffs, N.J.: Prentice-Hall, 1960.

High, Dallas. *Language, Persons, and Belief: Studies in Wittgenstein's Philosophical Investigations and Religious Uses of Language.* New York: Oxford University Press, 1967.

Hodge, Alexander. *Outlines of Theology.* Grand Rapids, Mich.: Eerdmans, 1929.

Hodge, Charles. *Systematic Theology.* New York: Scribner & Armstrong, 1876.

Hollander, John. *The Untuning of the Sky.* Princeton, N.J.: Princeton University Press, 1961.

Hudson, Donald. *Ludwig Wittgenstein: The Bearing of His Philosophy on Religious Belief.* Richmond, Va.: John Knox Press, 1968.

Jansen, John Frederick. "Glossolalia." *The Oxford Companion to the Bible.* Edited by Bruce M. Metzger and Michael D. Coogan. Oxford, Eng.: Oxford University Press, 1993.

Johnson, Samuel. "Preface." *A Dictionary of the English Language.* New York: AMS Press, 1967.

Kepel, Gilles. *The Revenge of God: The Resurgence of Islam, Christianity, and Judaism in the Modern World.* Translated by Alan Braley. University Park: Pennsylvania State University Press, 1994.

Kisley, Lorraine. "The Sacred World of the Other: An Interview with Seyyed Hossein Nasr." *Parabola* 30, no. 40 (Winter 2005).

Lakoff, George, and Mark Johnson. *Metaphors We Live By.* Chicago: University of Chicago Press, 1980.

MacCormac, Earl R. *Metaphor and Myth in Science and Religion.* Durham, N.C.: Duke University Press, 1976.

McFague, Sallie. *Metaphorical Theology: Models of God in Religious Language.* Philadelphia: Fortress Press, 1982.

Macquarrie, John. *God-Talk: An Examination of the Language and Logic of Theology.* New York: Harper & Row, 1967.

Manguel, Alberto. *A History of Reading.* New York: Viking, 1996.

Marsden, George M. *Understanding Fundamentalism and Evangelicalism.* Grand Rapids, Mich.: Eerdmans, 1991.

Marty, Martin, and R. Scott Appleby. *Fundamentalisms Observed,* vol. 1 of *The Fundamentalism Project.* Chicago: University of Chicago Press, 1991.

Moser, Bob. "The Crusaders." www.rollingstone.com/politics/story/_id/7235393 (accessed July 13, 2005).

Oberman, Heiko A. *Luther: Man Between God and the Devil.* New York: Doubleday Image, 1992.

Olmert, Michael. *The Smithsonian Book of Books.* New York: Wings Books, 1992.

Ong, S.J., Walter. *The Presence of the Word: Some Prolegomena for Cultural and Religious History.* New Haven, Conn.: Yale University Press, 1967.

Oxford University Press. *The Compact Edition of the Oxford English Dictionary.* Oxford, Eng.: Oxford University Press, 1971.

Padgen, Anthony. *The Fall of Natural Man: The American Indian and the Origins of Comparative Ethnology.* Cambridge: Cambridge University Press, 1986.

Pelikan, Jaroslav. *Luther the Expositor: Introduction to the Reformer's Exegetical Writings.* St. Louis, Mo.: Concordia House, 1959.

Ramsey, Ian T. *Religious Language: An Empirical Placing of Theological Phrases.* New York: Macmillan, 1957.

Ravenhill, Philip L. "Religious Utterances and the Theory of Speech Acts." In *Language in Religious Practice,* edited by William J. Samarin, 26–39. Rawley, Mass.: Newbury House Publishers, 1976.

Richardson, James T. "Psychological Interpretations of Glossolalia: A Reexamination of the Research." *Journal for the Scientific Review of Religion* 12:2 (June 1973): 199–207.

Ricoeur, Paul. *The Rule of Metaphor.* Translated by Robert Czerny with Kathleen McLaughlin and John Costello, S.J. Toronto: University of Toronto Press, 1977.

Samarin, William J., ed. *Language in Religious Practice.* Rawley, Mass.: Newbury House Publishers, 1976.

Sargent, Winthrop, trans. *The Bhagavad Gita.* Albany: State University of New York Press, 1984.

Schuon, Frithjof. *The Transcendent Unity of Religions.* Translated by Peter Townsend. New York: Harper Torchbooks, 1973.

Shelton, Austin J. "Controlling Capricious Gods." In *Language in Religious Practice,* edited by William J. Samarin, 63–71. Rawley, Mass.: Newbury House Publishers, 1976.

Silva, Moises. *God, Language and Scripture: Reading the Bible in the Light of General Linguistics.* Grand Rapids, Mich.: Zondervan, 1990.

Skeat, Walter. *An Etymological Dictionary of the English Language.* Oxford, Eng.: Clarendon Press, 1927.

Smith, Daniel J., and J. Roland Fleck. "Personality Correlates of Conventional and Unconventional Glossolalia." *The Journal of Social Psychology* 114 (1981):209–71.

Sontag, Susan. "The Aesthetics of Silence." *Styles of Radical Will.* www.susansontag.com/stylesofradicalwilexcrpt.htm (accessed September 19, 2005).

Swift, Jonathon. *A Proposal for Correcting, Ascertaining and Improving the English Tongue.* www.etext.library.adelaide.edu.au/s/swift/Jonathon/s97p (accessed January 11, 2006).

Van Bingsbergen, Wim. "Rupture and Fusion in the Approach to Myth." www.shikanda.net/ancient_models/myth%20mineke%20defdefdef.pdf (accessed January 11, 2006).

Van Buren, Paul M. *The Edges of Language: An Essay in the Logic of a Religion.* New York: Macmillan, 1972.

Wallis, Jim. *God's Politics: Why the Right Gets It Wrong and the Left Doesn't Get It.* San Francisco: HarperSanFrancisco, 2005.

Webster, John. "Eberhard Jüngel on the Language of Faith." *Modern Theology* 1 (4 July, 1985): 253–76.

Westfall, Richard S. *Science and Religion in Seventeenth-Century England.* Ann Arbor, Mich.: Ann Arbor Paperbacks, 1972.

Wickering, Deborah. *Negotiating Intimacy: Life Among Tarabiin Bedouins in the South Sinai.* Unpublished manuscript.

Wieman, Henry Nelson. *Man's Ultimate Commitment.* Carbondale: Southern Illinois University Press, 1958.

Wilder, Amos Niven. *Theopoetics: Theology and the Religious Imagination.* Philadelphia: Fortress Press, 1976.

Wilson, Peter Lamborn, and Nasrollah Pourjavady, trans. *The Drunken Universe: An Anthology of Sufi Poetry.* Grand Rapids, Mich.: Phanes Press, 1987.

Wisdom, John. *Philosophy and Psychoanalysis.* Berkeley: University of California Press, 1953.

———. "Gods." *Philosophy and Psychoanalysis.* Oxford, Eng.: Blackwell, 1953.

Wittgenstein, Ludwig. *Lectures and Conversations on Aesthetics, Psychology, and Religious Beliefs.* Edited by Cyril Barrett. Berkeley: University of California Press, 1967.

Index

aborigines, Australian, 88–89
Age of Reason, 49–51
"Agnosticism and Christianity"
    (Huxley), 61
Allah, 157, 158
American Civil Religion, 146
American Creed, 145
"American Solution," 18
Andre of Reivaulx, 191
animal communication, 171
Antoun, Richard, 12, 22
apocalyptic thinking, 73, 77
Aquinas, Thomas, 151, 153, 158,
    161–63, 178, 199
Aristotle, 160–61
Armstrong, Karen, 23, 26
art, 96–97
    vs. science, 64
Augustine, Saint, 34
Augustine of Hippo, 189
Austin, J. L., 133, 134

Babel, story of the tower of, 17,
    28–30
balance, need for, 30
Bambara tribe, 88
Baptism, 74
Beach, Henry, 70
Beckett, Samuel, 159
Being, 152
belief, xvii, 102–3
    language of, 170
Bernard of Clairvaux, 189
Bhagavad Gita, 181–84
Bible, 24, 33, 41–42. See also
    specific topics
    fundamentalism and the, 59
    Higher Criticism, 61–62, 68–70,
        90
    science and the, 52–53, 59–60,
        68
    truth and the, 56, 59–61
    versions and translations, 67–68
    as "Word of God," 78 (see also
        literalism)

biblical inerrancy, 69–71. *See also* literalism

biblical interpretation, 65–67. *See also* Higher Criticism; literalism; theology

Bickerton, Derek, 171, 172, 174

books, 43–44. *See also* printing and printing presses

"born again," 23, 117

Boyle, Robert, 52

Brahman, 157

breath, 191–92

Brooke, J. H., 67

Buddha, 116, 118

Buddhism, 114, 118–19, 149, 150, 159

Zen, 198–99

Bush, George W., 23, 79–80

"calling," religious, 170

Calvin, John, 58, 59

cathedrals, 17–18

Catholic Church, 90

printing and, 38–42

causality and God, 151–52, 154

Christian counterculture in 1960s, 74–75

Christian fundamentalism, 58. *See also* fundamentalism

Christian mystics, 190

Christianity. *See specific topics*

Chuang-tzu, 199–200

Church of England, 144

cities, modern, 17, 18

Cold War, 77

colonialism, 27

communism, 74, 77

"compassion test," 16

connaisance, 94

conscience, 64

Corbett, Lionel, 113, 123

"counterculture" movement in 1960s, 21

"creation science," 24–25

cults, 123, 124, 127

Darby, John Nelson, 66

Darwin, Charles, 70

On the Origin of Species, 53, 60

Declaration of Independence, 19

depression, 21

Diamond Sutra, 198, 199

dictionaries, 47–48

discernment commitment, 100

ecumenism, 143, 150

education, fundamentalist institutions of higher, 25

Eichhorn, J. G., 61

Eisenstein, Elizabeth, 40, 41, 43, 208n25

England, 144

enteleche, 152

evangelicals, Christian, 23, 24, 73, 80

evolution, 90–91. *See also* Darwin

Exodus, 156, 180

facts, 56

faith, 103, 170

falsifiability, 105–6

Falwell, Jerry, 82–83

family values, 3
Fiddler on the Roof (musical),
    138–39
Fitzgerald, Frances, 77, 78
Four Great Signs, 116
Four Noble Truths, 114
freedom, religious, 144–46
fundamentalism, xiii–xiv, 9–10, 85
    "fundamentals" of, 71
    God and, 153
    late-twentieth century upsurge
        in, 22, 26
    mass media and, 73
    meanings of, 72
    modernism and (*see specific
        topics*)
    psychology of, 123–24
    scientific challenges to scripture
        and, 60–62
    truth and, 32, 57, 84
fundamentalist movements
    history, 59–82
    as reactionary, 26–27
Fundamentals, The, 68, 69, 71

generativity, 116–17
Ghazali, Ahmad, 189
glossolalia, 195–97
God, xiv, xvii, 116, 177, 188, 189
    as attempt to name what is
        unnameable, 177
    being "called" by, 170
    etymology of the word, 155
    kingdom of, 193–94
    "masks" of, 184
    meanings and associations of the
        word, 4–5, 31, 146–47, 151,
        160

metaphor and, 160–69 (*see also*
    metaphor(s))
    names for, 155–58
    naming, 180–81, 198
    in Old Testament, 156–57, 160,
        180–81
    revealing and concealing himself,
        180–81
    Thomas Aquinas on, 151, 153,
        158, 161–63
    truth and, 55–56
    using language to talk about,
        154–55, 158–59
    "ways" that lead one toward the
        idea of, 151–54
God-language, xvi, 4. *See also
    specific topics*
Gosse, Edmund, 62
grammar, 46–50
Greeks, ancient, 37, 101
Gregory of Nyssa, 188, 197
Grey, James, 69–71
group solidarity and identity,
    128–30. *See also* "I," "we,"
    and "they"; tradition
Gutenberg, Johannes, 38, 39

Haldeman, Isaac M., 71–72
Harwood, Edward, 51–52,
    207–8n23
Heagle, David, 69
healing, 117
Higher Criticism, 61–62, 68–70,
    90
Hinduism, 157, 158, 169, 190. *See
    also Bhagavad Gita*
history
    art, 96–97

oral vs. written, 33–37 (*see also*
    printing and printing presses)
    religion and, xv
Hodge, Archibald Alexander, 63–65
Hodge, Charles, 63
holiness, 115–17, 130–32, 136
Holy Spirit, 191, 192, 195
Huxley, Thomas, 53, 61

"I," "we," and "they," 129–30,
    140–41. *See also* "others"
    and othering
idolatry, 185
imagery and the divine, 188–91. *See*
    also metaphor(s)
Index, 41
infidels, 147
information, definitions of, 37
ingroup/outgroup. *See* "I," "we,"
    and "they"
intelligences, multiple, 92
interfaith dialogue, 186–87. *See also*
    religions, connections
    between
interfaith services, 149
Inuit, 14
Islam, 17, 34, 157
Islamic fundamentalism. *See also*
    September 11, 2001 terrorist
    attacks
    colonialism and, 27
Israel. *See also* Palestine
    founding of the modern state
    of, 71, 73

James I, King, 144–45
Jefferson, Thomas, 144

Jesus Christ, 26, 33, 61, 96, 194
    and living a whole and holy
    life, 117–18
    Second Coming, 65–66, 71–72, 81
Jewish fundamentalists, 23, 27
Johnson, Mark, 176, 177
Johnson, Samuel, 47
Jung, Carl Gustav, 30, 97
Jüngel, Eberhard, 170

Kaaba, 17
Kena Upanishad, 169–71, 174,
    189
Kennedy, James, 81
"kingdom of God," 193–94
knowing, scientific and
    mythic/narrative modes of,
    93–95, 121
knowledge, tacit, 105
Koran, 34, 167–68

LaHaye, Tim, 81
Lakoff, George, 176, 177
Lamkin, Kurtis, 35
language, xiv, 3, 171–72
    changing, 46, 47
    culture and, 33–37
    defined, 33
    functions, 171, 172
    imprecision, 47
    mapmaking and, 172–76
    oral vs. written, 33–37, 45–49
        (*see also* printing and printing
        presses)
    phatic, 130
    refining, 50–51
    science and, 51–53

standard(ized), 46, 47
Le Saux, Henri, 200
liberals, 27–28, 78, 81–82
Lindsey, Hal, 75
literalism, 42, 56, 59, 65–67, 78, 94–95. *See also* metaphor(s); myth(s)
 truth and, 188
logic, 93
love, 103, 121, 190, 191
Lowth, Robert, 49
Lull, Ramon, 190
Luther, Martin, 39, 40, 58–59

MacCormac, Earl, 104, 106, 169, 177
Macquarrie, John, 102, 134, 154, 155, 177
Mahabharata, 182–83
mapmaking and language, 172–76
Mauro, Philip, 70
McFague, Sallie, 171, 195
Mencken, H. L., 72
metaphor(s), 104, 137, 171, 176–77, 188
 comparison view of, 164
 defined, 102
 etymology of the word, 168
 "experientialist" test of the truth of, 176
 God-language and, 160–69, 176–78, 188–95
 interactive view of, 164–67
 of Jesus, 194
 reading sacred, 192–93
 substitution view of, 163–64, 166
 as transgressive, 165–66

Miller, William, 65–66
modern cities, 17, 18
"Modern Philosophy" (Mauro), 70
modernism, 8, 10, 187
 and antimodernist movement, 66–67
 definitions, 11
 historical perspective on, 11, 19
 impact of, 12
 language and, 30
 "modern life" and, 11–16, 20–22
 secular, 139
 technology and, 20, 28–29
 World Trade Center and, 15–16, 28–29
monotheism, 147, 155
Moody Bible Institute, 67
Moody, Dwight, 67
Moses, 156, 180, 181
mystical participation, 98
mystical traditions, 188–90
 similarities amongst, 188
mythic vs. scientific modes of knowing, 93–95
mythology, 87–90, 99–102, 109
 names and naming in, 214n15
 psychology and, 97–98
mythopoesis, 107
mythos, 93
myth(s), 62, 63, 83–84, 86, 98, 105, 109
 "here/not here" and "now/not now" quality, 101
 meanings, 86–87, 210n1
 origin of the word, 86
 questions to ask when seeking the truth of, 107
 rituals and, 100

science and, 87–93, 100–101,
104–6
stories and, 99–101
"tacit knowledge" and, 105
truth and, 62, 84, 86, 90, 91,
160–61 (*See also* truth)

Nasr, Seyyed Hossein, 148
nature, mysteries of, 95–96
negation, way of, 159, 198
9/11 terrorist attacks. *See*
September 11, 2001 terrorist
attacks
nirvana, 192

Odin, 108
Ong, Walter, 34, 35, 51, 102, 175
Operation Save America, 83
oral history and transmission of
information, 33–37, 45. *See
also* printing and printing
presses
Origen, 188
orrery, 98–99
Orwell, George, xiv
"others" and othering, 140–41,
143, 147, 186
Oxford English Dictionary (OED),
54

Palestine, 193. *See also* Israel
parables, 194
participation mystique, 98
performative vs. informative
language, 133–37, 139–40,
147

phatic language, 130
Philosopher's God, 152, 153
Plato, 37
Plotinus, 215n23
poetry, 102, 188–91
politics and religion, xiv
premillennialism, 65–66, 72
presence and the spoken word,
34–35
Princeton Presbyterians, 71
printing and printing presses,
38–44, 46
Protestantism, 42. *See also*
Reformation
psychology
mythology and, 97–98
religion and, 116–17, 122–24

Ramsey, Ian, 121
randomness, 110–11
Rapture, 66, 81, 117, 124
rational life, 9
Ravenhill, Phillip, 150
Reagan, Ronald, 77–78
reason, 93
Reber, A. S., 105
Reconstructionists, 79
Reformation, 39–43
religion, xiv, xv, 125–26, 201. *See
also specific topics*
as action word, 112–13
effectiveness of, 116–17
etymology of the word, 111–13
goal of, 111
meanings of the word, 110, 126
message of, 118
misuse and debasement of the
word, 115

motivations for turning to, 122–24

need for, 124–25, 142, 201

psychology and, 116–17, 122–24

vs. randomness, 110–11

science and, 62–64, 68, 90–91, 105–6

sociological dimensions of, 129

as solitary journey vs. collective activity, 127–29

yoga and, 111, 112

religions

connections between, 147–50, 188 (*see also* interfaith dialogue)

as languages/dialects, 148–49, 185–86

religiosity, 121–23, 126. *See also under* United States

"religious," 113

religious discourse, 132

Religious Function of the Psyche (Corbett), 113–14

religious language, 4, 5, 7–9, 30–31, 52, 131–32. *See also specific topics*

death, crises, and, 118

distrust of, 121

fundamentalists and, 82, 83

metaphor, poetry, and, 102 (*see also* metaphor(s))

multilevel understanding of, 162–63

oral vs. written, 43, 46 (*see also* language, oral vs. written)

as performative vs. informative, 133–37, 139–40, 147

self, society, tradition, and, 130–31

religious questions, essential, 117, 169

religious right, 23–24

religious scriptures, 34, 36, 52. *See also* Higher Criticism; *specific topics*

Revelation, 65, 66

revelation, 102

reverence, 137

Ricoeur, Paul, 165, 166

Riley, William Bell, 72

ritual objects, 96–97

ritual time, 136–38

Roman Empire, 193

Royal Society of London, 44–47

"sacred," 136, 137

salvation, 117

Sana'i, 178

savoir, 94, 114

science, 43–46. *See also under* myth(s)

definitions and meanings, 64–65

language and, 51–53

religion and, 62–64, 68, 90–91, 105–6

truth and, 43, 53, 55, 59–60

Scientific Revolution, 42–44, 104

Scofield Reference Bible, The, 67, 68

Scopes monkey trial, 72

Second Coming, 65–66, 71–72, 81

Secondary Reference System, 171

secular humanism, 76, 78–79

secular modernism, 139. *See also* modernism

self. *See* "I," "we," and "they"

self-actualization, 116–17

Self (archetype), 113–14
self-transformation, 117
semantic collision, 166
semantic space, 174
September 11, 2001 terrorist
    attacks, 15–17, 28, 82–83
sexuality, 20–21
Shakespeare, William, 47
silence, 197–200
sin, 115
Sontag, Susan, 200
sovereignty, 145
Soviet Union, 77
speaking in tongues. *See* glossolalia
spelling, 49
spirit, 191–92
spiritual beliefs, xv
spirituality, 113
Sprat, Thomas, 44, 45
suffering, 114–15
Sufi poets, 188–90
suicide, 21
Swift, Jonathan, 47, 51

etymology of the word, 128
individual identity, group
    solidarity, and, 128–30,
    139–41
"Tradition" (*Fiddler on the Roof*),
    138
"traditional values," 139
truth, xiv, xvii, 3–4, 31, 57
    definitions and meanings, 53–57,
        86, 103, 106
    fundamentalism vs. modernism
        and, 32
    "literal," 56
    literalism and, 188
    modernist definition, 58, 142–43
    myth and, 62, 84, 86, 90, 91,
        160–61 (*see also* myth(s))
    religion and, 55, 142–43
    science and, 43, 53, 55, 59–60
        (*see also* science)
    shift in our understanding of the
        word, 32–33
    spellings of the word, 54

Tabernacle, 69
taboo, 132, 135
tacit knowledge, 105
Taosim, 158, 199
Tarabiin, 14
technology and modernism, 20,
    28–29
terrorism. *See* September 11, 2001
    terrorist attacks
theolinguistics, 5
theology, 63–65
tolerance, 143, 147
Tolstoy, Leo, 199
tradition

United States. *See also specific
    topics*
    founders of, 144–47
    religiosity, 18–19, 24, 25, 74–76,
        145–47 (*see also*
        fundamentalist movements,
        history)
    1960s and, 21, 74, 138, 139
Upanishad. *See* Kena Upanishad
Ussher, James, 59

value(s), 3, 19, 137
    "traditional," 139

Van Buren, Paul, 158, 181
verbs (religious), performative, 132, 135
Viguerie, Richard, 76

Wallis, Jim, 81, 83
Ward, W.G., 65
"we." *See* "I," "we," and "they"
Wellhausen, Julius, 61
wholeness, need for and pursuit of, 30, 115–17
Wieman, Henry, 117
Wilberforce, Samuel, 53

"Word of God," 78, 188. *See also* literalism
words, 3–7. *See also specific topics*
  Latin and Greek roots, 50
World Trade Center (WTC), 15–16, 28–29. *See also* September 11, 2001 terrorist attacks
worship, 137

yoga, 111, 112, 192

zazen, 199